Pro EDI in BizTalk Server 2006 R2

Electronic Document Interchange Solutions

■ ■ ■

Mark Beckner

Apress®

Pro EDI in BizTalk Server 2006 R2: Electronic Document Interchange Solutions

Softcover re-print of the Hardcover 1st edition 2007

ISBN-13: 978-1-4842-2097-9

ISBN-10: 1-4842-2097-8

DOI 10.1007/978-1-4302-0530-2

Lead Editor: Jonathan Hassell
Technical Reviewer: Tony Bernard

Project Manager: Kylie Johnston
Copy Editor: Jennifer Whipple
Associate Production Director: Kari Brooks-Copony
Production Editor: Katie Stence
Compositor: Susan Glinert
Proofreader: Patrick Vincent
Indexer: Carol Burbo
Artist: April Milne
Cover Designer: Kurt Krames
Manufacturing Director: Tom Debolski

Distributed to the book trade worldwide by Springer-Verlag New York, Inc., 233 Spring Street, 6th Floor, New York, NY 10013. Phone 1-800-SPRINGER, fax 201-348-4505, e-mail orders-ny@springer-sbm.com, or visit http://www.springeronline.com.

For information on translations, please contact Apress directly at 2855 Telegraph Avenue, Suite 600, Berkeley, CA 94705. Phone 510-549-5930, fax 510-549-5939, e-mail info@apress.com, or visit http://www.apress.com.

The source code for this book is available to readers at http://www.apress.com.

This book is dedicated to my mother, who taught me to drink tea, and my father, who brought a TRS-80 into the house.

Contents at a Glance

Contents

Foreword

At the beginning of the sci-fi movie classic *Star Trek II: The Wrath of Khan*, there is a scene where new Star Fleet trainees blow up the bridge of the starship U.S.S. Enterprise, or so they think (it turns out later to simply be a training simulation). Crew members are blown to bits and thrown helplessly around the bridge, including our favorite Star Fleet officers Spock, Sulu, Uhura, and Dr. McCoy. After the training simulation has ended and Admiral Kirk strides off the bridge, he turns to look at the now resurrected Spock and quips "Aren't you dead?"

The same has been said many times about Electronic Data Interchange (EDI). In early 2000, when XML-based e-commerce exploded onto the scene at the height of the Internet boom, nearly all analysts and vendors alike predicted that the rise of XML B2B technologies would lead to the rapid demise of EDI. Turns out we were only half right. While XML B2B traffic has indeed increased significantly over the past seven years, it hasn't in any way killed off the significant mainstream use of EDI by businesses to automate their business transactions (now accounting for more than one-third of the U.S. gross domestic product). In fact, according to a recent study by Forrester Research ("B2B Integration Trends: Message Formats—Alternatives Grow, but EDI Standards Remain the Leading Option for B2B Messaging"), EDI traffic is still the leading form of B2B e-commerce (representing 85%–90% of total B2B traffic, and growing at a rate of 3%–5% year over year).

It turns out that most businesses, having sunk considerable portions of their IT budgets into EDI over the past 30 years, are fairly reluctant to rip and replace proven, stable supply-chain technologies (even if the newer technology options are superior in many ways). Instead, enterprises are looking for ways to extend the life of the existing EDI infrastructure (often embedded tightly into their mission-critical applications). This might include adding on newer real-time event processing (replacing traditional nightly batching), shifting to transmitting EDI over the Internet (to reduce VAN charges), and applying business process management techniques for automating end-to-end supply-chain collaboration processes (to reduce manual exception handling processes and shrink response times). These IT strategies can all be incrementally deployed around existing EDI applications to enhance business visibility and control, while still offering rapid returns on investment.

With the release of BizTalk Server 2006 R2, Microsoft's fifth-generation integration and business process server, we're hoping to make it even easier and more cost-effective for companies to extend the value of their EDI investments. By integrating comprehensive EDI support (both X12 and EDIFACT standards) as part of our unified platform for building next-generation business process applications, Microsoft is helping customers bridge the worlds of their older and proven EDI applications with the latest cutting-edge innovations such as radio frequency identification (RFID) and service-oriented architecture (SOA).

The result? We think this will allow customers to more easily extend the life of their aging applications and drive greater profitability for their businesses. Or as Spock might say, "Live long and prosper."

Burley Kawasaki
Director of Product Management, Connected Systems Division
Microsoft Corporation

About the Author

MARK BECKNER is a technical consultant specializing in business development and enterprise application integration. He runs his own consulting firm, Inotek Consulting Group, LLC, delivering innovative solutions to large corporations and small businesses.

His projects have included engagements with numerous clients throughout the United States and range in nature from mobile application development to complete integration solutions. He is the coauthor of *BizTalk 2006 Recipes: A Problem-Solution Approach* (Apress, 2006), has spoken at a number of venues, including Microsoft's BizTalk Server 2004 in a Service-Oriented World conference, and is certified in Microsoft technologies, including MCSD.NET.

Mark resides with his wife, Sara, and their dog Rosco, the Adventure Mutt, in western Colorado. He can be contacted at `mbeckner@inotekgroup.com` for any questions regarding the concepts in this book, or for advice on integration projects, BizTalk 2006 implementations, or other consulting endeavors.

About the Technical Reviewer

TONY BERNARD currently serves as a senior program manager in the Connected Systems Division of Microsoft's Server and Tools Business. In this role he is responsible for driving the business-to-business (B2B) strategy and feature set for BizTalk Server, Microsoft's enterprise integration platform. Prior to joining Microsoft, Tony served as the vice president of technology for TrueCommerce. In this role he was responsible for all software product development, information systems management, and technical operations at the company.

Prior to joining TrueCommerce, Tony served as senior director of systems architecture for FreeMarkets Inc. In this role, he was responsible for the overall application, data, and technical architecture of FreeMarkets' customer-facing software products. He was an early member of the FreeMarkets team and was with the company for more than six and a half years, helping to guide it through three consecutive years of 300% head count and revenue growth. During that time he held several development, architecture, research and development, and technical management roles. He is also listed as a co-inventor on several patents in the FreeMarkets intellectual property portfolio and prior to his departure was a member of the FreeMarkets/Ariba merger integration team.

Before joining FreeMarkets, Tony was employed as a senior manager at Ernst and Young LLP, where as a member of the information technology consulting practice, he assisted Fortune 500 companies with all aspects of designing, developing, and deploying information technology solutions to meet their business needs. Before that, Tony held several other technology-related positions, including systems coordinator for the Securities Lending group of Mellon Bank; project manager for CIScorp, a systems integration firm; and senior consultant for Accenture.

Tony holds a BS in applied mathematics with a concentration in operations research and management science from Carnegie Mellon University. He has also guest lectured at Duquesne University, the Katz Graduate School of Business at the University of Pittsburgh, and the Heinz School at Carnegie Mellon University.

Acknowledgments

I would like to thank the following individuals for their contributions to my professional life:

- Sara Ann, who allowed me to walk the road that led me to where I am today
- Stephen Roger, who kept me on full-time projects after I went independent
- Brandon Gross, who brought me on as a coauthor on the previous book
- Scott Jones and Brennan O'Reilly, who taught me how to code and how to eat
- Dan Allworth, for placing me on the first BizTalk 2006 R2 EDI project
- Long Duong, the only person I know who actually read my previous work

A great deal of gratitude is owed to the ever widening network of friends and colleagues who are bound for incredible successes, including the guys at Attunix Corporation; Altriva, LLC; Guardian ProStar Inc.; and EMC's Microsoft Practice.

Introduction

The EDI capabilities of BizTalk Server 2006 R2 are a new implementation of an old technology. EDI originated in the 1970s to facilitate the delivery of data between businesses. Rather than diminishing in scope, however, EDI continues to play a major role in commerce today. Because of this, an extensive engine has been added to BizTalk Server to provide for robust handling of EDI transmissions. This book will immerse the reader in working with the new EDI components and demonstrate how to successfully build and deploy a fully functional solution.

Who This Book Is For

The EDI implementation for R2 is unlike any previous incarnation of EDI in BizTalk. Because of this, there is material covered in this book that is equally useful to seasoned BizTalk architects and new developers alike. The intention of the material is to provide all of the detail necessary for any level of developer to envision, build, test, deploy, and support an EDI solution. There are several topics, such as exception handling, that are common to all BizTalk implementations and will prove useful in architecting any solution. The majority of the book, however, from the EDI schemas and party configurations to the new EDI reporting tools, is completely new material not covered in other mediums and will prove to be useful to anyone engaged in a BizTalk 2006 R2 EDI project.

How This Book Is Structured

There are a number of exercises throughout the course of this book illustrating how to work with different components. All chapters with exercises that require code begin with an exercise outlining how to set up the sample code that accompanies that chapter (available for download via the Apress website). All exercises can be worked through from scratch, or the code can simply be deployed and referenced. The following chapters provide end-to-end coverage of building, deploying, and supporting an EDI BizTalk Server 2006 R2 solution:

Chapter 1, "EDI Schemas": At the foundation of all BizTalk implementations are the schemas. BizTalk Server 2006 R2 ships with thousands of predefined EDI schemas, each representing a different EDI document type. These serve as a starting point and are to be refined—based on the trading partner requirements—to define the final structure of the EDI document. This chapter outlines how to work with these schemas and how to validate their accuracy.

Chapter 2, "Trading Partner Configuration": Using BizTalk parties to implement the details for a trading partner includes setting the header and footer information for an EDI document and specifying details around the delivery and acknowledgement of documents. Party configuration and EDI schemas are both used to define the outcome to the final EDI text document.

Chapter 3, "Retrieving and Mapping Data": Determining the source of data for an EDI document and how that source data is manipulated to create the appropriate data is an essential step in the formation of EDI documents. This chapter outlines how to use the BizTalk SQL Receive Adapter to retrieve data from a source database, and how to use the BizTalk map components to do standard EDI document mapping.

Chapter 4, "EDI and Orchestrations": Many times, if more than a single step is needed for the creation of an EDI document, orchestrations will play an important role in the creation and delivery of EDI documents. One of the most important features covered in this chapter is the concept of a common exception handling infrastructure.

Chapter 5, "Transporting Documents": There are a variety of BizTalk components that may be used to send and receive data. Both AS2 and VAN infrastructures are used in the delivery of EDI documents. This chapter describes how to configure parties to deliver using AS2, how to use the FTP adapters for sending and receiving data, and how to work with a third-party AS2 adapter.

Chapter 6, "Trading Partner Testing": Once a solution has been developed, it must be tested. This generally requires extensive interaction with trading partners to ensure that the data being delivered is valid and complete. This chapter outlines the most common approaches to testing, how to determine where documents are in the overall creation and delivery process, how to work with administrative BizTalk tools, and how to use the new EDI reporting.

Chapter 7, "Deployment and Production Support": This chapter walks through the different deployment options available for BizTalk R2 EDI solutions. It also demonstrates how to keep a solution supported and optimized in a production environment.

Prerequisites

This book demonstrates the functionality of BizTalk Server 2006 R2 EDI; therefore, it is essential that this version of BizTalk is available, and that the EDI components are installed. EDI can be added to a BizTalk installation through the use of the configuration.exe file located in the root Microsoft BizTalk Server 2006 folder. When this utility is run, the final option in the list is BizTalk EDI/AS2 Runtime. The features associated with this option must be successfully installed.

Downloading the Code

The source code for this book is available to readers at `http://www.apress.com` in the Source Code/Downloads section. The exercises in this book assume that this code has been extracted to the C:\ drive. The sample code includes all of the code used in the exercises throughout the book. However, it is possible to work through all of the solutions in this book without the use of this supporting code.

Contacting the Author

Mark Beckner can be contacted via email at `mbeckner@inotekgroup.com`, or via standard mail at the following address:

Inotek Consulting Group, LLC
P.O. Box 4890
Grand Junction, CO 81502

Visit Inotek Consulting online at `http://www.inotekgroup.com`. All inquiries, comments, and feedback are appreciated.

CHAPTER 1

EDI Schemas

This chapter provides an overview of working with EDI documents and BizTalk schemas. It introduces where the information for EDI schemas comes from, how to modify the schema based on a trading partner's requirements, how to validate the schema and document content, and how to deploy the schema once it has been completed. This chapter should be read along with the content of Chapter 2 on trading partner configuration, as it is essential to understand both concepts to be able to define and complete a full EDI schema and create a full EDI instance, with all header, context, detail, and footer (summary) information.

Schemas are considered the foundation of a BizTalk implementation—all other components are dependent on them being in place. The primary steps in defining and working with EDI schemas are the following:

- **Using an EDI implementation guide**: The EDI implementation guide is the starting point for all EDI solutions. It defines all of the documents that a trading partner uses, how those documents are formed (e.g., what segments and data elements are available), and what data is expected to be present when the document is delivered.
- **Determining the right BizTalk schema**: Based on the implementation guide, the appropriate BizTalk schema can be determined. There will likely be multiple schemas in any EDI solution, some specific to trading partners, others shared by multiple trading partners.
- **Modifying the BizTalk schema based on the trading partner**: Once the correct schema has been determined and added to a BizTalk project, the next step is to modify the schema to fit the requirements of the individual trading partner. Often this involves removing unneeded nodes (segments), modifying field lengths, and determining whether data elements are mandatory or optional.
- **Promoting fields**: Field promotion becomes a factor in implementations that will be using send port filtering or orchestration logic based on the content of an EDI document.
- **Validating and generating EDI instances**: During schema development, existing EDI instances will need to be validated and new file instances may need to be created. Validation generally involves taking a known instance of an EDI document that works for a given trading partner and validating it against the BizTalk schema. Based on the results, the schema may need to be further revised.

Schema Overview

All documents processed in BizTalk Server, whether they are EDI or otherwise, adhere to a schema. There are numerous EDI documents in existence, ranging from invoices and bills of lading to functional and technical acknowledgements, and all of these documents have their own schema. On top of that, each EDI trading partner may have its own variation on an individual EDI document: Company A may expect slightly different information in a slightly different format for its invoice than Company X does. Each of these unique documents is defined by a different BizTalk schema (also known as an *XSD*).

Figure 1-1 shows an example of an EDI document. The document has been split into the different parts that will be referred to throughout the course of this book.

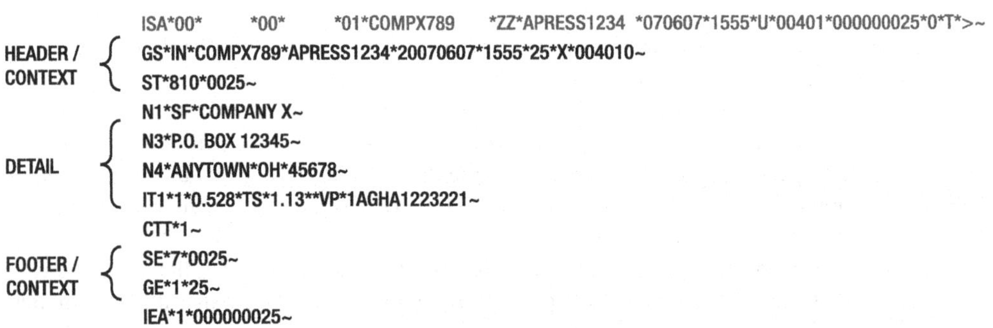

Figure 1-1. *Diagram of an EDI document representing an X12 810 invoice*

Because of the nature of EDI implementations, document structure, and trading partner requirements, it is common practice to have one BizTalk schema for every EDI document type per trading partner. On occasion, however, a schema may be shared between multiple trading partners; in this case, defining a "common schema project" can be helpful. Figure 1-2 illustrates a sample BizTalk project schema structure for two trading partners that both have unique invoice schemas and a shared bill of lading schema. One of the trading partners also has its own unshared purchase order schema.

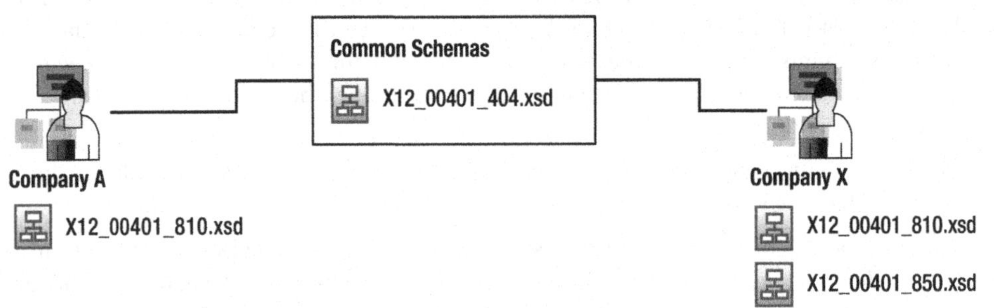

Figure 1-2. *Schema project structure*

Exercise 1-1 walks through setting up the sample code provided for this chapter. This chapter uses the files located in C:\Apress.Integration\Chapter 1.

Exercise 1-1. Preparing the Solution Files

Use the steps in this exercise to prepare the environment on the local machine without having to work through each of the exercises individually:

1. Make sure that the Chapter1 sample files have been extracted and placed on the C:\ drive.
2. The components can be deployed in a single package by importing the Chapter1.MSI file available in C:\Apress.Integration\Chapter 1\BizTalk Application. Open BizTalk Administration Console and right-click the Applications folder. Select Import ➤ MSI File. This will create the EDI.Demonstration.Chapter1 BizTalk application and all of the send and receive ports used in this chapter. It will also import the schemas. Alternatively, there are two solutions that can be deployed manually (rather than using the MSI):
   a. Open the solution contained in C:\Apress.Integration\Chapter 1 called Apress.Integration.EDI810.CompanyX.sln. This solution contains two items: a modified version of the X12 810 schema, tailored to Company X, and a property schema containing information about promoted fields. Deploy this by right-clicking the solution in Visual Studio and selecting Deploy.
   b. Open the solution called Apress.Integration.EDIFACT.ServiceExtension.sln. This solution contains the X12 service schema with modifications. This can also be deployed by right-clicking the solution in Visual Studio and selecting Deploy.

EDI Implementation Guide and Document Layout

The single most important component in determining information about the trading partner is the EDI implementation guide. An implementation guide is available from virtually any company using EDI. This guide outlines all of the documents being exchanged and all of the segments and fields that are used within each document. Implementation guides are generally comprised of the following sections:

- **Transaction set specification**: The transaction set specification is very similar to a title page—it simply defines what document is being covered and gives some high-level information about that document. Figure 1-3 shows a sample transaction set specification page.
- **Introduction**: The introduction is an overview of all the segments that are used within the given transaction set. The segments are defined and it is noted whether they are mandatory or optional and how many times they are expected to appear in a document; any notes associated with the segment are outlined. The introduction is comprised of three parts: header, detail, and footer.
- **Segment definitions**: After the introduction, each segment is presented, including all of the data elements (or *fields*) that are available on the segment, the length, and whether they are mandatory or optional. Any notes associated with each data element are defined in the segment definitions.

EDI Implementation Guide

Transaction Set

810 – Invoice to Customer

Version 4010

January 1st, 2007

Figure 1-3. *The transaction set specification page in the implementation guide*

The following figures are representations of what should be found in the introduction of an EDI implementation guide. Figure 1-4 shows the header segments, whether the segment is mandatory or optional, and how many times the segments will appear in the document. Note that there are two looping segments, N1 and N9, both appearing up to 200 times in a given EDI instance.

Seg ID	Name	Mandatory/Optional	Max Use
ISA	Interchange Control Header	M	1
GS	Functional Group Header	M	1
ST	Transaction Set Header	M	1
BIG	Beginning Segment for Invoice	M	1
REF	Reference Identification	O	12
Loop ID – N1			200
N1	Name	O	1
N2	Additional Name Information	O	2
N3	Address Information	O	2
N4	Geographic Location	O	1
ITD	Terms of Sale/Deferred Terms of Sale	O	1
BAL	Balance Detail	O	1
PAM	Period Amount	O	1
Loop ID – N9			200
N9	Reference Identification	O	1
MSG	Message Text	O	10

Figure 1-4. *Header segment in the introduction*

Figure 1-5 shows all of the detail segments and whether they are optional and what their usage is. The IT1 loop can appear one to many times, whereas the N1 loop can appear zero to many times.

Seg ID	Name	Mandatory/Optional	Max Use
Loop ID – IT1			200000
IT1	Baseline Item Data (Invoice)	M	1
MEA	Measurements	O	40
REF	Reference Identification	O	1
DTM	Date/Time Reference	O	10
SAC	Service, Promotion, Allowance, or Charge Info	O	25
Loop ID – N1			200
N1	Name	O	1
N3	Address Information	O	2
N4	Geographic Location	O	1

Figure 1-5. *Detail segment*

The final section of the implementation guide is the definition of the footer (or summary) segments. These segments are shown in Figure 1-6.

Seg ID	Name	Mandatory/Optional	Max Use
TDS	Total Monetary Value Summary	M	1
Loop ID – SAC			200
SAC	Service, Promotion, Allowance, or Charge Info	O	1
TXI	Tax Information	O	10
CTT	Transaction Totals	O	1
SE	Transaction Set Trailer	M	1
GE	Functional Group Trailer	M	1
IEA	Interchange Control Trailer	M	1

Figure 1-6. *Footer (summary) segment*

Figure 1-7 shows a sample version of a segment definition from an EDI implementation guide. The introduction states that the ST header (transaction set header) segment will be in the 810 EDI document, that it is a mandatory segment, and that it will appear one time. The segment definition for the ST segment shows the specific implementation information for that segment. For example, the first field, Transaction Set Identifier Code, has a constant value of 810 and must be exactly three characters long. The second field, ST02, is a number that will be automatically set by BizTalk, ensuring that it is a unique value.

Ref	Data Element Summary	Value	Length
ST01	Transaction Set Identifier Code	810	3/3
ST02	Transaction Set Control Number	[Unique ID]	4/9

Figure 1-7. *ST segment*

Note The ST segment is different from the majority of segments in that it must be part of the EDI X12 schemas, but at the same time it has some values that are set by the EDI send pipeline. Most segments are either completely set by the pipeline (such as the ISA segment via trading partner configuration) or are completely handled in mapping.

Schema Development and Deployment

BizTalk Server 2006 R2 is packaged with thousands of EDI schemas that can be used as starting points for a BizTalk EDI implementation (accessing these schemas is shown in Exercise 1-2, later in this section). These schemas are designed to contain a superset of all the nodes that may be required by any trading partner for the specified document type. There will frequently be fields that need to be modified (i.e., changing a "required" field to "optional," changing the maximum length of a field, or changing the type of data that can be stored in a field), and there will frequently be the need to eliminate a number of the nodes that do not pertain to the trading partner in question.

EDI schemas have an additional tab available to them in the Visual Studio Editor, shown in Figure 1-8. This tab gives quick access to some of the most prominent properties that are set for EDI data elements. Aside from this tab, working with EDI schemas is no different than working with any other type of BizTalk schema.

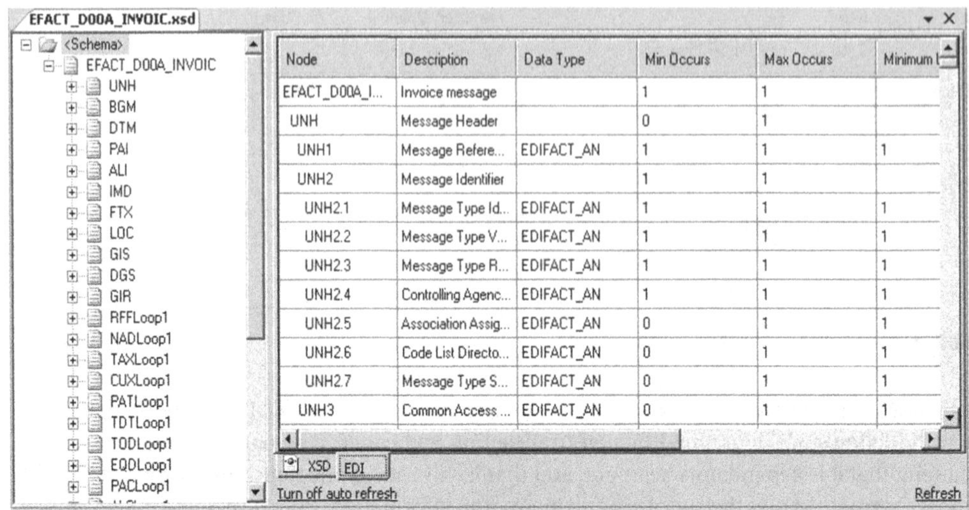

Figure 1-8. *The BizTalk schema EDI tab in Visual Studio*

Figure 1-9 shows all of the properties that can be set in an EDI schema. The most important properties to pay attention to are as follows:

- **Base Data Type and Data Type**: These properties indicate what type of data is expected to be present in the field. There are standard types, such as string and int, but there are also a large number of EDI-specific fields, such as X12_ID. Each of the EDI-specific fields has different properties associated with it (such as enumerations) and will automatically set these values when selected. Generally, the value of the element is set appropriately by default. If a trading partner needs a different type of data in this field, it is easiest to simply set this to xs:string, which allows anything to be present. Of course, by doing this, any EDI validation will be removed from this field.
- **Notes**: This is a description property that states what the field represents. It can be helpful during development and testing.
- **Max and Min Occurs**: These represent how many times the node or element can occur in the document. Occasionally it may be necessary to change these values, especially when a node is marked as "mandatory," but the trading partner does not expect it to be present on every document.
- **Length, Maximum Length, and Minimum Length**: These three fields dictate how long the data in the field can be. It is frequently necessary to modify these values for a given element, since different trading partners expect different lengths of data.
- **Enumeration**: This field contains an array of values that can be entered and compared against a schema. If the value in the field does not match a value in the enumeration, it will not be valid. See Exercise 1-3 (in the "X12 and EDIFACT Schemas" section, later in this chapter) on changing these values.

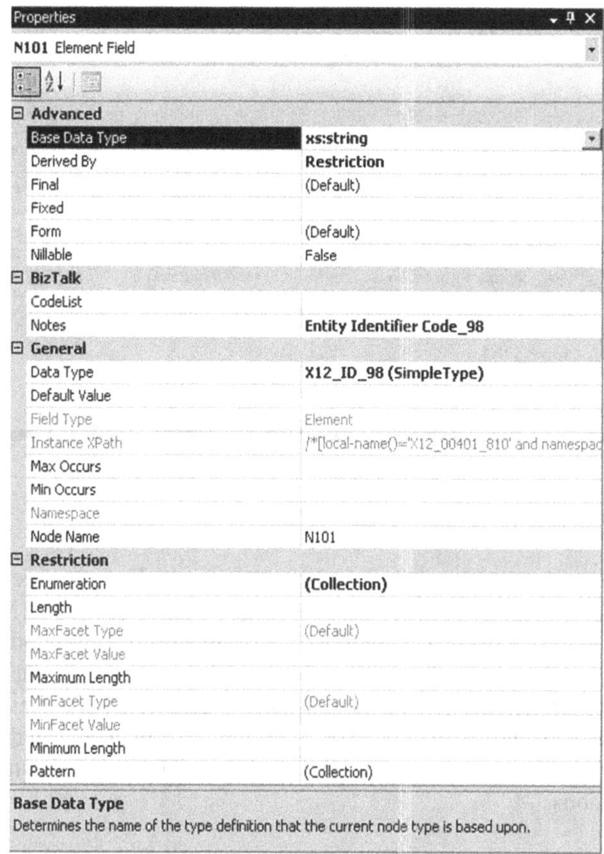

Figure 1-9. *EDI schema element properties*

Exercise 1-2 demonstrates how to access the default EDI schemas that ship with BizTalk Server 2006 R2.

Exercise 1-2. Accessing Default BizTalk EDI Schemas

There are a large number of EDI schemas that ship with BizTalk Server 2006 R2 and are made available when the EDI components are installed. They can be accessed as follows:

1. Browse to the directory c:\Program Files\Microsoft BizTalk Server 2006\XSD_Schema\EDI.
2. Before schemas are extracted, there is a single file: MicrosoftEdiXSDTemplates.exe. This is a compressed file that contains thousands of EDI schemas. Run this file to extract all of the schemas to the local path. Figure 1-10 shows the location of this file in Windows Explorer.

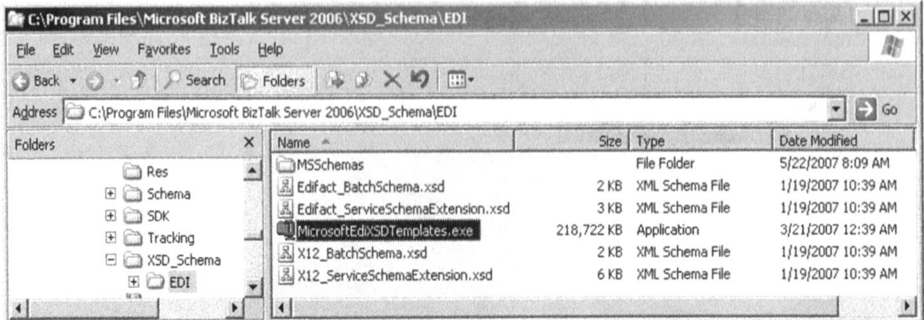

Figure 1-10. *BizTalk EDI schemas*

X12 and EDIFACT Schemas

There are two EDI standards: X12 and EDIFACT. Briefly stated, the X12 standard is for United States/North American markets, and EDIFACT represents documents exchanged in European/United Nations markets. While the segments and elements within each standard differ greatly from one another, the basic structure of the document itself is similar, with header, detail, and footer segments. All of the exercises throughout this book are interchangeable between the X12 and EDIFACT schemas; the nomenclature and the BizTalk party EDI properties are the only things that differ between the two types. Figure 1-11 shows an instance of an invoice schema for both X12 and EDIFACT, illustrating the difference in naming conventions.

■ **Note** The default EDI schemas provided with BizTalk Server 2006 R2 can be used as is—without modification—for any trading partner. However, in most cases, some amount of modification will be necessary; different partners often have minor changes in their requirements that do not match the default instances. Removing unneeded nodes from the schema also simplifies the schema and mapping and will reduce the overall size of the file.

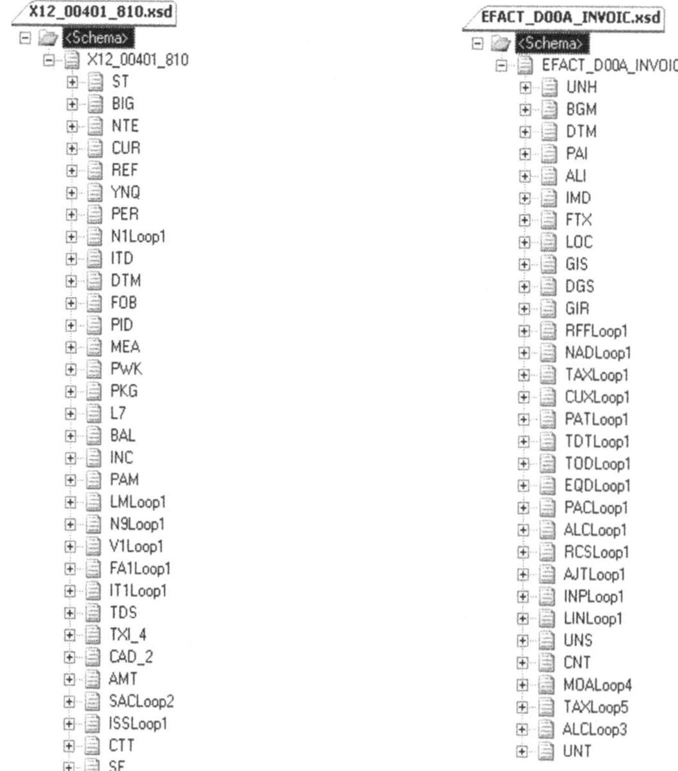

Figure 1-11. *Comparing X12 to EDIFACT*

The steps in Exercise 1-3 illustrate how to work with an EDI schema in Visual Studio.

Exercise 1-3. Modifying and Deploying a BizTalk EDI Schema

This exercise walks through the steps necessary to modify a BizTalk EDI 810 schema based on information obtained from an EDI implementation guide. It also demonstrates how to change an enumeration on a specific node. Once the schema is complete, it will be deployed to a specific BizTalk application:

1. Create a new Visual Studio project that will contain one schema for trading partner Company X.
   a. Add an existing schema to the project. Right-click the project and select Add ➤ Existing Item. Browse to c:\Program Files\Microsoft BizTalk Server 2006\ XSD_Schema\EDI\X12\00401. Add the file X12_00401_810.xsd (this is an X12 810 invoice) and click OK.
   b. Rename the schema to X12_00401_810_CompanyX.xsd. In solutions where multiple trading partners may be receiving the same type of document, adding the name of the trading partner to the filename will help eliminate confusion.

2. Open the schema so that it is visible in Visual Studio and can be edited. The schema will now be modified to more closely match the needs of this trading partner. The implementation guide is shown in Figures 1-12, 1-13, and 1-14. Remove all nodes from the schema that do not appear in the header, detail, or footer section of the implementation guide. Nodes can be removed by right-clicking the node or element in the schema and selecting Delete.

Seg ID	Name	Mandatory/Optional	Max Use
ISA	Interchange Control Header	M	1
GS	Functional Group Header	M	1
ST	Transaction Set Header	M	1
Loop ID – N1			200
N1	Name	O	1
N2	Additional Name Information	O	2
N3	Address Information	O	2
N4	Geographic Location	O	1

Figure 1-12. *Header in implementation guide*

■ **Note** The X12 ISA, GS, GE, and IEA segments never appear in a schema (UNA, UNB, UNG, and UNZ for EDIFACT). These fields are either configured via trading partner settings or are automatically set by the BizTalk EDI pipeline. When creating and modifying a BizTalk EDI schema, ignore these segments.

Seg ID	Name	Mandatory/Optional	Max Use
Loop ID – IT1			200000
IT1	Interchange Control Header	M	1
Loop ID – N1			200
N1	Name	O	1
N3	Address Information	O	2
N4	Geographic Location	O	1

Figure 1-13. *Detail segment in implementation guide*

Seg ID	Name	Mandatory/Optional	Max Use
CTT	Transaction Totals	O	1
SE	Transaction Set Trailer	M	1
GE	Functional Group Trailer	M	1
IEA	Interchange Control Trailer	M	1

Figure 1-14. *Footer (summary) segment in implementation guide*

The final schema in Visual Studio should look like that shown in Figure 1-15.

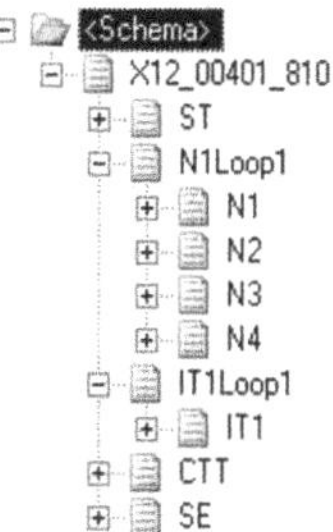

Figure 1-15. *Modified 810 invoice schema based on implementation guide*

3. This step illustrates how to change the values in an enumeration. Often additional values will need to be added to support a trading partner. To illustrate this, expand the N1Loop1 loop, and click N101. This is an identifier code and has an associated list of valid enumerations.

    a. In the properties for N101, click the ellipsis next to Enumeration, as shown in Figure 1-16.

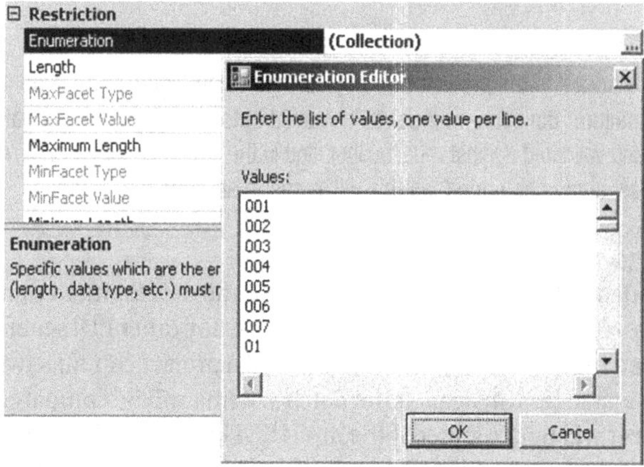

Figure 1-16. *Enumeration window*

    b. In the window that opens, add an additional value (or remove a value). Only those values that are available in this window will be allowed when validating the data against this schema.

4. Set the schema to deploy to a specific project and set a reference to a strong name key.

    a. Right-click the project and select Properties.

    b. Expand Configuration Properties and click Deployment.

    c. In the Application Name property, enter EDI.Demonstration.Chapter1.

    d. Expand Common Properties and click Assembly. Scroll down and click the Assembly Key File property and browse to a strong name key. One has been created in C:\Apress.Integration\Chapter 1 and is called Apress.Integration.Chapter1.snk.

5. Build and deploy the project by right-clicking the project and selecting Deploy.

6. Once the schema has been deployed, it will be shown in the BizTalk Administration Console under the EDI. Demonstration.Chapter1 application. Click Schemas to view all schemas that are part of the application, as shown in Figure 1-17.

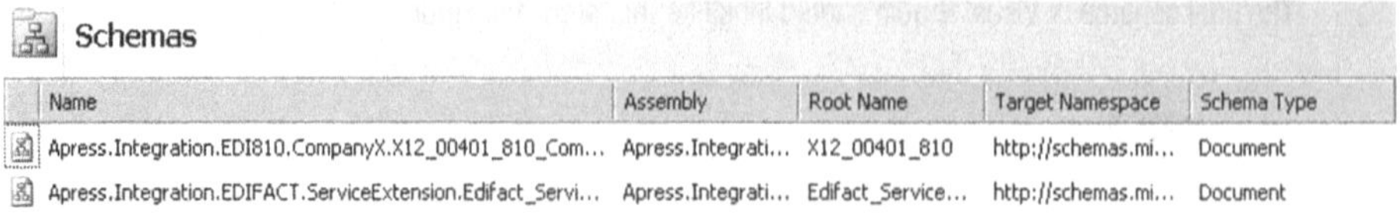

Schemas

Name	Assembly	Root Name	Target Namespace	Schema Type
Apress.Integration.EDI810.CompanyX.X12_00401_810_Com...	Apress.Integrati...	X12_00401_810	http://schemas.mi...	Document
Apress.Integration.EDIFACT.ServiceExtension.Edifact_Servi...	Apress.Integrati...	Edifact_Service...	http://schemas.mi...	Document

Figure 1-17. *Schema list in the BizTalk administration console*

Batch Schemas

The primary purpose of the EDI batch schemas for X12 and EDIFACT is that they are to be used when validating EDI document instances during schema development. For instance, if a full EDI instance exists, with the header and footer information included, it will not validate directly against a schema of the same type; the X12 and EDIFACT schemas do not support the header and footer segments. However, validating the same document against the batch schema, which is associated with the EDI schema of the same type as the document, will allow the header and footer nodes to be present in the input instance.

Note The batch schema must be added to the project, but only during design time. Trying to deploy a project that contains this project will end in failure; the schema must be removed before deployment. For validation, both the batch schema and the schema being validated against must be included in the project. Also note that no nonschema files, such as orchestration (.odx) files, should be added, as this will result in an error.

The batch schema is intended to be added to a project during the development phase to ease validation. When a document is validated against the batch schema, any other EDI schema that is in the same project will be included in the validation. For instance, if a project contains two schemas, an 810 and an 864, any EDI file instances run against the batch schema will be compared against both the 810 and the 864. An error will be generated if the input EDI instance fails validation against any of the schemas within the project. The EDIFACT batch schema is shown in Figure 1-18. A full demonstration of using a batch schema for instance validation is outlined in Exercise 1-6, in the "Validation and Generation of EDI Documents" section, later in this chapter.

```
<?xml version="1.0" encoding="utf-16" ?>
- <xs:schema xmlns:b="http://schemas.microsoft.com/BizTalk/2003"
    xmlns="http://schemas.microsoft.com/Edi/tet" targetNamespace="http://schemas.microsoft.com/Edi/tet"
    xmlns:xs="http://www.w3.org/2001/XMLSchema">
  - <xs:annotation>
    - <xs:appinfo>
        <schemaEditorExtension:schemaInfo namespaceAlias="btsedi"
          extensionClass="Microsoft.BizTalk.Edi.SchemaEditorExtension.EdiSchemaExtension"
          standardName="EDI"
          xmlns:schemaEditorExtension="http://schemas.microsoft.com/BizTalk/2003/SchemaEditorExtensions" />
        <b:schemaInfo standard="EDI" root_reference="EdifactInterchangeXml"
          xmlns:b="http://schemas.microsoft.com/BizTalk/2003" />
      </xs:appinfo>
    </xs:annotation>
    <xs:element name="EdifactInterchangeXml" type="xs:anyType" />
  </xs:schema>
```

Figure 1-18. *The EDIFACT batch schema*

Service Schema Extensions

The service schemas contain those elements within the EDIFACT and X12 schemas that can have additional enumerations specified. Occasionally it may be necessary to add additional enumerations to support trading partner requirements. Trading partner configuration is covered in great detail in the next chapter, but while discussing schemas it is important to understand that several of the header, context, and footer segments are set as EDI properties on the BizTalk party, and these values are added on during document processing in the EDI send pipeline. The values for a number of these fields are controlled by the service schemas and are never part of the transaction set schema. Exercise 1-4 demonstrates how to work with the service extension schema and illustrates its role in party configuration.

Exercise 1-4. Modifying and Deploying a Service Extension Schema

The steps in this exercise demonstrate how to add additional options in the drop-down fields for several elements in a service schema. This exercise works with an EDIFACT service schema and demonstrates how to add a new value to the UNB2.2 element in the trading partner EDI properties:

1. Ensure that the BizTalk Administration Console is closed. The values in the drop-down will only be refreshed when the Administration Console is first opened.
2. Open Visual Studio to create a new project that will contain the modified service schema and will allow the schema to be easily deployed. Add the EDIFACT service schema to the project. Right-click the project and select Add ➤ Existing Item. Browse to c:\Program Files\Microsoft BizTalk Server 2006\XSD_Schema\EDI. Add the file Edifact_ServiceSchemaExtension.xsd and click OK. Ensure that the project has a strong name key associated with it so that it can be deployed.
3. Open the schema in Visual Studio. There are two elements present that contain enumerations. They are UNB2.2 and UNB3.2. Add an additional value to the enumeration of UNB2.2:
    a. Right-click UNB2.2 and select Properties.
    b. In the Properties window, find the Enumeration property and click the ellipsis next to the (Collection) value.
    c. In the window that opens, enter the value DEMO. There will already be a value SGG. Make sure that the values are on different lines, as shown in Figure 1-19. Additional values can be entered.

Figure 1-19. *Property enumeration values*

    d. Click OK.

4. Deploy the schema by right-clicking the project and selecting Deploy. This will make the new enumerations available, in addition to the default service schema that is part of the BizTalk EDI engine.

5. Open BizTalk Administration Console and click the Parties folder. The new enumeration(s) will be available both on the global EDI properties and all individual parties.

   a. Right-click the Parties folder and select EDI Global Parties.

   b. Click the UNB Segment Definition.

   c. View the list of enumerations in the drop-down next to UNB2.2. The new enumerations will appear as shown in Figure 1-20.

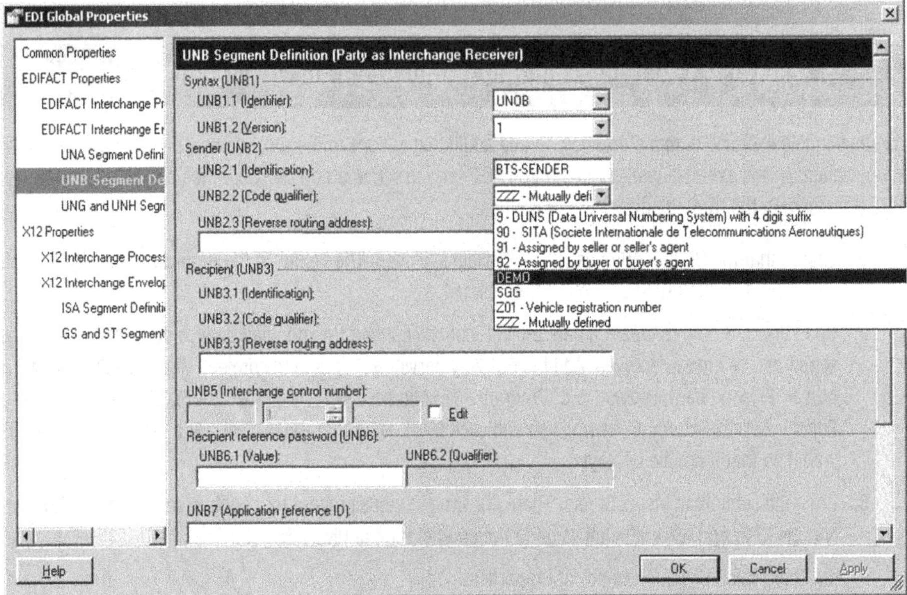

Figure 1-20. *EDI Global Properties dialog with modified UNB2.2 enumerations*

Promoting Fields

The promotion of properties on a schema allows the data within the promoted field to be accessible to external components, such as send ports and orchestrations. Promotion comes in two flavors: *distinguished* and *property*. Distinguished fields are those that are available within a certain context, such as an expression shape within an orchestration, and are accessible for determining conditional flow, much like properties on an object. Distinguished fields are not available on send ports and cannot be used for document routing on the MessageBox. A property field is one that is accessible by all BizTalk components and can be used for routing within the MessageBox and within orchestrations.

There is extra overhead with property fields, as they require a property schema (which can be automatically generated); distinguished fields do not require any additional schema. The property schema allows fields to be accessible to external components and is deployed along with the standard EDI schema. To illustrate this, work through the steps in Exercise 1-5 and then deploy the project (this includes the 810 schema and the property field). Once the schemas have been deployed, they will be accessible as a filter on a send port, as shown in Figure 1-21.

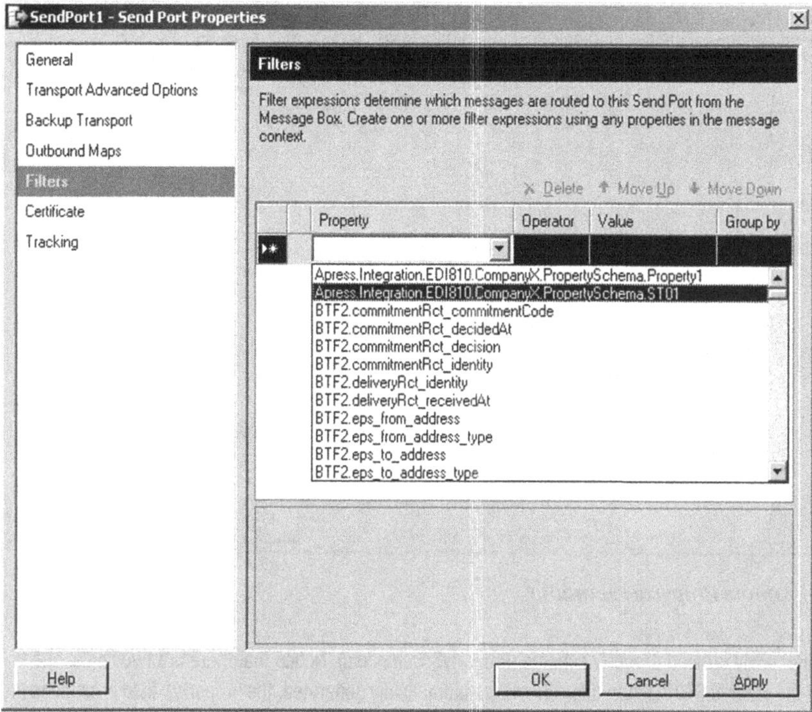

Figure 1-21. *Send port filter showing promoted property as an option*

Exercise 1-5. Promoting Properties

This exercise illustrates how to promote both distinguished and property fields in a schema:

1. In Visual Studio, open the project created in Exercise 1-3.
2. In the schema editor, right-click the ST01 node and select Promote ➤ Quick Promotion. In the dialog box that asks whether to create a property schema, click OK. This will promote the field as a property field, create a property schema, and make the field available to external components once it has been deployed. Figure 1-22 shows a schema with the ST01 field promoted.

Figure 1-22. *Promoted property on a schema*

3. Right-click the ST01 field again and select Promote ➤ Show Promotions. There are two tabs: Distinguished Fields and Property Fields. The Property Fields tab will show the ST01 field that was just promoted.
4. Add a distinguished field by clicking the Distinguished Field tab, selecting ST02, and clicking Add. This would make the ST02 field available in an orchestration (if one is used). Figure 1-23 shows what the promotion of this field looks like. Click OK when complete.

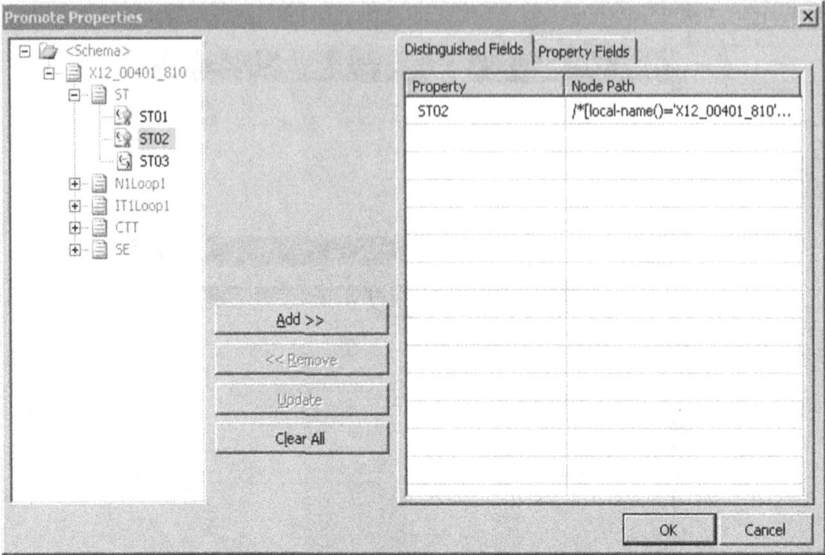

Figure 1-23. *Promote Properties window*

5. Double-click the newly created property schema (PropertySchema.xsd). Notice that there are two fields: one is Property1 and the other is ST01. When this schema is automatically generated, the Property1 field is included (it is always included when creating a schema via Quick Promotion). It can be removed by right-clicking and selecting Delete.

■ **Note** This exercise uses ST01 for demonstration purposes. By default, this field is already promoted in the EDI engine and is available without setting the field as a promoted property on the schema.

Validation and Generation of EDI Documents

Once a schema has been created, it will always be necessary to validate individual EDI instances, ensuring that the schema and document instances match requirements for the trading partner. It may even be helpful to generate an instance of the EDI document in its native flat file format. There are a variety of items that a schema can validate, including the following:

- **Existence of all expected nodes (complete hierarchy)**: Schema validation can ensure that the segments are in the correct order, that all expected segments exist, and that all of the mandatory data elements within a segment are present.
- **Proper formatting and naming**: Ensuring that all of the segments are named properly, that they have the expected data element separators, and that the segment terminators are correct are part of validation.
- **Content type and length**: The data within each data element in a segment is controlled by the schema. Items such as the expected length and whether the data is in the correct format (int vs. string) can be validated.

Throughout the development and test phases of any EDI implementation, file instances need to be validated. The steps shown in Exercise 1-6 outline the simplest way to validate a document. Once mapping becomes part of the picture, more complex document validation techniques may need to be incorporated (this is explained in Chapter 5).

Exercise 1-6. Validating an EDI Instance Against a Schema

The following steps introduce the validation of an instance of an EDI document with the header and footer segments included:

1. In Visual Studio, open the project created in Exercise 1-3.
2. Adding the batch schema to this project will allow full EDI documents, with header and footer segments, to be validated and created. To add this schema, take these steps:
   a. Right-click the project and select Add ➤ Existing Items. Browse to the directory c:\Program Files\Microsoft BizTalk Server 2006\XSD_Schema\EDI.
   b. Select the schema X12_BatchSchema.xsd and click OK.
3. This exercise demonstrates an invalid instance first. Right-click the newly added schema and select Properties. Point the Input Instance Filename property to the Invalid-Input.txt file in the directory C:\Apress.Integration\Chapter 1\Test Documents. The content of this file is shown in Listing 1-1. Figure 1-24 shows the appropriate settings for the different properties.

Listing 1-1. *Invalid EDI Instance*

```
ISA*00*            *00*            *01*COMPX789         *ZZ*APRESS1234
*070607*1555*U*00401*000000025*0*T*>~
GS*IN*COMPX789*APRESS1234*20070607*1555*25*X*004010~
ST*810*0025~
N1*SF*COMPANY X~
N3*P.O. BOX 12345~
N4*ANYTOWN*OH*45678~
IT1*1*0.528*TS*1.13**VP*1AGHA1223221~
REF*INVALID
CTT*1~
SE*100*0025~
GE*1*25~
IEA*1*000000025~
```

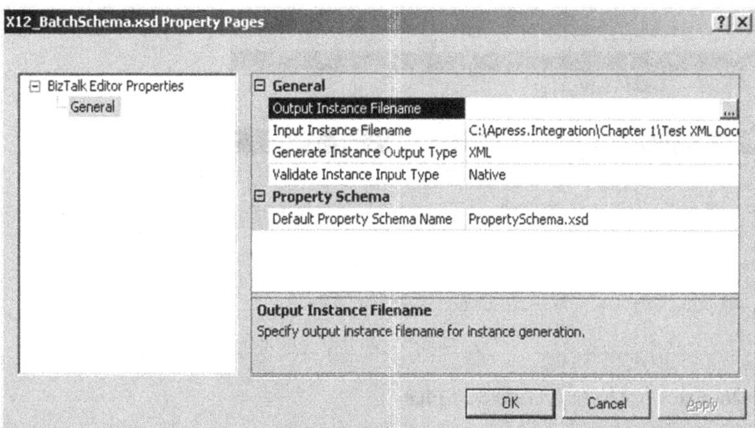

Figure 1-24. *Setting properties on the batch schema for validation*

4. Right-click the batch schema in Visual Studio and select Validate Instance.
5. In the EDI Instance Properties window (shown in Figure 1-25), accept all of the defaults and click OK. The EDI Instance Properties window allows different formats of the EDI document to be validated. For instance, if the document contains all of the segments, but their line end separator is a > instead of a line feed (CR LF), the value can be set in this window.

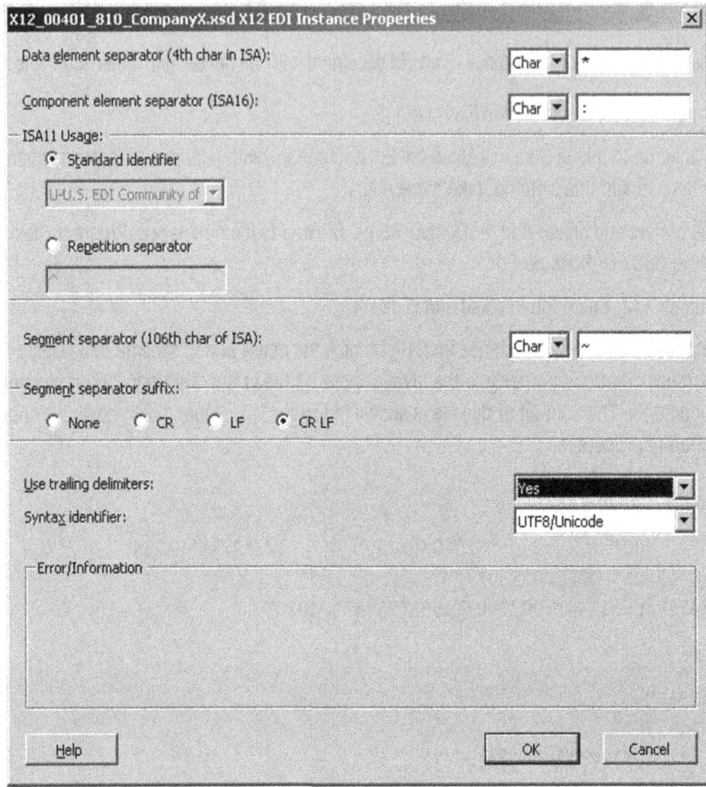

Figure 1-25. *EDI Instance Properties window*

A number of errors will be generated, as shown in Figure 1-26. These errors are as follows:

- **"Number of included segments do not match"**: This refers to the value in SE01, which is 100. The value should be an accurate count of all of the detail lines, which in this case is 7.

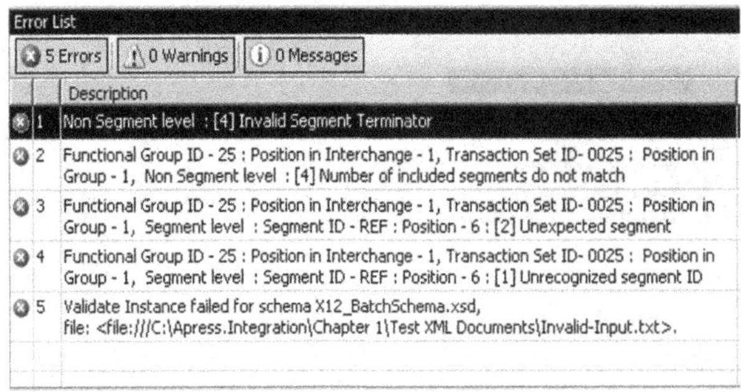

Figure 1-26. *Error list from invalid instance*

- **"Unexpected segment"**: The REF node is not included in the schema and is not part of the EDI implementation guide for this trading partner. The node should not exist in the sample EDI instance.

There are several other errors shown in this document, but they overlap those already discussed. Once the items in the previous two exceptions are fixed, the other errors will disappear.

6. Now validate a valid instance of the same EDI document. Right-click the batch schema and select Properties. This time set the input filename to the Valid-Input.txt file in the directory C:\Apress.Integration\Chapter 1\Test Documents. The content of this file is shown in Listing 1-2. The REF segment that caused the errors has been removed.

Listing 1-2. *Valid Version of the EDI Instance*

```
ISA*00*          *00*          *01*COMPX789       *ZZ*APRESS1234
*070607*1555*U*00401*000000025*0*T*>~
GS*IN*COMPX789*APRESS1234*20070607*1555*25*X*004010~
ST*810*0025~
N1*SF*COMPANY X~
N3*P.O. BOX 12345~
N4*ANYTOWN*OH*45678~
IT1*1*0.528*TS*1.13**VP*1AGHA1223221~
CTT*1~
SE*7*0025~
GE*1*25~
IEA*1*000000025~
```

The previous exercise demonstrates the validation of an instance of an EDI document. It is also possible to generate a new file instance, using the same basic approach, as shown in Exercise 1-7. Generating a document can be useful when no existing version of the EDI document exists in its native format (text file) or when trying to generate test data for development purposes.

Exercise 1-7. Generating an EDI Instance

It is useful to be able to create sample instances of an EDI document from a schema, and this can be easily accomplished by using the batch schema, as shown in these steps:

1. In Visual Studio, open the project created in Exercise 1-6.
2. Right-click the batch schema and select Properties.
3. Set the Output Instance File Name to a path on the local machine, and give the output file a name (such as output.txt).
4. Set the Generate Instance Output Type to Native.
5. Click OK to save the settings.
6. Right-click the batch schema again and select Generate Instance. This will create a dummy instance of the schema in EDI format.

Final Discussion

As the foundation to all BizTalk implementations, development of the schema can be a complex and time-consuming process. However, using the EDI implementation guide for a trading partner and understanding how to transfer the content of that guide to the development of an EDI schema will eliminate much of the complexity. Using property promotion to make fields in the schema available to external BizTalk components, such as ports and orchestrations, can aid in the simplification of the solution as a whole. Once the schema is fully defined, knowing how to validate existing EDI documents will ensure that the schema developed will match the requirements of the trading partner.

With an understanding of EDI schemas and how to work with them in BizTalk Server 2006 R2, the next step is to work through the configuration of the trading partner. Schema development and trading partner configuration are often intermixed since an EDI document consists of header, detail, and footer segments, many of which are defined in the trading partner properties (rather than the schema). Some of these segments are present in the schemas, some are present in the trading partner configuration, and some cross over between the two. Without knowledge of trading partner configuration, an EDI schema is incomplete, and without knowledge of EDI schemas, trading partner configuration cannot be completed.

CHAPTER 2

Trading Partner Configuration

Configuring trading partners in BizTalk Server 2006 R2 can be a complex endeavor, and the intent of this chapter is to approach this configuration in a systematic way, outlining the techniques necessary for EDI implementations. This chapter introduces the steps needed for the configuration of a *party* (the BizTalk equivalent of the trading partner), which consist of setting the EDI header and other context information and setting up any type of acknowledgments that may need to be sent or are expected to be received. It also introduces basic concepts around document delivery and how this delivery corresponds with trading partner configuration and creation of the EDI document. The chapter closes with a short discussion on how to validate the trading partner settings to ensure that an EDI document is wrapped with the proper header and footer data.

The following are the primary steps in trading partner configuration:

- **Creating trading partners:** EDI documents are resolved to BizTalk parties, which represent a relationship that is set up between BizTalk and a trading partner. There is generally one party set up for every trading partner relationship that exists (i.e., one party for each partner). Parties contain all of the information that is specific about doing business with a trading partner, including how the header and other context information will appear in an EDI document and what acknowledgments will be sent (if any).
- **Configuring parties as "Trading Partner As Receiver" and configuring acknowledgments:** A Trading Partner As Receiver is a trading partner that receives an EDI document from BizTalk Server. All of the header and context settings must be set appropriately for party resolution and document routing to succeed.
- **Configuring parties as "Trading Partner As Sender" and configuring acknowledgments:** If a trading partner is the initiator of a document, sending the EDI instance to the BizTalk Server that contains the configured parties, it is known as a *sender*. The party must have its header and context information configured appropriately for party resolution and document routing, and all needed acknowledgments must be set up.
- **Configuring AS2 properties:** When EDI documents are delivered using the AS2 protocol (HTTP), they are wrapped in an envelope. This envelope contains information describing the data within it, how the data is encrypted, and what certificates to use to accept and read the data. After reading the document and interpreting the information in the envelope, the enclosed EDI document is extracted and dropped on the MessageBox when BizTalk acts as the receiver of an EDI document sent via AS2. When BizTalk acts as the sender of an EDI document over AS2, it wraps the EDI document and encrypts it prior to shipping to the trading partner.

Note AS2 is implemented in BizTalk Server 2006 R2 so that it uses the traditional HTTP adapter to transmit documents. However, there are a number of properties related to this transmission that are essential to the delivery of the document but cannot be set on the standard HTTP adapter. Therefore, these properties have been moved to the party. Because much of the trading partner configuration consists of properties specific to how the document is delivered, setting up party properties for AS2 requires that an adapter be set up and that all of the certificates be made available. To truly understand AS2, it will be necessary to work through the AS2 delivery exercises outlined in Chapter 5. This chapter touches on AS2 configuration, but deals mainly with standard EDI transmissions.

- **Validating settings:** Once a trading partner has been configured, the settings should be validated by creating a sample EDI instance and validating that the header, context, and footer information matches expectations (as defined in an EDI implementation guide, or based on requirements gathered from the trading partner). This can be done by generating a sample instance of the document and comparing it against a known instance or documented requirements.

Configuration Overview

Trading partners are set up and configured in BizTalk Server 2006 R2 as parties. As EDI documents are delivered to BizTalk, they pass through the receive pipeline (EDIReceive or AS2EDIReceive) where they are validated and their party is resolved. This resolution is based on contextual information—information within the envelope or header data—that matches settings that have been set for the party. When documents are sent out of BizTalk, key data is added in the outgoing pipeline based on how the party to which the document resolves has been configured.

There are two types of configurations available on a BizTalk party through the BizTalk Administration Console: EDI and AS2. EDI documents are resolved primarily using the trading partner IDs (basically, the UNB2 and UNB3 for EDIFACT documents and ISA05 through ISA08 for X12 documents), whereas AS2 transmissions use the AS2-To and AS2-From properties (for the purposes of EDI, AS2 is an envelope that contains a traditional EDI document, such as that shown in Figure 2-1). Trading partners can be configured as senders, receivers, or both.

```
HEADER /    ISA*00*      *00*      *ZZ*APRESS1234    *01*CA000CA      *070609*0947*U*00401*000000002*0*T*>~
CONTEXT   { GS*FA*APRESS1234*CA000CA*20070609*0947*2*X*004010~
            ST*997*0002~
DETAIL    { AK1*IN*25~
            AK9*A*1*1*1~
            SE*4*0002~
FOOTER /  { GE*1*2~
CONTEXT     IEA*1*000000002~
```

Figure 2-1. *Diagram of an EDI document (Functional Acknowledgment, 997)*

The flow of documents through BizTalk Server can be confusing, especially with the configuration of acknowledgments, as a single trading partner can be configured as both a sender and a receiver. The diagram shown in Figure 2-2 attempts to outline how BizTalk parties are configured for party resolution on documents flowing in and out of the system. It also shows how the *home party* is set up; this is the party that is configured as the default in the EDI global properties (the home party is rarely used in a BizTalk EDI configuration but is covered in this chapter to demonstrate its functionality). The exercises in this chapter follow the party configuration shown in this diagram.

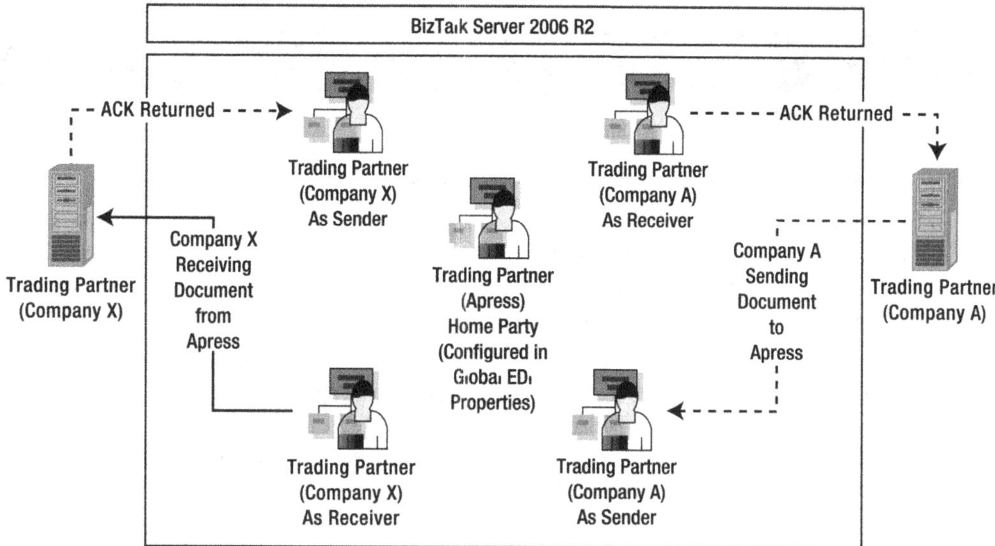

Figure 2-2. *Trading partner flow*

Acknowledgments are also introduced in this chapter, as they are configured through the party settings. EDI acknowledgments come in two varieties; *standards-based* and *business-level*. Standards-based acknowledgments are those that can be configured for a trading partner and are sent automatically when an EDI transmission is received. Business-level acknowledgments, such as the purchase order acknowledgment (also known as an X12 855 4010), are common EDI documents and require no special configuration, therefore, these will not be covered in any detail.

Standards-based acknowledgments are actual EDI documents that indicate that the document being delivered has been received and is compliant with the requirements of the trading partner. There are two types of standards-based acknowledgments that can be automatically generated by BizTalk 2006 R2: *functional acknowledgments* and *technical acknowledgments*. Functional and technical acknowledgment documents are handled like virtually any other EDI document in BizTalk, except that (1) they are automatically generated (if configured) by BizTalk Server 2006 R2, and (2) they are automatically correlated back to the trading partner that sent the initial document. Acknowledgments are sent using send ports, received using receive ports, and routed through the MessageBox like any other EDI document.

Note A trading partner (BizTalk party) must be configured as both a sender and a receiver when acknowledgments are part of the solution. Acknowledgments create Business Activity Monitoring (BAM) activities, and these activities are correlated such that an acknowledgment can be linked back to the original document that was sent.

To prepare a development environment to work through the exercises in this chapter, review the steps outlined in Exercise 2-1. The exercises in this chapter use the files located in C:\Apress.Integration\Chapter 2 and rely on the application, parties, and schemas being imported and deployed.

Exercise 2-1. Preparing the Environment

Use the following steps to prepare the environment on the local machine:

1. Make sure that the Chapter2 sample files have been extracted and placed on the C:\ drive.
2. Import the Chapter2.MSI file available in C:\Apress.Integration\Chapter 2\BizTalk Application. Open BizTalk Administration Console and right-click the Applications folder. Select Import ➤ Bindings. This will create the EDI.Demonstration.Chapter2 BizTalk application, all of the parties and party configurations, and all of the send and receive ports used in this chapter. Alternatively, the Chapter 2 binding file, located in the same directory, could be imported through the BizTalk Administration Console.
3. Open the solution contained in C:\Apress.Integration\Chapter 2 called Apress.Integration.EDI810.CompanyX.sln. This solution contains two files: a modified version of the X12 810 schema, X12_00401_810_CompanyX.xsd, tailored to Company X; and a reference to Microsoft.BizTalk.EDI.BaseArtifacts.dll, which contains all of the acknowledgment schemas that are generated by BizTalk.

■ **Note** For functional and technical acknowledgments to function properly, Microsoft.BizTalk.EDI.BaseArtifacts.dll must first be deployed. This can be added in to the BizTalk application through the BizTalk Administration Console, or it can be deployed in a Visual Studio project deployment. It is located in the root folder of the BizTalk Server program files (C:\Program Files\Microsoft BizTalk Server 2006).

---

4. Deploy the solution by right-clicking it in Visual Studio and selecting Deploy.

Additional files and folders used in this chapter include C:\Apress.Integration\Chapter 2\Test Documents, containing two sample instances of documents used in various exercises; and C:\Apress.Integration\Chapter 2\Drops, containing a number of input and output folders used by send and receive ports in various exercises.

Creating Trading Partners (BizTalk Parties)

The creation of trading partners usually begins with an examination of the EDI implementation guide for a given partner. The guide contains information about how to configure the sender or receiver ID, what the header and context information should be, and other specifics about the partner settings. Exercise 2-2 demonstrates how to create a party; later exercises in this chapter demonstrate the configuration of the party.

Exercise 2-2. Creating a Trading Partner

Follow these steps to create a trading partner (BizTalk party):

1. Open BizTalk Administration Console and right-click on the Parties folder. Select New ➤ Party.
2. Name the party appropriately. For this exercise, the trading partner will be named Company X.

3. The Aliases box is used primarily with parties configured for AS2 but can be set for non-AS2 transmissions. The properties consist of the primary party identifiers. For non-AS2 transactions, the EDI identifiers that are used are those that have been configured in the EDI properties. Use the following settings for the properties in this box:
   a. Set the Name (Organization) to the appropriate organization. In this case, set it to Mutually Defined. The value in Organization Name (Qualifier) will be automatically set, depending on what is selected in the Organization column.
   b. Set the last column (the Value property) to the trading partner ID. In this case, it is COMPX789. This value will be available from the trading partner and will be shown in the EDI implementation guide. The settings should correspond to the UNB2.1 and UNB2.2 (when it's a sender) or the UNB3.1 and UNB3.2 (when it's a receiver) segment fields for EDIFACT. For ISA, they will correspond to the equivalent entries in ISA05, ISA06, ISA07, and ISA08.
4. Click OK.

Some EDI trading partner configuration information can be set at a global level. The most appropriate use of these settings is for a home party. Generally, this would be the company where the BizTalk implementation was put into place. In cases where there is no default trading partner, or the BizTalk implementation is used solely to route messages between external trading partners, there is no reason to set the global properties. Exercise 2-3 outlines how to work with the global EDI settings.

Note Global EDI properties are used only when a document cannot be matched to a specific party that has been created. The global properties do not override what is set for individual parties. In true EDI implementations, there is little use for configuring the global properties as they relate to the different segments, unless there is only one trading partner that is being engaged with. The use of these properties will likely be revised in future BizTalk EDI functionality.

Exercise 2-3. Accessing the Global EDI Settings

This is a simple exercise demonstrating how to access the global EDI settings:

1. Open BizTalk Administration Console and right-click the Parties folder. Select EDI Global Properties.
2. Set the default settings as appropriate. For a home party, instead of creating a separate party as shown in Exercise 2-2, the values can be set at this level. Whichever values are set will be used when a document is received and cannot match the values set in any individual party. An example of setting these properties is shown in Figure 2-3.

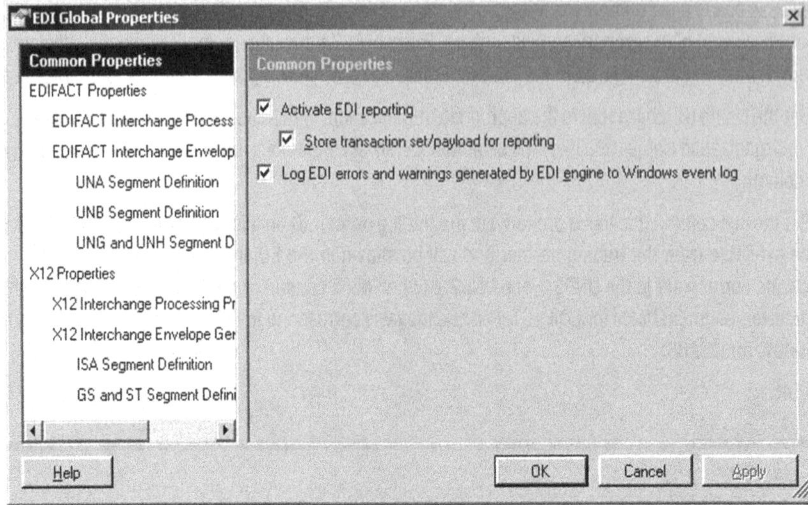

Figure 2-3. *EDI global properties*

Configuring a Trading Partner As Sender

A trading partner is considered a *sender* when it sends a document to BizTalk Server. The document can be any type of EDI instance, including an acknowledgment. When BizTalk receives a document from an external source, the source would be configured as a BizTalk party set up to be a Trading Partner As Sender. Any acknowledgments that would be sent back to this trading partner would require that the partner be configured as a Trading Partner As Receiver. Exercise 2-4 describes the steps necessary to configure a trading partner as a sender and to deliver acknowledgments back to the partner. Figure 2-4 illustrates the flow of a Trading Partner As Sender.

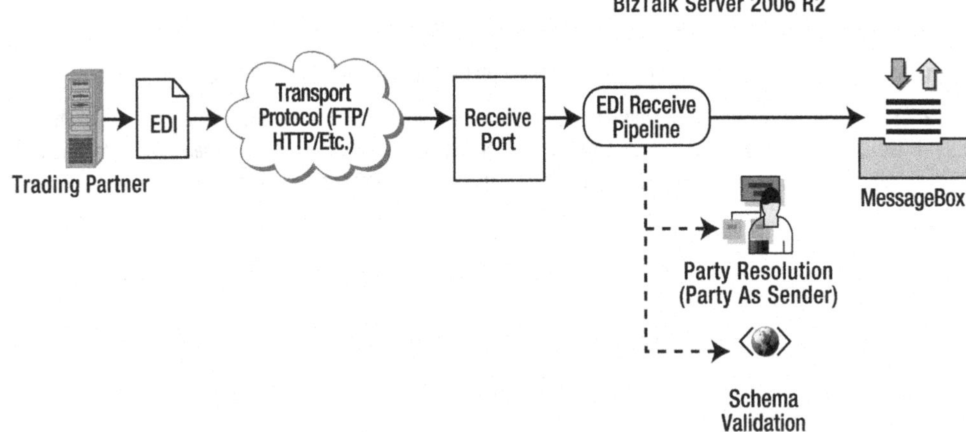

Figure 2-4. *Trading Partner As Sender*

EDI Receive Pipeline Flow

The flow of the EDI receive pipeline will now be outlined, as this is where party resolution occurs, providing insight into how a document travels from the receive port to the MessageBox. The steps in the pipeline are as follows:

1. **Examine document type**: The pipeline first determines whether the incoming document is EDIFACT or X12 (or neither) and inspects the character sets. Certain properties within the document are promoted.
2. **Resolve party**: The document is then inspected to determine which party to resolve against. The steps for resolution are executed in the following order:
   c. **Check IDs**: The pipeline first inspects the header values (ISA05-08, or UNB2 and UNB3 segments) to see if any parties have been configured with matching values. If so, the party is resolved.
   d. **Global EDI properties**: Next, if the pipeline could not be routed based on an ID (no parties match the values in the document), it will use the global EDI properties.
3. **Schema resolution and validation**: The document is now validated against the schemas that are available. If the schema cannot be resolved, or the document does not pass validation, the document will be suspended.
4. **Create acknowledgment**: If the party has been configured to send an acknowledgment, the pipeline will generate an acknowledgment document and drop it on the MessageBox (a send port must be configured separately to deliver this acknowledgment back to the party).

Note The flow of the AS2 EDI pipeline is similar to the steps described here but resolves the party in a slightly different way, looking at what is configured in the AS2-To and AS2-From properties for the trading partner instead of the ISA/UNB segments. The AS2 pipeline is outlined in detail in Chapter 5.

Configuring Acknowledgments (Trading Partner As Sender)

Once a trading partner has been configured to receive EDI documents, the next step is to determine the type(s) of acknowledgments that need to be returned to the party that sent the EDI document. Recall that there are two types of acknowledgments that indicate successful receipt of an EDI transmission: technical and functional. Acknowledgment documents are treated as any other EDI document, except that they can be configured to be automatically generated. The trigger to create these documents is automatic, but the delivery of the documents to a specific location requires the same components to be in place as other types of documents, namely, send ports and pipelines. Figure 2-5 illustrates the flow of an acknowledgment for a trading partner configured as a sender, while Exercise 2-4 demonstrates how to configure this type of acknowledgment.

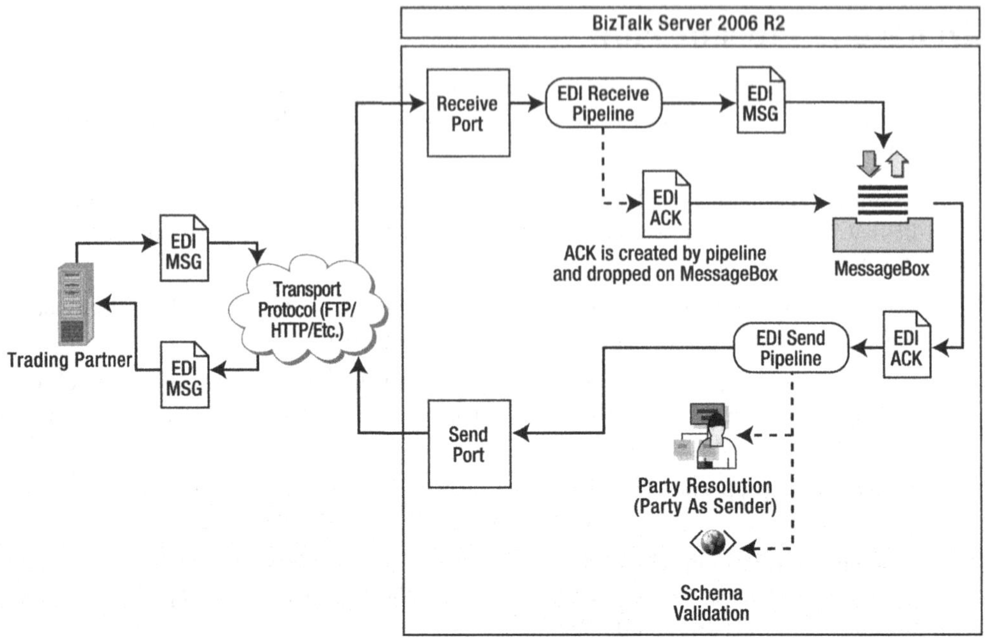

Figure 2-5. *Trading Partner As Sender with acknowledgment*

Exercise 2-4. Configuring Acknowledgments—Trading Partner As Sender

This exercise demonstrates the creation and configuration of a Trading Partner As Sender. The full solution will demonstrate the flow of the EDI document from this trading partner through BizTalk. The exercise also outlines how to configure functional and technical acknowledgments, and how to deliver these documents back to the trading partner (which then becomes a Trading Partner As Receiver). Figure 2-6 illustrates the components used in this exercise.

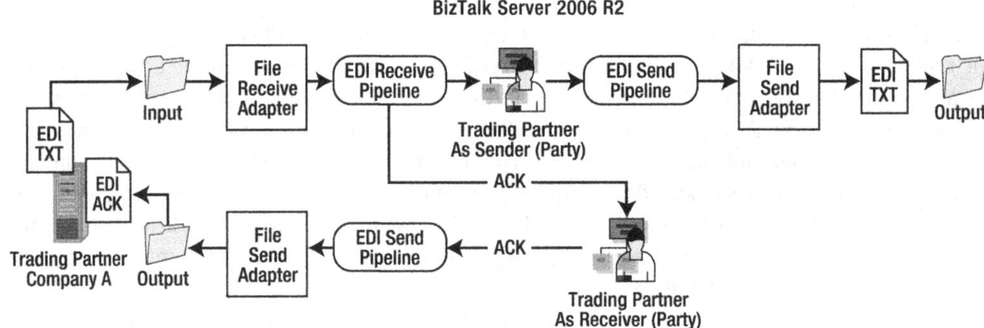

Figure 2-6. *Overview of exercise components*

1. In BizTalk Administration Console, right-click the Parties folder and select New ➤ Party. Note that these properties are not used for standard EDI processing, only for AS2. However, it helps to define these values for ease of reference for an administrator (for organization). Configure the properties as follows:

   a. Set the name of the trading partner as Company A.

   b. In the Name column, under Organization, select D-U-N-S (Dun & Bradstreet).

   c. The Organization Name property in the Qualifier column should be set to 1.
   d. Set the Value property for Company A as CA000CA. This is an identifier used to identify this trading partner for this example.

2. Set up the receiver trading partner (home party). In this exercise, this will use the global EDI settings that have been set to Apress in Exercise 2-3. This represents the party that will be receiving the EDI documents from Company A, which, in this case, is BizTalk Server.
3. Right-click the party Company A created in the first step and select EDI Properties. This party will be configured to be a Trading Partner As Sender. Click the X12 Interchange Processing Properties and set the properties as shown in the following set of steps (the final outcome is shown in Figure 2-7). Generally, all of this information will be available from a trading partner in the EDI implementation guide:
   a. ISA01–ISA04: Set these values to the default 00 – No Information Present setting.
   b. ISA05: Set this to 01.
   c. ISA06: This value identifies the current party; set it to CA000CA.
   d. ISA07: Set this to ZZ. This must match the value of the company that is set up as the receiver; again, this would typically be in the implementation guide.
   e. ISA08: Set this to APRESS1234, which matches the trading partner ID for Apress, configured in the global EDI properties.
   f. Uncheck all of the boxes in the configuration window. This will simplify testing the EDI documents. These settings allow BizTalk to validate whether the document has already been received and processed based on the identifiers in the various incoming fields in the segments.
   g. Set the target namespace to match the schema for the trading partner. In this case it should be set to http://schemas.microsoft.com/BizTalk/EDI/X12/2006. If incoming documents have a target namespace different than the default, the following two fields will be used to resolve the document:
      i. Set GS02 to CA000CA.
      ii. Set ST01 to 810-Invoice. This represents the expected document type that will be delivered.

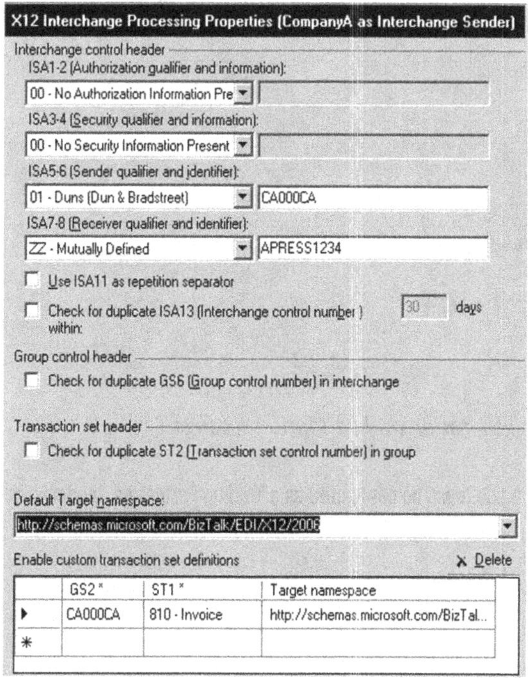

Figure 2-7. *X12 interchange processing properties*

4. Click the ACK Generation and Validation Settings tab. Set the properties on this screen as follows (any properties not listed can remain as their default value (the final outcome is shown in Figure 2-8):

   a. Uncheck Route ACK to Send Pipeline on Request-Response Receive Port. This exercise demonstrates sending the acknowledgment out via a one-way send port.

   b. Check Generate TA1. This is a technical acknowledgment and will be sent in parallel with the functional acknowledgment.

   c. Check the box next to Do Not Batch TA1.

■ **Note** Technical acknowledgments are generally not used in most EDI implementations. These acknowledgments are outlined in this exercise only to demonstrate how BizTalk uses them.

---

   d. Check Generate 997. This is the functional acknowledgment.

   e. Check Do Not Batch 997.

   f. Check EDI Type.

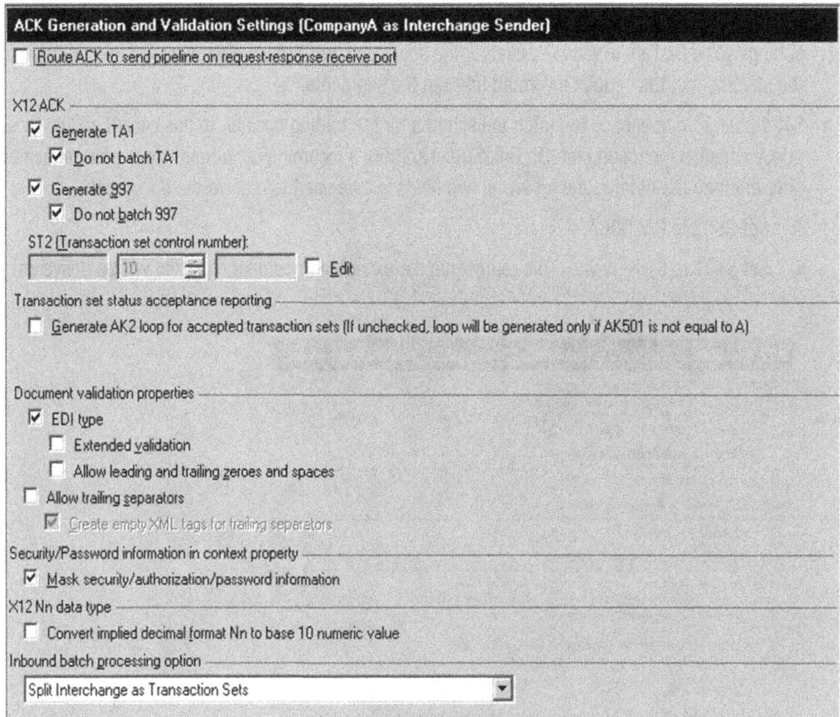

Figure 2-8. *Acknowledgment generation and validation settings*

5. Click OK. This will save Company A and it will be configured as a Trading Partner As Sender, with technical and functional acknowledgments.

6. This step deals with creating a receive port and receive location that will simulate receiving the document from Company A (the trading partner that is sending the document). Generally, EDI transmissions will be over FTP or HTTP (AS2), but for this exercise they will be delivered via a file adapter. Begin by expanding the EDI.Demonstration.Chapter2 BizTalk application (if this does not exist, it will need to be created), right-click Receive Ports and select New ➤ One-Way Receive Port. Set the properties of the port as follows:
   a. Name the port EDI.Demonstration.Example.TradingPartnerAsSender.FILE.810.
   b. Click the Receive Locations tab and create a file receive location named TradingPartnerAsSender, pointed to C:\Apress.Integration\Chapter 2\Drops\Incoming - Trading Partner As Sender - EDI.
   c. Set the Receive Pipeline property to EDIReceive.
7. This step creates a send port that simulates the processing of the document once it has arrived in BizTalk Server. All documents that arrive on the MessageBox must have a subscriber or else they will fail. In this case, the send port is being created solely for purposes of this exercise and simply ensures that the incoming document is processed without throwing an error. In the same BizTalk application, right-click Send Ports and select New ➤ Static One-Way Send Port and set the properties of the port as follows:
   a. Name the send port EDI.Demonstration.Example.TradingPartnerAsSender.FILE.810.
   b. Set the send port to be a file transport, writing documents to C:\Apress.Integration\Chapter 2\Drops\Outgoing - Trading Partner As Sender - EDI\.
   c. Set the send pipeline to EDISend.
   d. Click the Filter tab and set the filter as BTS.ReceivePortName == EDI.Demonstration.Example.TradingPartnerAsSender.FILE.810. This will cause the send port to subscribe to all documents that arrive on the specified receive port.
   e. Click OK to save the settings.
8. The next step is to create the send port that will send acknowledgments. Create a new send port with the following properties:
   a. Name the port EDI.Demonstration.Example.TradingPartnerAsSender.FILE.ACK.
   b. Set it as a file transport with the output document sent to C:\Apress.Integration\Chapter 2\Drops\Outgoing - Trading Partner As Sender - ACK\.
   c. For now, leave the send pipeline as PassThruTransmit. This will write the acknowledgments in XML, without the header and footer information present in an EDI document, and will help demonstrate the party settings. It will be changed to EDISend in a later step.
   d. The Filters tab is the key to getting the send port to subscribe to acknowledgments. All acknowledgments are written to the MessageBox. The send port can subscribe to the documents in a variety of ways. In this exercise, the port will be set up to subscribe to the message type associated with the functional and technical acknowledgments. Click the Filters tab and set the following properties (shown in Figure 2-9).
      i. Set the first filter to subscribe to functional acknowledgments by setting the BTS.MessageType == http://schemas.microsoft.com/Edi/X12#X12_997_Root.
      ii. Set the second filter to subscribe to technical acknowledgments by setting the BTS.MessageType == http://schemas.microsoft.com/Edi/X12#X12_TA1_Root.

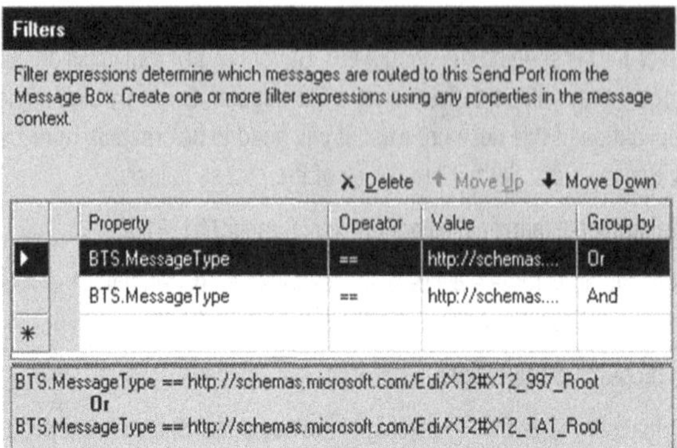

Figure 2-9. *Acknowledgment send port filter settings*

e. Click OK to save the settings.

9. Test that all of the settings thus far are correct. Enlist and start all of the send and receive ports created in the exercise. Once they are started, work through the testing process by doing the following:

   a. Copy the document named TradingPartnerAsSender-Input.txt located in C:\Apress.Integration\Chapter 2\Test Documents and paste it in the folder being monitored by the receive location - C:\Apress.Integration\Chapter 2\Drops\Incoming - Trading Partner as Sender - EDI.

   b. Validate that the document was picked up from the folder by BizTalk. Check the Windows Event Viewer for any errors that may have occurred.

   c. Check for the existence of the output 810 file in C:\Apress.Integration\Chapter 2\Drops\Outgoing - Trading Partner as Sender - EDI.

   d. Check that both of the acknowledgments were written out to the acknowledgment folder in C:\Apress.Integration\Chapter 2\Drops\Outgoing - Trading Partner as Sender – ACK. The functional acknowledgment should appear as shown in Figure 2-10.

```
- <ns0:X12_997_Root IsGeneratedAck="true" InterchangeActivityId="8d466ccab5884680aac6f711b04a476e"
    xmlns:ns0="http://schemas.microsoft.com/Edi/X12">
  - <ns0:ST>
      <ST01>997</ST01>
      <ST02>0022</ST02>
    </ns0:ST>
  - <AK1>
      <AK101>IN</AK101>
      <AK102>25</AK102>
    </AK1>
  - <AK9>
      <AK901>A</AK901>
      <AK902>1</AK902>
      <AK903>1</AK903>
      <AK904>1</AK904>
    </AK9>
  - <ns0:SE>
      <SE01>4</SE01>
      <SE02>0022</SE02>
    </ns0:SE>
  </ns0:X12_997_Root>
```

Figure 2-10. *Functional acknowledgment in XML format*

10. The final step is to set up the trading partner to receive the acknowledgments in EDI format. This is done by configuring the Trading Partner As Receiver properties. Since acknowledgments are exactly like any other EDI document, they get their header and footer segments from what is configured in the party settings.

    a. Open the EDI Properties of the Company A party in BizTalk Administration Console.

    b. Click the ISA Segment Definition tab and set properties as shown in Figure 2-11. For full details about configuring a Trading Partner As Receiver, see Exercise 2-5 in the next section.

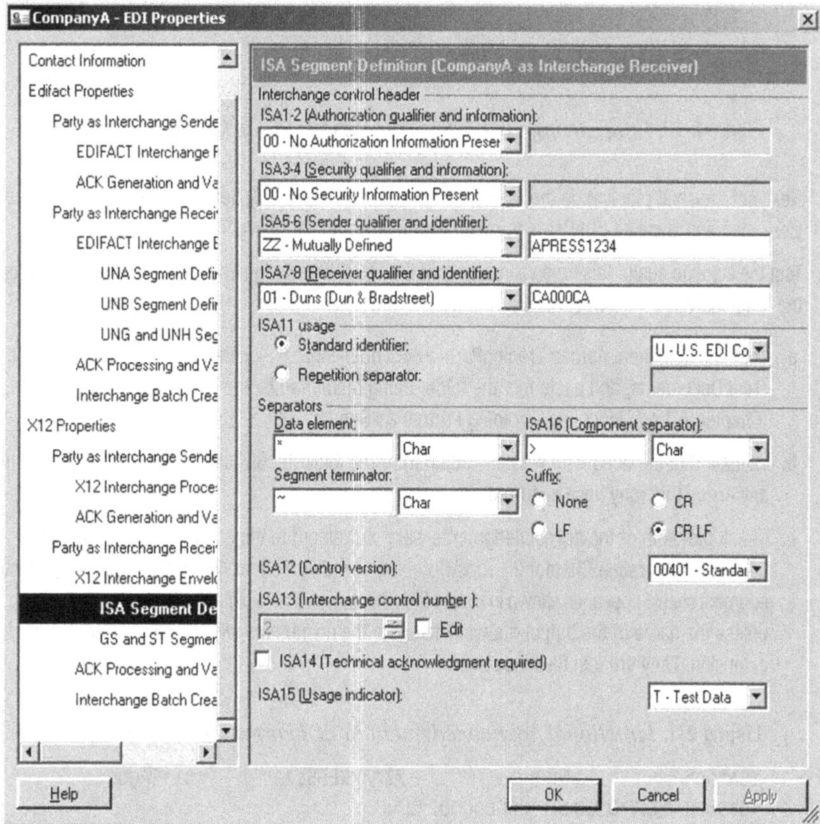

Figure 2-11. *Configuring the ISA segment for EDI acknowledgments*

    c. Now configure the GS and ST segment definition as shown Figure 2-12. See Exercise 2-5 for full details on configuring this segment for a Trading Partner As Receiver.

    d. Save all of the party settings by clicking OK. Company A is now configured as both a Trading Partner As Sender and a Trading Partner As Receiver.

■ **Note** If the only types of documents a trading partner is receiving are functional and/or technical acknowledgments, there are only a few fields in the GS and ST segments that are used (primarily for resolution). However, all of the fields are required to be set in the BizTalk Administration Console before the properties can be saved. For fields such as ST01, the value can be set to anything; this value will be overridden by the EDI send pipeline with the appropriate value (e.g., a 997 acknowledgment's ST01 field will be overridden with the value 997, while the GS01 would be set to FA, regardless of what is selected in the BizTalk Administration Console.)

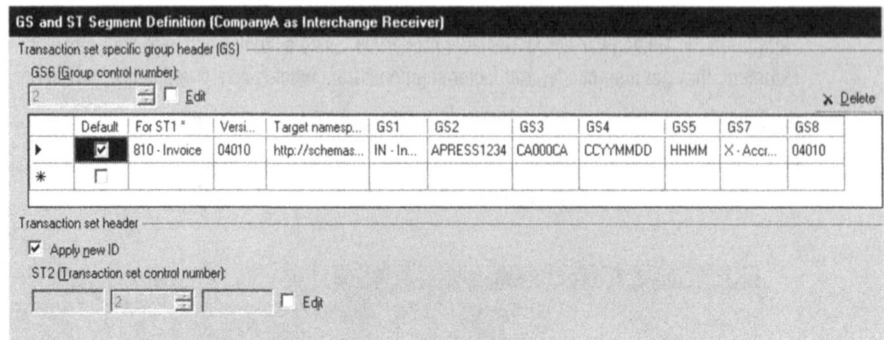

Figure 2-12. *Configuring the GT/ST segments for EDI acknowledgments*

11. Next, set the send pipeline on the acknowledgment send port to EDI Send. The send port was created in a previous step and is called EDI.Demonstration.Example.TradingPartnerAsSender.FILE.ACK.

12. Test the solution again, this time validating that the EDI acknowledgment documents are written out (rather than the XML equivalent shown earlier):

    a. Copy the document named TradingPartnerAsSender-Input.txt located in C:\Apress.Integration\Chapter 2\Test Documents, and paste it in the folder being monitored by the receive location - C:\Apress.Integration\Chapter 2\Drops\Incoming - Trading Partner As Sender - EDI.

    b. Validate that the document was picked up from the folder by BizTalk. Check the Windows Event Viewer for any errors that may have occurred.

    c. Check that both of the acknowledgments were written out to the acknowledgment folder in C:\Apress.Integration\Chapter 2\Drops\Outgoing - Trading Partner As Sender – ACK. The functional acknowledgment should appear as shown in Listing 2-1; the technical acknowledgment is shown in Listing 2-2. Note that unless the name of the output file was changed, the documents will still be written out with the .xml file extension. They are text files, however.

Listing 2-1. *Functional Acknowledgment in EDI Format*

```
ISA*00*          *00*          *ZZ*APRESS1234     *01*CA000CA
*070609*0947*U*00401*000000002*0*T*>~
GS*FA*APRESS1234*CA000CA*20070609*0947*2*X*004010~
ST*997*0002~
AK1*IN*25~
AK9*A*1*1*1~
SE*4*0002~
GE*1*2~
IEA*1*000000002~
```

Listing 2-2. *Technical Acknowledgment in EDI format*

```
ISA*00*          *00*          *ZZ*APRESS1234     *01*CA000CA
*070609*0947*U*00401*000000003*0*T*>~
TA1*000000025*070607*1555*A*000~
IEA*0*000000003~
```

Configuring a Trading Partner As Receiver

A trading partner is considered a *receiver* when it receives a document from BizTalk. This document can be any type of EDI instance, including an acknowledgment. When sending documents from BizTalk Server 2006 R2 to an external trading partner, all segments and acknowledgments related to setting a party as a receiver (configured in the EDI properties of the party) must be configured. This section outlines the flow of a Trading Partner As Receiver, contains an exercise demonstrating how to configure the party settings, and includes information about subscribing to any acknowledgment documents that are returned. Figure 2-13 illustrates the flow of an EDI document to a trading partner configured as a receiver.

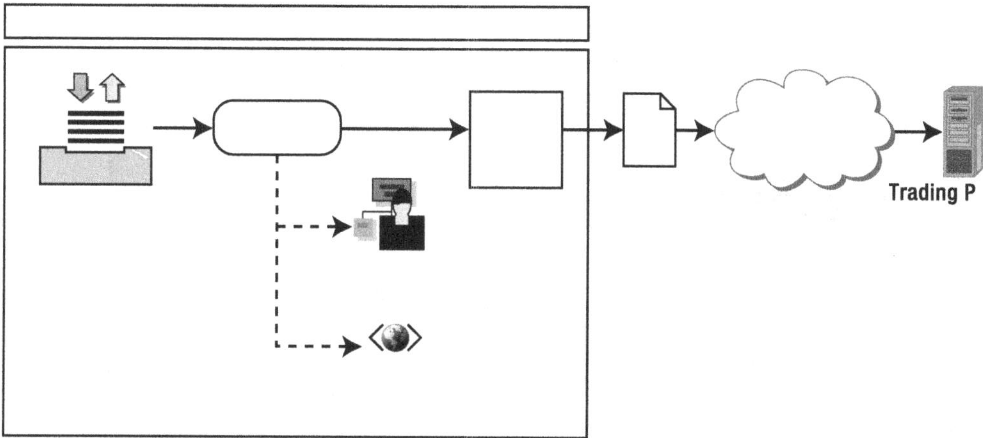

Figure 2-13. *Trading Partner As Receiver*

Exercise 2-5. Configuring a Trading Partner As Receiver

Follow these steps to configure a trading partner as a receiver:

1. Right-click the Company X party created in Exercise 2-2 and select EDI Properties.
2. Click the ISA Segment Definition to configure the settings shown in Figure 2-14. In an actual implementation, these values would be set based on trading partner requirements (usually defined in the EDI implementation guide provided by the partner (shown in Figure 2-15).

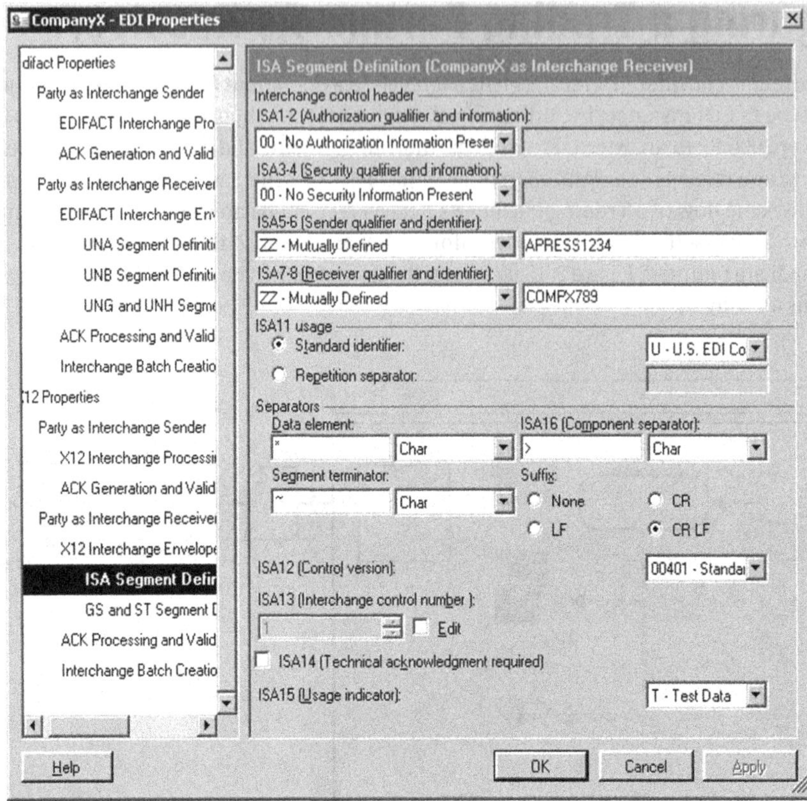

Figure 2-14. *ISA segment configuration settings*

Ref	Data Element Summary	Value	Length
ISA01	Authorization Information Qualifier	00	2/2
ISA02	Authorization Information	N/A	10/10
ISA03	Security Information Qualifier	00	2/2
ISA04	Security Information	N/A	10/10
ISA05	Interchange ID Qualifier	ZZ	2/2
ISA06	Interchange Sender ID	APRESS1234	15/15
ISA07	Interchange ID Qualifier	ZZ	2/2
ISA08	Interchange Receiver ID	COMPX789	15/15
ISA09	Interchange Date	[Date]	6/6
ISA10	Interchange Time	[Time]	4/4
ISA11	Interchange Control Standards Identifier	U	1/1
ISA12	Interchange Control Version Number	00401	5/5
ISA13	Interchange Control Number	[Unique ID]	9/9
ISA14	Acknowledgement Requested	1	1/1
ISA15	Usage Indicator	[T]est, [P]roduction	1/1
ISA16	Component Element Separator	>	1/1

Figure 2-15. *ISA interchange control header in implementation guide*

a. ISA01 and ISA03 can be set as 00, indicating that there is no authentication information needed.

b. Set ISA05 to ZZ – Mutually Defined.

c. Set ISA06, the sender ID, which represents the company where the source data is coming from, to APRESS1234. This value is static; all EDI trading partners have a unique ID.

d. Set ISA07 to ZZ – Mutually Defined.

e. Set ISA08 to COMPX789. The sender and receiver IDs are always 15 characters or less in length.

f. Set ISA11 to U.

g. Set ISA16 to the > character.

h. Set the separator suffix to CR LF. This will make the resulting document more "user friendly" for demonstration purposes by adding a line return between each segment. Different trading partners will have different requirements around what separators are needed.

i. Set ISA12 to 00401. This is based on the version of the standard being used for the interchange envelope.

j. Validate ISA13. It will be automatically generated. The configuration window allows the "seed" number to be set to any value. This value will increment by 1 for each document that is run through the system.

k. ISA14 can be set to indicate whether an acknowledgment is expected. Check this box.

l. Set ISA15 to indicate whether the data is test or production data. In this case, it is test.

3. With the ISA segment configured, click the GS and ST segment definition and set the properties as outlined in the figures showing the sample implementation guides (the GS segment is shown in Figure 2-16, and the ST segment is shown in Figure 2-17). Follow these steps to configure these properties.

Ref	Data Element Summary	Value	Min/Max
GS01	Functional Identifier Code	IN	2/2
GS02	Application Sender's Code	APRESS1234	2/15
GS03	Application Receiver's Code	COMPX789	2/15
GS04	Date	[Format CCYYMMDD]	6/6
GS05	Time	[Format HHMM]	4/8
GS06	Group Control Number	[Unique ID]	1/9
GS07	Responsible Agency Code	X	1/2
GS08	Version/Release Identifier Code	004010	1/12

Figure 2-16. *GS functional group header*

Ref	Data Element Summary	Value	Min/Max
ST01	Transaction Set Identifier Code	810	3/3
ST02	Transaction Set Control Number	[Unique ID]	4/9

Figure 2-17. *ST transaction set header*

a. The GS6 value is automatically incremented for each document that is processed. The "seed" value can be changed, if desired. For this exercise leave it set to the default value.

b. Only one row will be configured; enable the Default check box on the first row.

c. The ST1 property should be set to 810 – Invoice.

d. Version/release should be set to 00401.

e. The Target Namespace property is set to the value of the target namespace in the schema that represents the EDI document that will be delivered to the trading partner. In cases where the trading partner's schema may have been altered, along with the target namespace, the schema must first be deployed for this value to be present in the drop-down. For this exercise, select the http://schemas.microsoft.com/BizTalk/EDI/X12/2006 option from the drop-down.

f. Set GS1 to IN – Invoice Information (810).

g. Set GS2 to APRESS1234.

h. Set GS3 to COMPX789.

i. GS4 represents the format for the date, while GS5 represents the format for the time. In this case, the format is CCYYMMDD HHMM. Enter this format into the two properties.

j. Set the value of GS7 to X.

k. Set the value of GS8 to 004010. Note that this contains an extra 0 on the end but still represents the version/release.

l. The setting for ST2 represents the transaction set control number. This value can be set in a map (generally to a unique identifier that can be used in the source system, BizTalk processing, and the target system) or can be set to a unique value, overriding anything that may have been mapped. This can be set with the check box next to Apply New ID.

EDI Send Pipeline Flow

The flow of the EDI send pipeline is where party resolution and schema validation occurs. The steps in the pipeline are as follows, in the order shown:

1. **Destination party name context property matching:** The pipeline tries to match the party on the exact name specified in the context property. This property will not always be set (generally, it is only set by BizTalk in the case of acknowledgment generation and by code that has been entered within custom orchestrations) but enables quicker processing for known types.
2. **ID matching:** If the party name property is not available, the pipeline will look for the header values (ISA05-08, or UNB2 and UNB3 segments) to try and resolve the party. If the IDs are present, the pipeline will try and match all of the IDs with a party. If no party is found with exactly the same configuration, the message will be suspended.
3. **Send port affiliation:** Once the party has been resolved, the document will be sent to the send port that is affiliated with the party. If no port is associated with the party, documents will be routed based on send port filters or orchestrations that subscribe to the document. If no filters or subscribers are configured, the document will suspend on the MessageBox.
4. **Schema resolution and validation:** The document is now validated against the schemas that are available. If the schema cannot be resolved, or the document does not pass validation, the document will be suspended.

Configuring Acknowledgments (Trading Partner As Receiver)

Exercise 2-4 outlines all of the steps necessary to send an acknowledgment to a trading partner when that partner has been set up as a sender. When the trading partner is a receiver, the process is inverted. Essentially, the configuration consists of setting up the BizTalk party to expect that a document will be delivered from the trading partner that was just delivered to. When an acknowledgment is expected from an external party, BizTalk will await a response to correlate back to the original sent message (using BAM activities).

The key item to understand about acknowledgments set up for a Trading Partner As Receiver is that the trading partner returns the acknowledgment to BizTalk—just like any other document would be returned—and BizTalk must subscribe to the document and process it. This means that a receive port and a receive location must be set up to listen to where the trading partner will return the document.

■ **Note** When configuring BizTalk to expect an acknowledgment from a trading partner, a BAM activity is created the moment the EDI document is sent, and this activity is what the returned acknowledgment is correlated to. Without this activity, there is no way to determine which acknowledgment is a result of which original EDI document, unless a custom orchestration has been created that manages this correlation itself. This correlation process is performed automatically by the BizTalk engine.

Figure 2-18 illustrates the full cycle of the acknowledgment and the creation of the BAM activity.

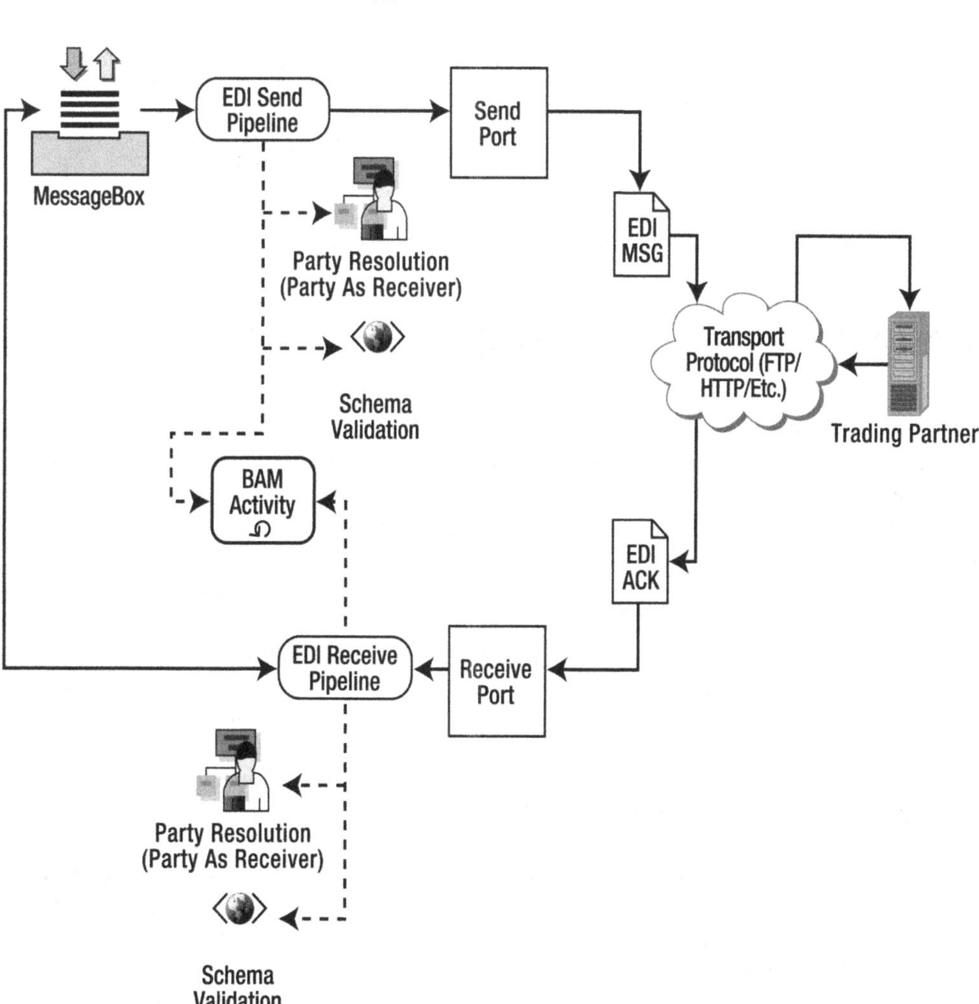

Figure 2-18. *Trading Partner As Receiver with acknowledgment*

Outlined in Figure 2-19 is a sample implementation of an EDI interchange with an acknowledgment configured for a Trading Partner As Receiver. As soon as the acknowledgment is returned, the trading partner must be viewed as a sender, and the document must be subscribed to by a BizTalk receive port to be processed. The acknowledgment will automatically be routed and correlated without any additional custom components. Make sure and refer to Exercise 2-4 for an in-depth look at configuring acknowledgments and configuring the BizTalk components.

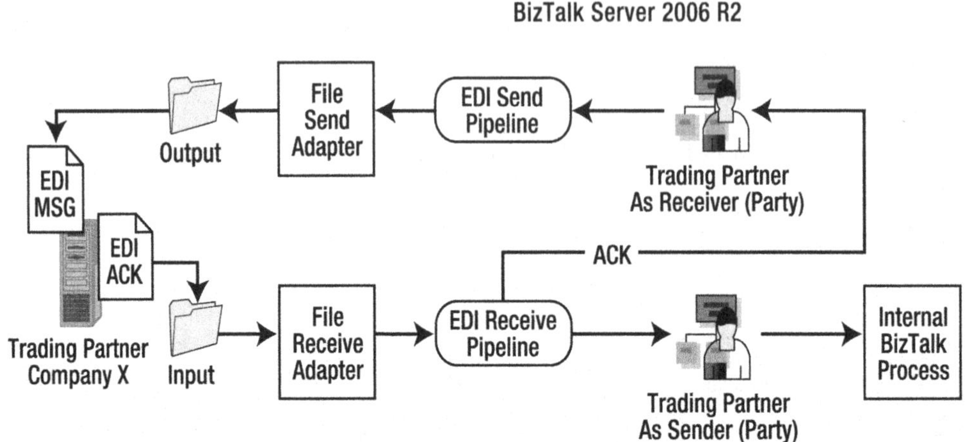

Figure 2-19. *Sample implementation of acknowledgment flow from receiver*

Configuring AS2 Properties

The discussions and exercises up to this point have dealt with parties configured to handle EDI documents delivered via traditional file-based transmission methods (FTP, email, file, etc.). AS2 (also known as EDIINT) is the process for delivering EDI documents over the Internet, using the HTTP protocol rather than traditional protocols. Acting as an envelope containing the traditional EDI document, AS2 provides additional layers of security with capabilities around document encryption and contains information about how to resolve a document against a party. Documents are resolved to BizTalk parties using data within the AS2 envelope rather than the data within the EDI header data.

The purpose of this section is to introduce the concept of AS2 and how it is related to a trading partner, but not to introduce information specifically related to the actual delivery of the document using this protocol. A full description of how to use the standard AS2 functionality that ships with BizTalk, and how to work with a third-party AS2 adapter, is described in detail in Chapter 5.

The key differences in processing EDI documents delivered using AS2 are that the AS2 EDI pipelines are used (rather than the standard EDI pipelines referred to up to this point) and that the majority of transmissions are encrypted (through the use of certificates). Documents are resolved to parties based on what is entered into the alias of the party (this is largely ignored by standard EDI transmissions). The alias information must match the AS2-To and AS2-From settings in the AS2 envelope sent from a trading partner and the properties in the Party As Receiver tab. Before documents can be resolved, they must first be decrypted using certificates stored in the certificate store (external to BizTalk).

AS2 properties can be accessed on a party by right-clicking and selecting AS2 properties. In the window that opens, there are three basic tabs:

- **General**: Information regarding AS2 reporting and how the HTTP connection will be processed is here. The default way in which BizTalk handles AS2 transmissions is via a standard HTTP adapter. Properties that are related to the transmission, but that cannot be set in the adapter, are set within the party properties.
- **Party As Sender**: When an AS2 transmission is sent to BizTalk, it is generally encrypted using a certificate. The properties on this screen allow the user to configure the appropriate way to decrypt the incoming document and how to send the Message Disposition Notification (MDN) acknowledgment back to the sender. Note that an MDN acknowledgment is not related to EDI acknowledgments, meaning an MDN can be sent on a 997 (an acknowledgment of the reception of an acknowledgment). It is used primarily as a receipt to eliminate any argument that the transmission was received.
- **Party As Receiver**: When BizTalk initiates the AS2 transmission, the party is the receiver of that transmission. The properties around how to sign and encrypt the message, which only the receiver knows how to decrypt, are set on the Party As Receiver tab. The most important settings on this tab include configuring whether MDN acknowledgments are expected back and the settings for AS2-To and AS2-From (which correspond to what is configured for the party alias, as shown in Figure 2-20).

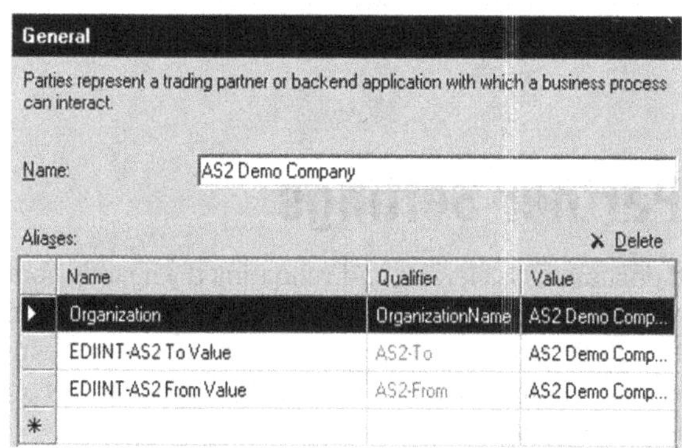

Figure 2-20. *AS2 uses aliases in party resolution (standard EDI largely ignores aliases).*

Note Many of the properties available on these tabs are overridden when using third-party BizTalk AS2 adapters, especially the way certificates are set up. For example, certificate resolution may be configured directly on the third-party AS2 adapter, whereas the standard BizTalk AS2 functionality sets certificate resolution on the party.

Figure 2-21 is a screen shot of typical AS2 settings configured in the BizTalk Administration Console.

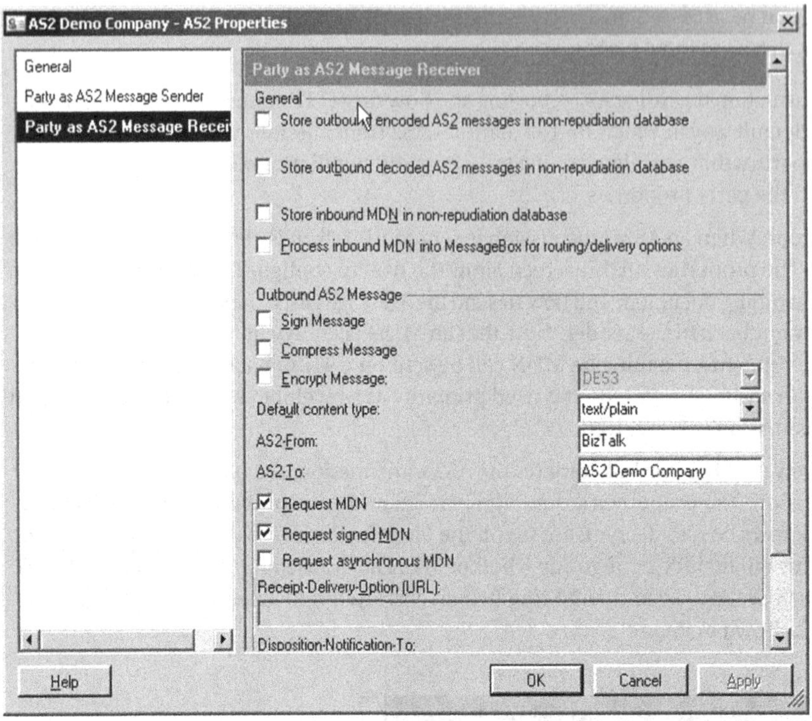

Figure 2-21. *AS2 properties*

Validating Trading Partner Settings

One of the most elusive portions of EDI documents is viewing and validating the header, context, and footer information set based on how the party is configured. In most cases, this information is only available once the document has been fully processed, run through the EDI send pipeline, and delivered to an external location. This section outlines how the header, context, and footer are added to the document and demonstrates with Exercise 2-6 the full validation process.

As EDI documents flow through the MessageBox, the header (such as ISA/UNB) and footer (such as GE/IEA/UNT) segments are contained outside of the EDI document itself; they are set as context information, a wrapper around the message itself. As BizTalk routes messages (EDI or otherwise) around, there is the message (the *body*), and all of the context information about that message (such as where the message first came from, its schema, any promoted fields, etc.). Not until the EDI document is sent through an EDI pipeline do the header and footer information actually become part of the document. Because of this, it is not possible to see the full EDI document as it would appear to an external trading partner until the document has been fully sent through an EDI send port.

To illustrate the message body vs. the context properties of an EDI document, Figure 2-22 shows the GS and ISA segment information in the message context window, while Figure 2-23 shows the EDI message content itself (in XML). This is prior to being processed by the EDI send pipeline. All of this information is accessed via the BizTalk Group Hub on a suspended message (details of using the Group Hub and working with messages appears in Chapter 6).

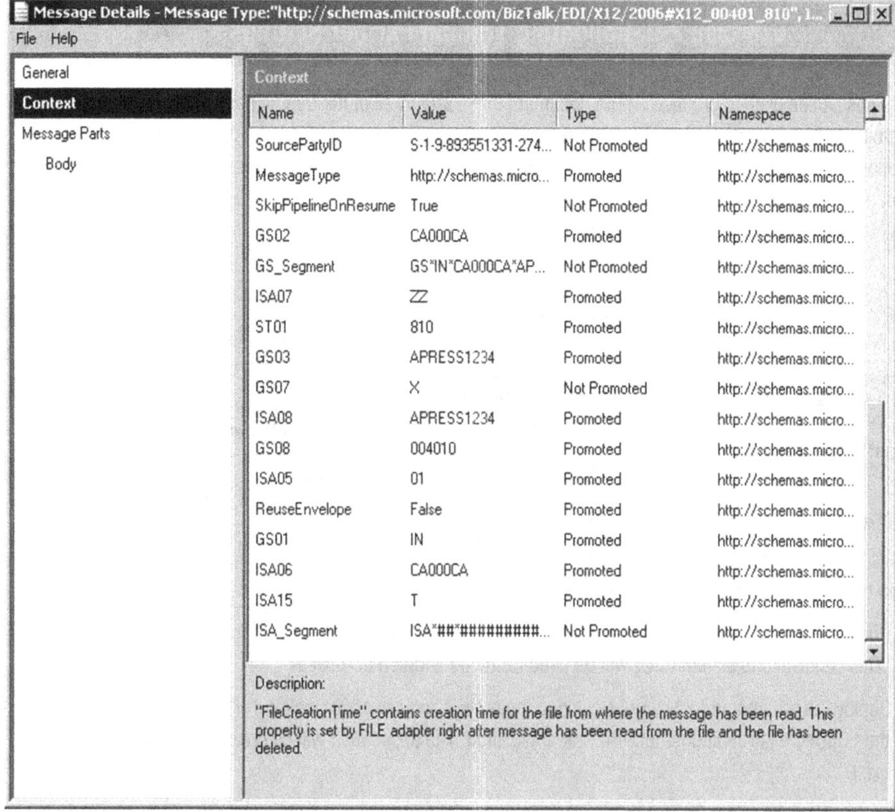

Figure 2-22. *Message context properties showing ISA and GS segment information*

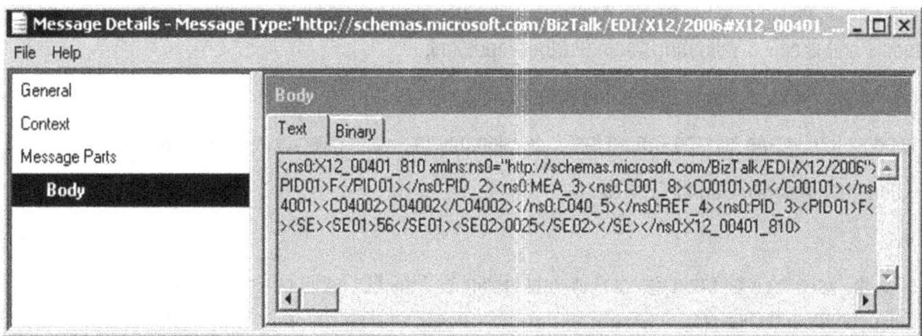

Figure 2-23. *Message body showing content prior to processing by EDI send pipeline*

Exercise 2-6 demonstrates the minimum number of components needed to create a full EDI file instance. The components that are built can be used for any EDI document and are generic enough that they could be set up at the beginning of an EDI development project and reused throughout the project to validate documents.

Exercise 2-6. Validating Trading Partner Settings

The following steps can be used to produce an EDI document that contains all of the trading partner settings configured in the BizTalk Administration Console. The contents of the document will not contain valid data, but the header, detail, and footer information will be valid. This exercise will walk through creating a sample XML instance, a receive location where this instance can be dropped, and an output location where the EDI output will be written. Figure 2-24 outlines the flow of a document through the components of this exercise.

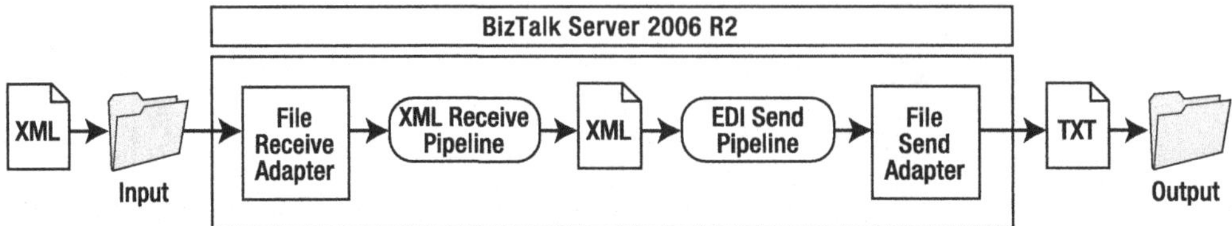

Figure 2-24. *Validating trading partner settings exercise flow*

1. Begin by creating the BizTalk application and deploying the schema, using these steps:
   a. Open the solution file Apress.Integration.EDI810.CompanyX.sln located in C:\Apress.Integration\Chapter 2. This contains one schema that will be used for demonstration purposes.
   b. Deploy the schema project by right-clicking the project and selecting Deploy. This will deploy the schema to the EDI.Demonstration.Chapter2 BizTalk application. The application will be created if it does not already exist.
   c. Add a reference to the BizTalk EDI application, which stores all of the control schemas. This can be done by right-clicking the BizTalk application EDI.Demonstration.Chapter2 and selecting Add ➤ References. Click BizTalk EDI Application.
2. Next, create a sample instance to work with. A version of this has been created in C:\Apress.Integration\Chapter 2\Test Documents and is called ValidatingTradingPartner-Input.xml:
   a. Right-click the schema in Visual Studio and select Properties.
   b. In the window that opens, set the Output Instance Filename to a valid directory on the local computer.
   c. Set the Generate Instance Output Type to XML.
   d. Click OK.
   e. Right-click the schema again and select Generate Instance. If the EDI Instance Properties dialog box opens, accept all defaults and click OK.
   f. Validate that the sample instance is written to the specified location. This represents the EDI document before it is run through any EDI pipelines that format it as a flat file. Using this instance will allow the creation of a simple receive/send process to output the file in a valid format.
3. Create a receive adapter and a file receive location where the sample XML instance will be dropped by working through these steps:
   a. In the BizTalk Administration Console, expand the EDI.Demonstration.Chapter2 BizTalk application.
   b. Right-click Receive Ports and select New ➤ One-Way Receive Port. Give the receive port a name (for this demonstration, it is named EDI.Demonstration.Example.ValidatingTradingPartner.FILE.810).
   c. Click the Receive Locations tab and click the New button. A fully configured receive location is shown in Figure 2-25.

i. Name the receive location (the sample is named FileReceive).

ii. Set the Type property to FILE and configure it to listen to a file drop. The demonstration has it configured at C:\Apress.Integration\Chapter 2\Drops\Incoming - Validating Trading Partner - XML. Ensure that all files with the extension of *.xml are being listened for.

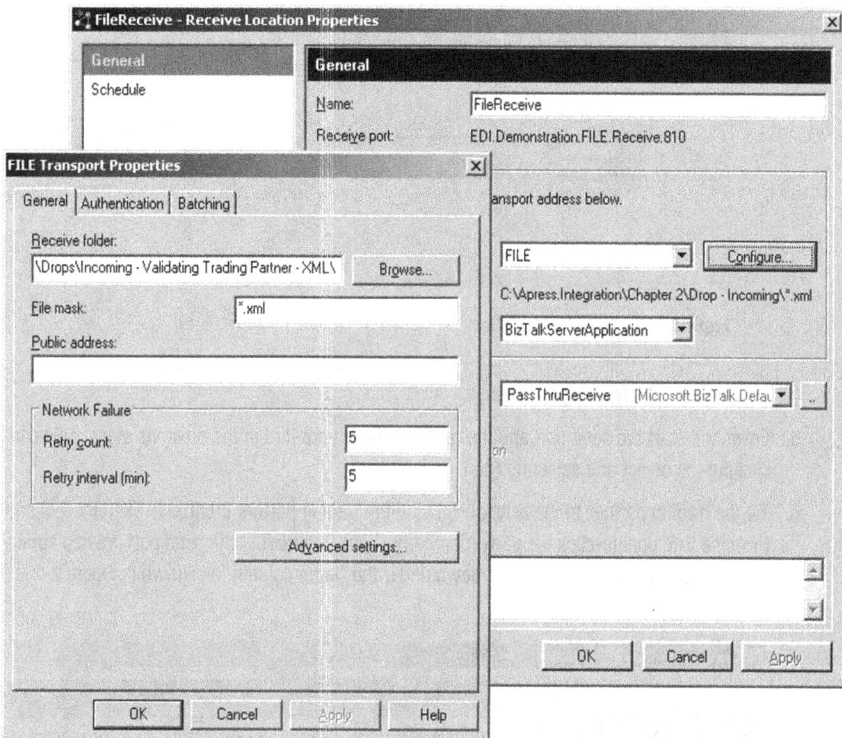

Figure 2-25. *Configure file receive location*

4. Create a file send adapter that will listen for documents coming in on the receive port created in the previous step and will run them through the EDI send pipeline, converting the XML into an EDI document and adding the header, detail, and footer information configured for the trading partner by working through these steps:

   a. In the BizTalk Administration Console, expand the EDI.Demonstration.Chapter2 BizTalk application.

   b. Right-click the Send Ports folder and select New ➤ Static One-Way Send Port.

   c. Name the port appropriately. This exercise uses EDI.Demonstration.Example.ValidatingTradingPartner.FILE.810.

   d. Set the type as FILE and configure an appropriate output folder and file name:

      i. Set the output folder for this exercise as C:\Apress.Integration\Chapter 2\Drops\Outgoing - Validating Trading Partner - EDI\.

      ii. Set the file name to %MessageID%.txt.

   e. Click the Filters tab and set the Filter to the BTS.ReceivePortName property equal to EDI.Demonstration.Example.ValidatingTradingPartner.FILE.810 (the name of the receive port created earlier in this exercise). This will force all documents received by the receive port to be routed through this send port. See Figure 2-26.

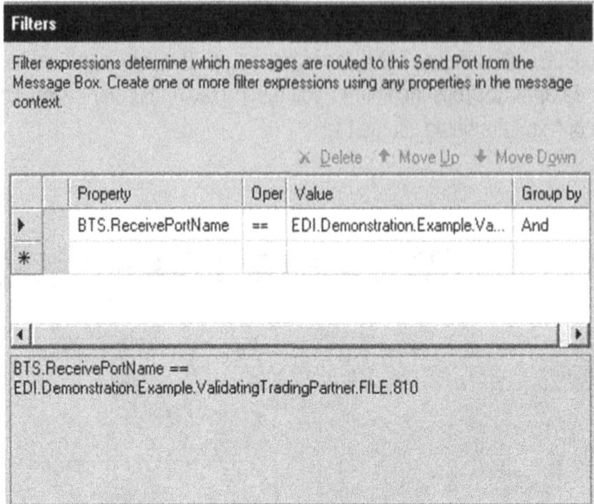

Figure 2-26. *Send port filter*

f. Click OK to save the port settings.

5. Enlist and start the send port and the receive location created in the previous steps. This can be done by right-clicking the object and selecting Start.

6. Tie the trading partner to the send port. Using the trading partner created in Exercise 2-2 and configured in Exercise 2-5, double-click the party (Company X) and ensure that the send port created appears in the send port list (ports can be selected via drop-down under the Name column, as shown in Figure 2-27).

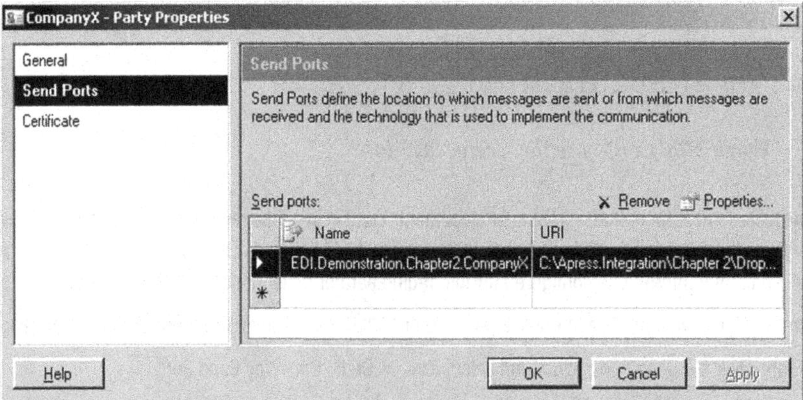

Figure 2-27. *Tie send port to trading partner*

7. Drop the sample XML document (ValidatingTradingPartner-Input.xml) on the input receive location. Look for the output document in the file directory configured for the output location. The header, detail, and footer information will be visible (as shown in Listing 2-3), and can be compared to the expected settings for the trading partner. If the document does not appear, check the Windows Event Viewer for error information.

Listing 2-3. *Sample Output with Header, Detail, and Footer Segments*

```
ISA*00*          *00*          *ZZ*APRESS1234     *ZZ*COMPX789
*070606*1508*U*00401*000000002*0*T*>~
GS*IN*APRESS1234*COMPX789*20070606*1508*2*X*004010~
ST*810*0002~
........
........
........
SE*56*0002~
GE*1*2~
IEA*1*000000002~
```

Final Discussion

There are a number of different concepts to understand when performing trading partner configuration. This chapter looked in detail at setting up trading partners and working with acknowledgments. The process begins with determining whether the trading partner settings should be based on the EDI implementation guide (if one exists). Setting the header and footer segment information is the first step, regardless of whether the partner is a sender or a receiver. After this has been configured, any needed acknowledgments should be set up. Depending on the flow of the document, send or receive ports will need to be prepared to be able to deliver the acknowledgments back to the partner. If an EDI document is being transported using AS2, additional properties must be configured on the party. The chapter concluded with an overview of how to validate and test that the BizTalk party has been configured correctly by demonstrating how to output a full EDI document with header and footer information included within it.

CHAPTER 3

Retrieving and Mapping Data

Data retrieval and EDI document mapping are essential to all EDI implementations. The goal of this chapter is to introduce a logical approach to determining how to define and structure the source and target data, how to retrieve the source data and deliver it to BizTalk Server, how to map the source data to the target trading partner schema, and how to test that the map produces the expected (an EDI text file). The following topics are covered in this chapter:

- **Defining the mapping components**: Mapping includes three primary BizTalk components: the source schema, the target schema, and the map. This section describes how to define these components based on the requirements of the trading partner's EDI document and the structure of the source data.
- **Retrieving the source data**: With the components defined, the source data must be returned to BizTalk Server for processing. This section outlines how to query the source data and return it to BizTalk using the SQL Receive Adapter.
- **Mapping the document**: The actual mapping of data from the source schema to the target schema is done through a combination of analyzing business requirements (determining how fields are related in the source and destination schemas) and implementing the logic to accomplish this (through actual map development). Generally, mapping requirements are outlined in the EDI implementation guide supplied by the trading partner. The section on mapping covers in detail some of the more common mapping tasks for EDI documents.
- **Testing the map**: Throughout the development process, the map will need to be tested. This section outlines a step-by-step approach to testing EDI maps and understanding how to correct errors that may be encountered.

Preparing the Solution Files

The exercises in this chapter assume a general understanding of EDI schemas and trading partner configuration. The first exercise (Exercise 3-1) introduces how to set up the sample code files that accompany this book, for use in later exercises.

Exercise 3-1. Preparing the Solution Files

The exercises in this chapter use the solution files located in Apress.Integration\Chapter 3\Apress.Integration.EDI810.sln. Use the following steps to deploy the solution files to a local machine:

1. Open the solution file in Visual Studio on the local computer. The solution file contains two projects:
   a. **Apress.Integration.EDI810.Common**: This project contains the source data schema and is placed into a separate project so that it can be referenced by any trading partner project.
   b. **Apress.Integration.EDI810.CompanyX**: This project contains the map and target EDI schema specific to the EDI810 implementation for trading partner Company X.
2. Add the database to SQL Server. There are two options for creating the database (this assumes the use of SQL Server 2005).
   a. The database and log file can be attached using the following steps. This is the only option to obtain the full database with all test data populated:
      i. Open SQL Server Management Studio.
      ii. Right-click the Databases folder and select Attach.
      iii. In the window that opens, click the Add button and browse to the location of the MDF file. It is located in the folder Apress.Integration\Chapter 3\Database Files\Attach and is called Apress.EDI.Custom.mdf.
      iv. Click OK.
   b. Alternatively, the SQL scripts can be run (no data will be included). There are a total of six scripts, all contained in the folder Apress.Integration\Chapter 3\Database Files\Scripts.

In addition, there are two versions of the target schema and target map for Company X. The original map and schema (as used in Exercise 3-4, later in the "Mapping the Document" section) are included in the project and are in the folder Apress.Integration.EDI810.CompanyX. The modified map and schema (as used in Exercise 3-5) are located in the folder Apress.Integration\Chapter 3\Company X Final Schema and Map.

Finally, there is a sample document located in Apress.Integration\Chapter 3\Test Documents. This is used as a test map input for Exercise 3-5, later in the "Testing the Map" section. The content of this represents what is returned by the stored procedure. The contents can be modified using a text editor.

Defining the Mapping Components

The first step in the process of document mapping is to determine the flow of the document(s) being mapped. This includes defining where the source data is coming from, how it will be retrieved and delivered to BizTalk, what the format of the data will be, and what the target schema (or schemas, in the case of multiple trading partners) will be. Figure 3-1 gives a high-level overview of the document flow that is covered in detail in this chapter.

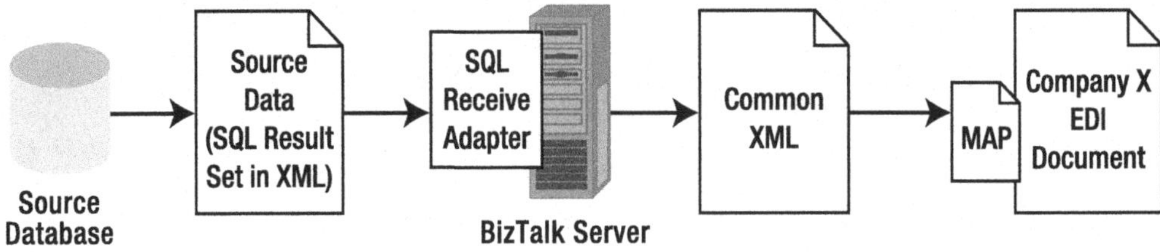

Figure 3-1. *Data mapping flow*

Defining the Target Schema

Schema creation and definition are covered in Chapter 1. At this point, it is assumed that the process for selecting a schema is understood and that the trading partner's requirements have been assessed for whichever type of EDI document is to be delivered. For the sample implementation outlined in this chapter, a modified version of the X12_00401_810.xsd (which represents an invoice) will be used. Many nodes in the schema that are not needed by the trading partner have been removed. This not only simplifies the document for illustration purposes but is good practice when preparing a schema for an actual implementation.

Note It is important to understand that the data being delivered to trading partners will frequently not adhere to the standard version of the EDI schema provided with BizTalk Server 2006 R2. It is a necessary step to make modifications to the schema where necessary. For instance, a trading partner may be using a specific segment to contain data that does not commonly belong there. The schemas should be modified on a per-partner basis, and should generally include only those nodes that the trading partner is interested in. Always refer to the EDI implementation guide when working with mapping requirements.

Company X represents the trading partner to which EDI documents will be delivered. The sample EDI document being used for demonstration purposes has been greatly simplified but represents a valid version of an X12 810 invoice document. The document shown in Listing 3-1 is a sample instance of the final EDI document that will be delivered to the trading partner (Company X) after each of the components in this chapter is put into place.

Listing 3-1. *Sample 810 EDI Document for Company X*

```
ST*810*1000~
N1*ST*Company Y~
N4*City R*State B*23456~
IT1*1*2**12~
IT1*2*2**10~
CTT*2*44~
SE*7*1000~
```

Note For X12 documents, the ISA, GS, GE, and IEA segments are never included in the map; these are configured through the BizTalk Administration Console and are automatically generated on outgoing documents. The same holds true for the UNA, UNB, UNG, and UNZ segments for EDIFACT documents. Configuring these segments is covered in Chapter 2.

It will prove to be helpful to define the target document (an actual instance of what is to be delivered to a trading partner) prior to creating or modifying the target schema. Working with the trading partner to determine the format and content of the document is essential in the early stages of requirements gathering and will eliminate a great deal of work during the development stage. Generally, trading partners will have recorded the specifications of EDI documents in an EDI implementation guide. Company X will use a modified version of the standard 810 schema, as shown in Figure 3-2.

Figure 3-2. *Trading partner target schema (modified from standard schema)*

Defining the Source Data and Schema

The *source data* is defined as all data being extracted from the source data store. It includes all data needed by any trading partner, such as billing and shipping address data, details about the contents of a message (e.g., in the case of 810 documents, invoicing information), and other pertinent information. It also includes all data that may be used during processing by BizTalk Server (such as IDs for tracking) and any other data that may be extracted—used or unused. This data may come from multiple sources, or it may come from a single source. For successful mapping, it is essential to define what the source data is, where it is coming from, and what the delivery format will be.

For the purposes of this section, the source data will come from a single data store (SQL Server 2005) and from a sample database that is intended to mimic a fractional subset of information housed in an accounting application. From this data, invoices will be generated, resulting in 810 EDI documents.

Generally, defining the source data and source schema go hand in hand; the schema is often a "work in progress," evolving throughout the course of the project as requirements are defined and additional data is needed for calculations and EDI document generation. In some rare instances, all of the needed data is known at the start of the project, and the complexities of defining where the data comes from are greatly diminished. In either case, whether the data is fully defined or whether it is being defined in parallel with development, implementing the structure of the data and encapsulating it into a source schema is a task that requires a great deal of thought to ensure that the long-term requirements of the trading partners are met.

The creation of the source schema begins with determining how best to structure the data. This is most easily accomplished by assessing how the data is set up in the source data store (i.e., in the case of databases, how the tables and the data within them are related), and from that, setting up the relational hierarchy that will be most easily constructed and matches, to some degree, the target EDI schema (to simplify mapping, if possible). In the case of the sample implementation, the source database is structured as defined in Figure 3-3.

With the data model of the source database known, and the target EDI document schema defined, the next step is to determine which of the fields are of interest to the external systems (including BizTalk and its components: maps, orchestrations, ports, etc.) and trading partners. The source data store will always contain proprietary information used within the data store itself (such as unique identifiers and metadata); this data is generally not needed by external systems and should not be included in the source schema.

For the sample implementation, the proprietary information includes most of the GUIDs (e.g., uidAddressID) which are primary keys within the database but are not generally useful for most purposes outside of the database. However, for this discussion one of the GUIDs will be included in the source schema (uidInvoiceID). It is intended to be used for tracking purposes within BizTalk Server. No trading partner is typically interested in this type of data, but it often makes sense to include it to be able to track the document through BizTalk.

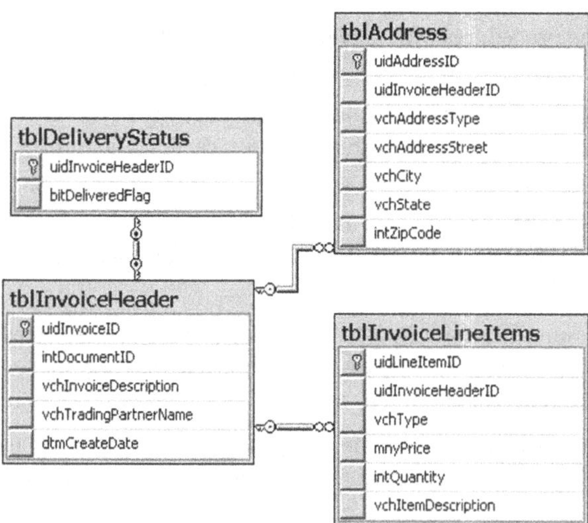

Figure 3-3. *Source database diagram*

From understanding the database diagram (what data is available) and knowing the target trading partner data requirements (what data is needed), it can be determined that the source document schema should be as shown in Figure 3-4.

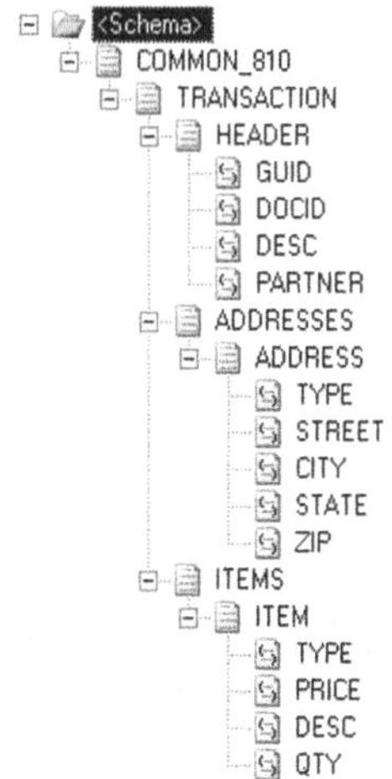

Figure 3-4. *Common source schema*

Retrieving the Source Data

This section outlines an approach to retrieving the data from the source data store, which will simplify schema development and the delivery of data to BizTalk Server. As with all integration projects, there are a large number of potential options in retrieving data that depend on a variety of factors:

- **Where the data is stored**: Different data stores have different methods for accessing the data they contain. This may be via stored procedures, web services, a custom API, flat files, or a number of other objects.
- **Amount of data**: The amount of information in a transaction, whether data will be batched or handled as individual transactions, and the size of data transmissions can have an impact on how the data will be retrieved (or delivered).
- **Frequency**: The frequency that data will be transmitted to BizTalk Server and whether this data will be delivered asynchronously or synchronously (real time) will help determine how best to implement the retrieval of source data.
- **Acknowledgements**: If two-way communication needs to occur between the source system and BizTalk Server (i.e., acknowledgement that delivery is successful/failed), it may make sense to implement one type of data retrieval process vs. another.
- **Network accessibility**: Occasionally the data store may be on a portion of the network that is not directly accessible to BizTalk Server. Security restrictions may require different approaches to retrieving data from the source.

For the purpose of discussion and demonstration, this section outlines the most common form of data retrieval from a data source housing EDI data: the retrieval of data via the BizTalk SQL Receive Adapter. From this process, more complex patterns can be implemented to suit the needs of any EDI implementation.The database component outlined here is the stored procedure, which returns the result set as an XML document. Rendering result sets in XML within the stored procedure (rather than trying to work with schemas on the SQL Receive Adapter to format the result sets after receiving the data) simplifies the data retrieval process, making the delivery of the data to BizTalk Server as seamless as possible. Figure 3-5 illustrates the flow and components used in retrieving data in XML, and shows that XML can be returned directly to the SQL Receive Adapter from the stored procedure.

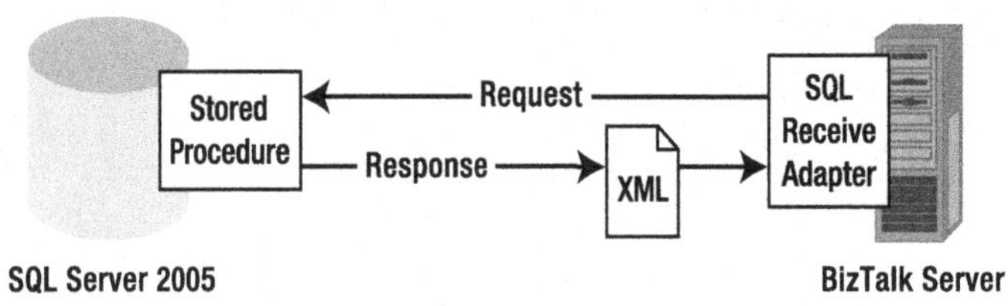

Figure 3-5. *Retrieving data as XML*

SQL Server 2005 has full support of XML and is readily available in the majority of BizTalk 2006 Server deployments (generally, BizTalk 2006 is deployed on SQL Server 2005; SQL 2000 has limited XML support, but can be used in a similar fashion to this implementation, if needed). A number of enterprise-level databases support some level of XML retrieval, and the approach outlined in this section can be used to process data directly from these systems. In many cases, the simplest approach to retrieving data from any external data source is to use linked servers from SQL Server 2005, which allows full flexibility in the stored procedure (on SQL 2005) to process data on external databases.

Creating the Stored Procedure

The steps to implementing the flow shown in Figure 3-5 begin with creating the stored procedure that will return a result set as an XML document. The function of the stored procedure is to return all of the fields needed in the creation of the target EDI schema. The stored procedure outlined in Listing 3-2 retrieves an XML document that matches the source schema defined earlier (see Figure 3-4). A sample instance of the XML document that will be generated by the stored procedure is shown in Figure 3-6.

■ **Note** When retrieving data using the BizTalk SQL Receive Adapter, a root node will always wrap the XML document retrieved from the database. In this case, the root node in the schema is <COMMON_810>, while the root node retrieved by the stored procedure is <TRANSACTION>. The <COMMON_810> node will be automatically added by the SQL Adapter.

Listing 3-2. *Stored Procedure to Return XML Document*

```
CREATE PROCEDURE [dbo].[spGetInvoice]
AS
BEGIN
 SET NOCOUNT ON;

 -- select invoice to be extracted
 DECLARE @uidInvoiceID As uniqueidentifier
  ,@intCounter As int

 -- get the first document returned that has not already
 -- been delivered.  Remaining documents will be processed
 -- on subsequent calls to this stored procedure.
 SET @uidInvoiceID =
  (SELECT TOP 1 uidInvoiceID
   FROM tblInvoiceHeader
   WHERE uidInvoiceID NOT IN
   (SELECT uidInvoiceHeaderID
    FROM tblDeliveryStatus
    WHERE bitDeliveredFlag = 1
   )
   ORDER BY dtmCreateDate
  )

 -- Only execute the code if an ID is present
 IF @uidInvoiceID IS NOT NULL
  BEGIN
   -- wrapping in a tran can be useful with multiple updates
   -- shown here for demonstration purposes only
   BEGIN TRAN
    BEGIN TRY
     -- generate XML document as result set
     -- note that BizTalk will add its own root node when
     -- extracted using the SQL Receive Adapter
```

```
    -- the DOCID is unique and can be used to trace
    -- document throughout entire process
    SELECT NULL
    ,(SELECT uidInvoiceID AS "GUID"
      ,intDocumentID AS "DOCID"
      ,vchInvoiceDescription AS "DESC"
      ,vchTradingPartnerName AS "PARTNER"
      FROM tblInvoiceHeader
      WHERE uidInvoiceID = @uidInvoiceID
      FOR XML PATH('HEADER'), BINARY BASE64, TYPE)
      ,(SELECT NULL
       ,(SELECT vchAddressType AS "TYPE"
                      ,vchAddressStreet AS "STREET"
                      ,vchCity AS "CITY"
                      ,vchState AS "STATE"
                      ,intZipCode AS "ZIP"
         FROM tblAddress
         WHERE uidInvoiceHeaderID = @uidInvoiceID
         FOR XML PATH('ADDRESS'), BINARY BASE64, TYPE)
        FOR XML PATH('ADDRESSES'), BINARY BASE64, TYPE)
        ,(SELECT NULL
         ,(SELECT vchType AS "TYPE"
                        ,mnyPrice AS "PRICE"
                        ,vchItemDescription AS "DESC"
                        ,intQuantity AS "QTY"
           FROM tblInvoiceLineItems
           WHERE uidInvoiceHeaderID = @uidInvoiceID
           FOR XML PATH('ITEM'), BINARY BASE64, TYPE)
          FOR XML PATH('ITEMS'), BINARY BASE64, TYPE)
         FOR XML PATH('TRANSACTION'), BINARY BASE64

    -- Now set the delivered flag in the table to "true"
    UPDATE tblDeliveryStatus
    SET bitDeliveredFlag = 1
    WHERE uidInvoiceHeaderID = @uidInvoiceID

   END TRY
   BEGIN CATCH
    -- error occurred, rollback
    ROLLBACK TRAN
    RETURN @@ERROR
   END CATCH
  -- success
 COMMIT TRAN
 END
END
```

```
- <TRANSACTION>
  - <HEADER>
      <GUID>4FA0B48B-ACCB-40F0-B1D2-7E22FFF820BA</GUID>
      <DOCID>2000</DOCID>
      <DESC>Sample Invoice for Company X </DESC>
      <PARTNER>Company X </PARTNER>
    </HEADER>
  - <ADDRESSES>
    - <ADDRESS>
        <TYPE>Billing</TYPE>
        <STREET>1234 A Road </STREET>
        <CITY>City G </CITY>
        <STATE>State A </STATE>
        <ZIP>12345 </ZIP>
      </ADDRESS>
    - <ADDRESS>
        <TYPE>Shipping</TYPE>
        <STREET>6789 F Road </STREET>
        <CITY>City G </CITY>
        <STATE>State A </STATE>
        <ZIP>12345 </ZIP>
      </ADDRESS>
    </ADDRESSES>
  - <ITEMS>
    - <ITEM>
        <TYPE>Standard</TYPE>
        <PRICE>100.0000</PRICE>
        <QTY>1</QTY>
        <DESC>Item A</DESC>
      </ITEM>
    - <ITEM>
        <TYPE>Hidden</TYPE>
        <PRICE>0.0000</PRICE>
        <QTY>3</QTY>
        <DESC>Service Charge </DESC>
      </ITEM>
    </ITEMS>
  </TRANSACTION>
```


Figure 3-6. *Sample XML result set generated by stored procedure*

Configuring the BizTalk SQL Receive Adapter

Once the stored procedure is created, it is necessary to set up a process that will call it and return the XML result to BizTalk Server for processing. The component that most easily accomplishes this is the BizTalk SQL Receive Adapter. It can be configured to run on a timed interval and will continue to call the stored procedure until all available invoices have been returned (the stored procedure shown in Listing 3-2 returns a single document each time it is called). The steps outlined in Exercise 3-2 provide all of the information needed to configure the SQL Adapter to return the result set in the format that matches the source data schema shown previously in Figure 3-4.

Exercise 3-2. Configuring the BizTalk SQL Receive Adapter

To create a BizTalk 2006 SQL Receive Adapter that is configured to execute a stored procedure on a timed interval and deliver the resulting XML to the BizTalk MessageBox, take the following steps:

1. Open BizTalk Administration Console and expand the EDI.Demonstration.Chapter3 application (or the application that contains the BizTalk components). Right-click Receive Ports and select New ➤ One-Way Receive Port.
2. On the General tab, name the port appropriately (the sample implementation names this EDI.Demonstration.SQL.Receive.810).

3. Click the Receive Locations tab. In the right-hand window, click New to create a receive location. Name the receive location appropriately (in this case, SQLReceive). The name will distinguish it from other receive locations that may be associated with this port.

4. Next to Type, select SQL. Click the Configure button. Figure 3-7 shows the window with each of the properties set in the following steps.

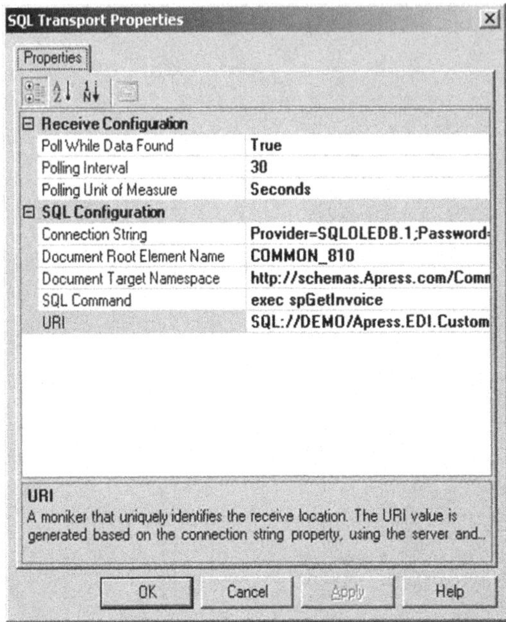

Figure 3-7. *Configuring the SQL receive location properties*

a. **Poll While Data Found**: This indicates whether the adapter will continue to call the stored procedure until no results are returned, or whether it will only be called once per execution period. For this solution, set this value to True. Each time the stored procedure is called, only one 810 document will be returned. By setting this value to True, the procedure will continue to execute until all 810 documents have been returned to BizTalk.

Note When using the Poll While Data Found property, it should be understood that if a SQL Receive Adapter is running on a BizTalk group, all of the BizTalk servers within the group may end up calling the stored procedure simultaneously. Depending on how the stored procedure is written, this may pose a problem. For instance, in the procedure called in this exercise, a flag is set indicating that a row has been delivered after the data has been returned. If the stored procedure is to be called simultaneously by multiple servers in a BizTalk Group, the result set may be returned more than once due to the fact that the flag will not be updated in time to prevent the second call from retrieving the same record. In a case such as this, the Poll While Data Found would need to be set to False, or a more robust way of determining whether data has already been retrieved would need to be added to the stored procedure.

---

b. **Polling Interval**: This setting indicates the amount of time to wait between executions of the stored procedure. The time will depend on the number of documents being returned and the frequency that these documents become available. For this demonstration, set the value to 60.

c. **Polling Unit of Measure**: Units are Hours, Minutes, or Seconds. Set this to Seconds.

d. **Connection String**: This is the connection string to the database where the stored procedure exists. Click the ellipsis to configure this setting. Once the values have been set, click the Test Settings button to ensure that the values are valid. Note that allowing the password to be saved will ensure that when exporting to an MSI file, the password will be stored. If it has not been saved, it will have to be set when imported to a new environment.

e. **Document Root Element Name**: This is the root element of the schema that the document being retrieved will adhere to. In this case, this will be set to COMMON_810. The root node of the document being retrieved by the stored procedure (<TRANSACTION>) will be wrapped by this node.

f. **Document Target Namespace**: This value must match the target namespace of the schema that the document being retrieved is set to. To find this value, open the schema in Visual Studio and find the Target Namespace property. For this solution, set the value to http://schemas.Apress.com/Common/810/v1.

g. **SQL Command**: When calling a stored procedure that returns a formatted XML document, all that needs to be set for this property is the SQL command to execute the stored procedure. In this case, set the value to exec spGetInvoice.

h. **URI**: The URI identifies this document from other documents. This must be a unique value and can generally be set to the default value that the receive location will be set to automatically. Even though this is set automatically, ensure that this value is unique when there is more than a single SQL receive location. For this solution, this property should be set to SQL://DEMO/Apress.EDI.Custom/Invoice. Note that each time this property comes into view (when the window is opened) BizTalk may automatically reset it to the default value. Make sure each time the SQL Transport properties are viewed (or modified), this value is set to the correct value.

5. Back on the main receive location configuration screen, set the Receive Pipeline property to XMLReceive.
6. On the Schedule tab, configure the receive location to execute during the appropriate hours. For example, there are frequently database backups that run during the early morning hours, networks are occasionally offline for maintenance, and so on. It may be appropriate to force the processing of documents to occur only during business hours. For this solution, the receive location will always be turned on (no modifications to the schedule are necessary).
7. Click OK. All values have been configured to call the stored procedure and return an XML document. Later chapters will discuss exception handling and tracking options.

Implementing Linked Servers

Generally speaking, data is stored in an enterprise-level database, which may or may not be SQL Server 2005. In cases where this is not SQL 2005, it is possible to use the same model discussed in the previous section, by implementing linked servers. Exercise 3-3 outlines the modifications that need to be made to the stored procedure shown in Listing 3-2 to allow it to interact with a linked server.

There are some limitations to linked servers that should be looked at prior to implementing them in a solution—most importantly, the increased demand on the network for the traffic generated between the database that houses the stored procedure and the database that is being linked to. For many EDI implementations, documents are retrieved from source systems on timed intervals (perhaps once a day, hourly, etc.), and the demand on the network is negligible; in such cases, linked servers are an ideal solution. In other cases, where large numbers of documents may be returned on a very frequent basis, it will likely make more sense to develop an interface directly between BizTalk Server and the source data store (such as through the use of a custom adapter). For purposes of discussion here, it is assumed linked servers will fulfill the requirements. Figure 3-8 depicts the components used when retrieving XML data from a linked server.

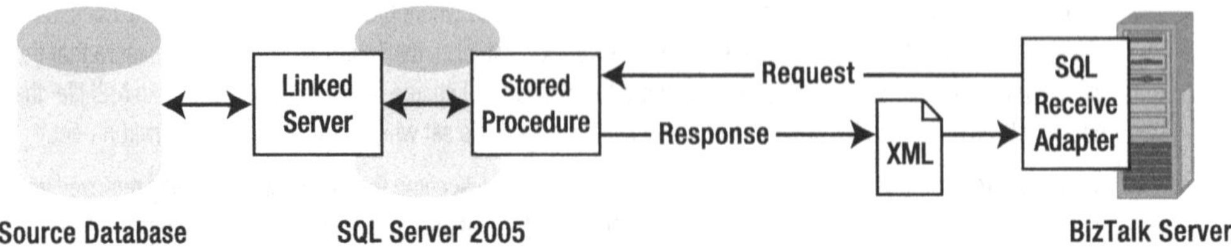

Figure 3-8. *Retrieving data using XML and linked servers*

Exercise 3-3. Using a Linked Server

The following steps indicate how to add a linked server to SQL Server 2005 and how to modify the stored procedure created earlier in this chapter (see Listing 3-2) to interact with this linked server (instead of with tables on the same database as the stored procedure):

1. Open SQL Server Management Studio. Expand Server Objects ➤ Linked Servers.
2. Right-click Linked Servers and select New Linked Server.
3. Name the linked server (this is how it will be referred to in the stored procedure) and configure all of the details about how to connect to it on the General tab. For this exercise, the name will be TestLinkedServer.
4. On the Security tab, indicate how to connect to the target system. This should be set to use the same BizTalk account as is configured to run the SQL Receive Adapter; when the stored procedure executes, it will run under the context of this account. In turn, the linked server connection will impersonate this account. The account that runs the SQL Receive Adapter is generally the BizTalkServerApplication, about which information can be obtained in the BizTalk Administration Console under Platform Settings ➤ Host Instances. Right-click the BizTalkServerApplication account and select Properties to see how this account has been configured.

   Once the linked server has been set up and verified, the stored procedure must be modified to be able to interact with it. This is a very simple modification, consisting primarily in changing the table names to the full linked server table name. Take the following steps:

   a. Add a new command at the top of the stored procedure as follows. This will ensure that connections to the linked server are handled properly:

   ```
   BEGIN -- this is existing in the original
    SET XACT_ABORT ON -- this is new for linked server
    SET NOCOUNT ON; -- this is existing in the original
   ```

   b. Change the names of the tables that stored the data to the full name of the linked server for all SELECT and UPDATE statements. For example, if the original select statement is

   ```
   SELECT vchType As "TYPE"
   FROM tblInvoiceLineItems
   ```

   For the linked server it would be

   ```
   SELECT vchType AS "TYPE"
   FROM TestLinkedServer.[database].[table name]

   -- or --

   SELECT vchType AS "TYPE"
   FROM TestLinkedServer.[instance].[database].[table name]
   ```

   c. Change any of the field names as appropriate for all UPDATE and SELECT statements.

Mapping the Document

Once the source and target schemas have been defined, and it is determined how the data will be retrieved, the actual mapping can take place. Mapping requirements can be simple or complex, depending on the requirements outlined in the implementation guide (or defined by the trading partner). In some cases, it may be as easy as dragging the source element and dropping it on the target element. In other cases, it may be more involved, requiring custom functoids, external .NET assemblies, and lookup tables. In any case, simple or complex, some amount of logic will need to be put into place to ensure that the document is mapped correctly.

This section outlines some common tasks that may be encountered during the mapping of EDI documents. Exercise 3-4 walks step-by-step through the creation of the map, including the configuration and placement of functoids. Before working through the exercise, however, it is important to look at several items. When mapping EDI documents, keep the following in mind:

- **Target node**: Information about the target element can be obtained from one of the properties on the target schema: the Notes property (see Figure 3-9). This property can be useful when trying to determine what different elements represent, as it describes the expected content of the node.

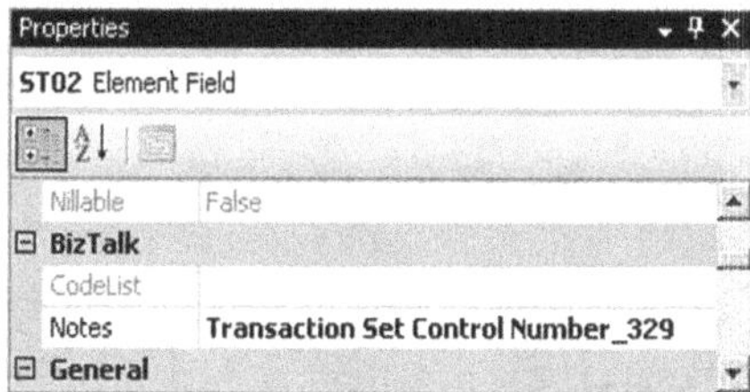

Figure 3-9. *The Notes property on the EDI schema*

- **Functoid input parameter order**: When configuring any functoid, ensure that the input fields are in the correct order. For example, when using a value mapping functoid, the first parameter must always return a boolean value, while the second parameter should always represent the value to be mapped when the boolean value is True.
- **Transaction ID**: The ST segment (or the UNH segment for EDIFACT documents) contains one element that can either be mapped or configured in the trading partner EDI settings. This element is ST02 (or UNH1 for EDIFACT), and it represents the unique identifier of the document (known as the *transaction set control/reference number*). For tracking purposes, it is very useful to take a unique document identifier from the source system and map it to this field; this way, the document can be tracked from the source system, through BizTalk Server, to the document that is delivered to the trading partner. However, in some cases it may make more sense to have BizTalk override this with a unique ID that is automatically generated by the system. The first approach is done through the use of a map, while the second can be set using BizTalk Administration Console in the EDI properties for a party using the GS and ST segment definition (or UNG and UNH segment definition for EDIFACT).

- **Conditional incremental counters**: The IT101 and CTT01 elements generally contain incremental counters indicating line item counts. These counters can be complex to calculate when there are line items in the source document that are not mapped, and therefore not counted. In simple cases, when all line items are mapped from the source document to the target document, an iteration functoid or record count functoid could be used to set these values. But in cases where there are unmapped line items, a global variable in the map is useful. A global variable allows a counter to be set and incremented for all items that are mapped, ignoring unmapped values. Listings 3-3 and 3-4 are used in the functoids included in the calculation of the IT101 and CTT01 elements.

The code in Listing 3-3 shows how to set and increment a global variable in a map each time the script functoid that the code is contained within is executed. In Exercise 3-4, this value is used in the IT101 element for each line item that is mapped.

Listing 3-3. *Iteration Counter Using a Global Variable Within a Map*

```
System.Collections.ArrayList _globalArrayList = new System.Collections.ArrayList();

public int intIterator(bool blnInput)
{
 int intRetVal = 0;
 if(blnInput == true)
 {
  // each time add 1 to the array
  int intCount = 1;
  globalArrayList.Add(intCount);

  for (int intI=0; intI<_globalArrayList.Count; intI++)
  {
   intRetVal += (int)_globalArrayList[intI];
  }
 }
 return intRetVal;
}
```

With the global variable (globalArrayList) incrementing each time a line item is mapped to the target schema, a running total is kept. Once all line items have been mapped, the final value can be reused to populate the CTT01 element, which represents the total number of line items mapped in the EDI document. Listing 3-4 shows the code used to access the count set in Listing 3-3. The full implementation of this code in a functoid within a map is outlined in Exercise 3-4.

Listing 3-4. *Accessing Total Iteration Counter*

```
public int intAccessTotal()
{
 int intRetVal = 0;
 for (int intI=0; intI<_globalArrayList.Count; intI++)
 {
  intRetVal += (int)_globalArrayList[intI];
 }
 return intRetVal;
}
```

Exercise 3-4. Creating an EDI Map

This exercise demonstrates how to add a new or existing map to a Visual Studio BizTalk 2006 project and create the mapping nodes needed for a sample EDI 810 (invoice) document. It is based on the EDI implementation guides shown in the figures throughout this exercise:

1. Open the Visual Studio solution. For this exercise, open Apress.Integration.EDI810.sln.
2. To add a new or existing map, right-click the project to which the map will be added. In this example, right-click Apress.Integration.EDI810.CompanyX.
   a. To add a new map, select Add ➤ New Item. In the window that opens, click Map Files and select Map from the right-hand window. This will add a new map to the project. In this case, create a new map named CommonXMLToCompanyX810.btm.
   b. To add an existing map, select Add ➤ Existing Item. Browse to the location of the map, select it, and click Add. This will add an existing map. The rest of this exercise assumes that the map does not already exist.
3. Once the new map is added, make sure that it is open in Visual Studio. Two links will appear: a link for the source schema, and a link for the target (or destination) schema.
   a. To add the source schema, click Open Source Schema. In the BizTalk Type Picker window that opens, select the document that will be the source schema. Because this solution uses a separate project to store the source schema, it appears under References. Expand References ➤ Apress.Integration.EDI810.CompanyX ➤ Schemas and select Apress.Integration.EDI810.Common.CommonXML. This will set the source schema for the map.
   b. To add the target schema, click Open Destination Schema. In the BizTalk Type Picker, select Schemas ➤ Apress.Integration.EDI810.CompanyX. X12_00401_810_CompanyX. This sets the target schema for the map.
4. Map the fields according to the trading partner requirements, as shown in these steps:
   a. All maps are created with a single tab. To aid in organizing a complex map, rename this tab to ST. Additional tabs will be created for different EDI document segments. The ST segment is known as the *transaction set header*. The map for the ST segment is shown in Figure 3-11 and is based on the requirements outlined in the implementation guide shown in Figure 3-10.

Ref	Data Element Summary / Mapping Details	Length
ST01	Transaction Set Identifier Code	3/3
	Code uniquely identifying a Transaction Set	
	Set to 810 Invoice	
ST02	Transaction Set Control Number	4/9
	Identifying control number - must be unique within functional group.	

Figure 3-10. *Mapping the ST segment*

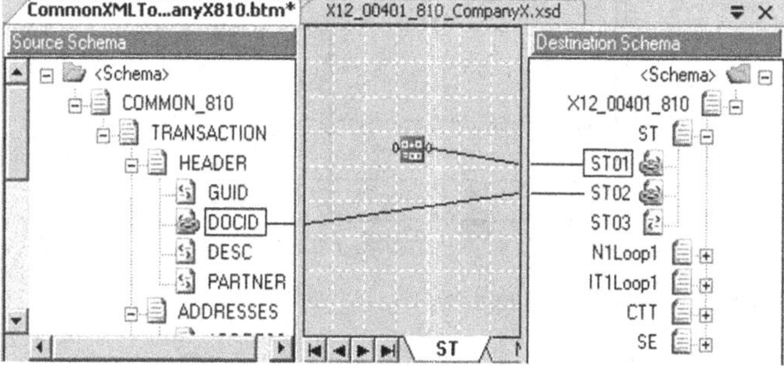

Figure 3-11. *ST segment (mapping details)*

i. **ST01**: Drag and drop a Concatenate functoid onto the map surface. Double-click the shape and set it to 810. Connect it to the ST01 node in the target schema. This segment indicates the Transaction Set Identifier Code, which in this case is the same as the document type.

ii. **ST02**: Map the DOCID element from the source schema to the ST02 element on the target schema. This is the unique document ID (transaction set control number) that can be used to identify a document in the source system, throughout BizTalk Server components, and with the trading partner once the document has been delivered.

b. Create a new tab on the map for the N1 loop. Right-click the ST tab (at the bottom of the map surface) and select Add Page. Name the new page N1 loop. The N1 loop contains segments with name, address, and other company contact information. Refer to Figure 3-12 and Figure 3-13 for the mapping specifications. The final map is shown in Figure 3-14.

Ref	Data Element Summary / Mapping Details	Length
N101	Entity Identifier Code	2/3
	Identify organization, physical location, property, or individual	
	ST or BT	
N102	Name	1/60
	Free form name of entity.	

Figure 3-12. *N1 segment (mapping details)*

Ref	Data Element Summary / Mapping Details	Length
N401	City Name	2/30
	Free form string representing city	
N402	State or Province Code	2/2
	Code defined by government agency.	
N403	Postal Code	3/15
	Exclude dashes and blanks. Example: 98765	

Figure 3-13. *N4 segment (mapping details)*

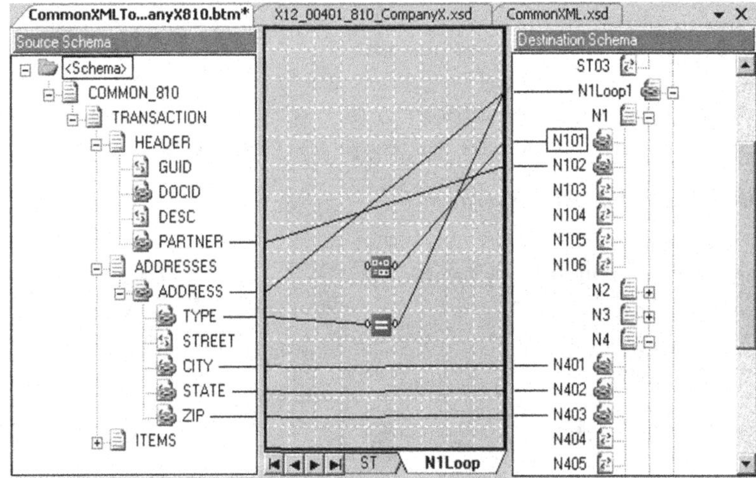

Figure 3-14. *Mapping the N1 loop segments*

To map the N1 loop segments, follow these steps:

i. **N1 loop**: In this demonstration, the source schema may contain multiple ADDRESS nodes. The only address that should be used for mapping the N1 node is the address with a Type = "Billing". The following steps ensure that no subnode to the N1 loop will be mapped in the target element unless the address type is appropriate:

   1. Drag and drop an Equals functoid onto the mapping surface.
   2. Double-click the Equals functoid and create a constant value of Billing.
   3. Drag the TYPE element from the source ADDRESS node to the Equals functoid.
   4. Drag the output of the Equals functoid to the N1Loop1 node on the target schema.
   5. Map the ADDRESS node from the source to the N1Loop1 node in the target.

ii. **N101**: Drop a Concatenate functoid on the map surface. Set the value of this functoid to ST. Drag the output of this functoid to the N101 node in the target schema. This represents the entity identifier code.

iii. **N102**: Drag the source schema element PARTNER to the target schema node N102. This represents the name of the trading partner.

iv. **N401**: Drag the source element CITY to the target N401 element. This represents the city name.

v. **N402**: Drag the source element STATE to the target N402 element. This represents the state name.

vi. **N403**: Drag the source element ZIP to the target N403 element. This represents the postal code.

c. Create a new tab on the map for the IT1 loop and CTT segment. Because the data in both is closely related, some of the functoids will be used to generate data for multiple elements. Right-click one of the page tabs at the bottom of the map and select Add Page. Name the page IT1Loop/CTT. The IT1 loop represents line item information, while the CTT loop contains information about the total transaction (summed from line items). The specification for the IT1 loop is shown in Figure 3-15. The CTT loop will be covered in later steps in this exercise.

Ref	Data Element Summary / Mapping Details	Length
IT101	Assigned Identification	1/20
	This is a line item counter - numeric	
IT102	Quantity Invoiced	1/10
	Numeric value	
IT104	Unit Price	1/14
	Two decimal places, numeric	

Figure 3-15. *IT1 segment (mapping details)*

i. **IT1 loop**: A line item will only be mapped if TYPE = "Standard". The following steps will ensure that only valid line items are mapped:

   1. Drop a Scripting functoid on the mapping surface.
   2. Right-click the functoid and select Configure Functoid Script.
   3. Select Inline C# for the Script Type property.
   4. Enter the code in Listing 3-5 into the script window (as shown in Figure 3-16).

Listing 3-5. *Item Mapping Functoid*

```
// if ITEM is Hidden, it will not be
// mapped or counted in the Iteration total

public string strItemType (string strTYPE)
{
 string strRetVal = string.Empty;
 switch (strTYPE) {
 case "Hidden":
  strRetVal = string.Empty;
  break;
 default:
  strRetVal = "Map";
  break;
 return strRetVal;
}
```

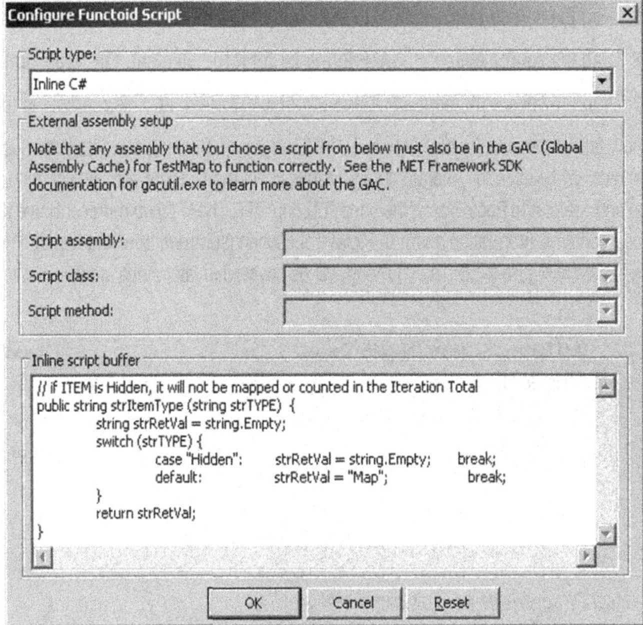

Figure 3-16. *Inline script for item type (scripting functoid)*

5. Click OK to save the code for the scripting functoid.
6. Drop an Equals functoid on the mapping surface, to the right of the Scripting functoid.
7. Right-click the Equals functoid and set a constant value of Map.
8. Drag the output of the Scripting functoid and drop it on the Equals functoid.
9. Drag the output of the Equals functoid and drop it on the It1Loop1 node in the target.

ii. IT101: This element represents the identifier for the line item. In this case, it will be a sequential number that begins at 1 and only increments for line items that are of a valid ("Standard") type. Figure 3-17 shows the mapping for the IT1 loop.

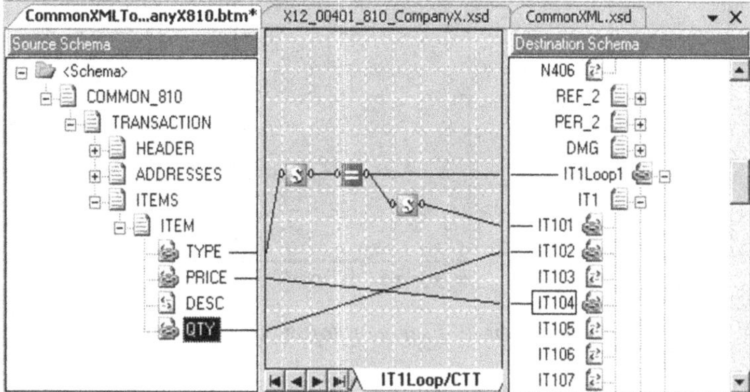

Figure 3-17. *Mapping the IT1 loop segment*

1. Drop a Scripting functoid on the mapping surface to the right of the Equals functoid.
2. Enter the inline C# code in Listing 3-3 for the scripting functoid. This will ensure that the line item is only incremented for valid line items.
3. Make the input for the Scripting functoid the output of the equals functoid.
4. Map the output of the Scripting functoid to the target schema element IT101.

iii. IT102: Drag the QTY element from the source document and drop it on the IT102 element in the target schema. This represents the quantity invoiced.

iv. IT104: Drag the PRICE element from the source document and drop it on the IT104 element in the target schema. This element is the unit price.

Using the same tab, the CTT mapping will now be added. Refer to Figure 3-18 for the implementation.

Ref	Data Element Summary / Mapping Details	Length
CTT01	Number of Line Items	1/6
	Sum of line items in IT1 Loop	
CTT02	Total value invoiced	1/20
	Sum of all line item prices multiplied by the quantity of that item.	

Figure 3-18. *CTT segment (mapping details)*

v. CTT01: This represents the total number of line items that are mapped in the IT1 loop. This must be a total of only valid line items (i.e., Type = "Standard"). Drop a Scripting functoid on the mapping surface and enter the inline C# code shown in Listing 3-4.

vi. CTT02: This represents a total of all line items. Some line items may indicate more than a single item as the quantity; therefore quantity and price are a factor in calculating this field. The completed map for the CTT01 and CTT02 segments is shown in Figure 3-19.

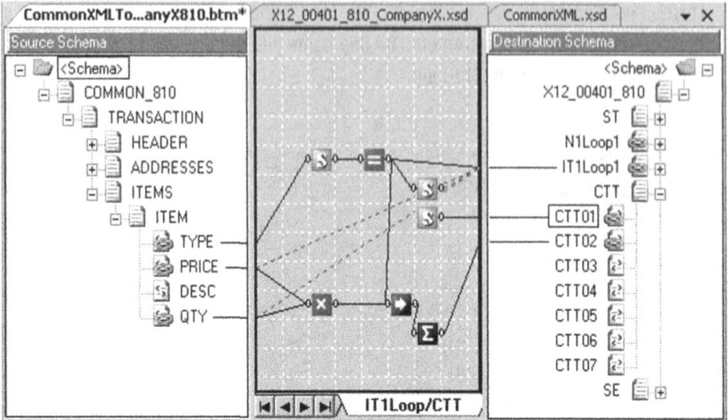

Figure 3-19. *Mapping the CTT segment (after IT1 loop mapping)*

1. Drop a Multiplication functoid on the mapping surface. Drag and drop two inputs to this functoid (in any order) from the source schema: the PRICE and QTY elements.
2. Drop a Value Mapping functoid on the map surface, to the right of the Multiplication functoid (and to the right of the Equals functoid created for the IT1 loop). This functoid has two inputs; the first is the output from the Equals functoid, ensuring that the line item is valid (equal to "Standard"); the second is the output from the Multiplication functoid. Validate that the output from the Equals functoid is the first input parameter, as it is a boolean value.
3. Drop a Cumulative Sum functoid on the map surface to the right of the others. The input to this functoid is the output of the Value Mapping functoid. The cumulative sum is a total of all line items mapped in the IT1 segment.
4. Drop the output of the Cumulative Sum functoid on the CTT02 element in the target.

5. All of the mapping steps have been completed, and the map is ready to be saved and tested. Save the map file in Visual Studio.

Testing the Map

Throughout the development of the map, it is essential to test the output. For the majority of mapping development, all map tests can be done within the Visual Studio environment. Working in Visual Studio, it is easy to test the map, giving a sample input instance and generating the output document. This section provides a detailed exercise demonstrating how to test the map created in the previous section.

There are several fields that have been configured to fail (in the exercise just completed) when testing the map. This is to demonstrate how to find and fix errors during testing. The errors occur on the following nodes:

- **IT104:** By default, this element is mapped with decimal places (from the source schema element PRICE), since the value in SQL Server is returned as SQL data type Money. The target schema has a restriction on this field that requires that it is a valid currency value (two decimals or less). A functoid will be used to solve this issue.

- **N402**: The target schema indicates that this should be a two-character code indicating the state or province. The source data contains the entire name of the state and is a standard string. The trading partner requires that the entire string be passed in the EDI document. The target schema will be modified to solve this issue.

The document shown in Listing 3-6 is a sample instance of a result set returned by the stored procedure configured earlier in this chapter. Testing a map is most easily done when using a valid input document (it can be done with an automatically generated instance, but this often does not adhere to valid data). This is why defining the source data and putting into place the components for retrieval are done before beginning any mapping development. Exercise 3-5 demonstrates how to test a map.

Listing 3-6. *Sample Input Instance*


```
<COMMON_810 xmlns="http://schemas.Apress.com/Common/810/v1">
<TRANSACTION>
  <HEADER>
    <GUID>8F97D20B-687F-4B82-A231-13BB30944E47</GUID>
    <DOCID>1000</DOCID>
    <DESC>Sample Invoice #1 for Company Y</DESC>
    <PARTNER>Company Y</PARTNER>
  </HEADER>
  <ADDRESSES>
    <ADDRESS>
      <TYPE>Billing</TYPE>
      <STREET>99 Highway R</STREET>
      <CITY>City R</CITY>
      <STATE>State B</STATE>
      <ZIP>23456</ZIP>
    </ADDRESS>
  </ADDRESSES>
  <ITEMS>
    <ITEM>
      <TYPE>Standard</TYPE>
      <PRICE>12.0000</PRICE>
      <DESC>Item K</DESC>
      <QTY>2</QTY>
    </ITEM>
    <ITEM>
      <TYPE>Standard</TYPE>
      <PRICE>10.0000</PRICE>
      <DESC>Item K</DESC>
      <QTY>2</QTY>
    </ITEM>
    <ITEM>
      <TYPE>Hidden</TYPE>
      <PRICE>100.0000</PRICE>
      <DESC>Item J</DESC>
      <QTY>1</QTY>
    </ITEM>
  </ITEMS>
</TRANSACTION>
</COMMON_810>
```

Exercise 3-5. Testing the EDI Map

Use the following steps to test the map created in Exercise 3-4:

1. Open the Apress.Integration.EDI810 solution that contains the Visual Studio map created in the previous section. This can be found in the sample files at Apress.Integration\Chapter 3\Apress.Integration.EDI810.sln.
2. Build the solution in Visual Studio (right-click the solution and select Build Solution).
3. In the Apress.Integration.EDI810.CompanyX project, right-click the map that is going to be tested (CommonXMLToCompanyX810.btm) and select Properties. Begin with an XML output that is not validated. Aside from the TestMap Input Instance, set the properties as shown in Figure 3-20.

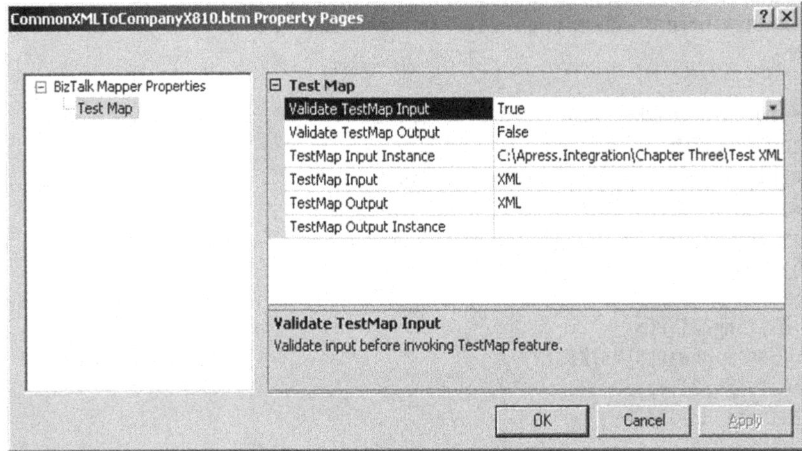

Figure 3-20. *The map property page with initial configuration*

4. Set the TestMap Input Instance to a valid source document. This is the document that is returned by the SQL Server stored procedure, along with the root node that wraps the document when the SQL Adapter retrieves the document. See Listing 3-6 for a valid instance, or open an actual instance from the sample files at Apress.Integration\Chapter 3\Test Documents\Source 810 XML.xml.
5. Click OK to save the settings and close the window.
6. Right-click the map and select Test Map. This will generate a nonvalidated XML instance of the map output. The output box will display a link to the output document. If the output box is not available, click View ➤ Output on the menu bar. Additionally, if the X12 EDI Instance Properties dialog box pops up, accept the default values and click OK. The output document can be viewed by holding the CTRL key and clicking the link next to the output: The Output Is Stored in the Following File. Figure 3-21 shows the instance as it appears after clicking this link.

```
C:\Documents and Settings\Administrator\Local Settings\Temp\_MapData\CommonXMLToCompan...
URL: C:\Documents and Settings\Administrator\Local Settings\Temp\_MapData\CommonXMLToCompanyX810_outpu

- <ns0:X12_00401_810
    xmlns:ns0="http://schemas.microsoft.com/BizTalk/EDI/X12/2006">
  - <ST>
      <ST01>810</ST01>
      <ST02>1000</ST02>
    </ST>
  - <ns0:N1Loop1>
    - <ns0:N1>
        <N101>ST</N101>
        <N102>Company Y</N102>
      </ns0:N1>
    - <ns0:N4>
        <N401>City R</N401>
        <N402>State B</N402>
        <N403>23456</N403>
      </ns0:N4>
    </ns0:N1Loop1>
  - <ns0:IT1Loop1>
    - <ns0:IT1>
        <IT101>1</IT101>
        <IT102>2</IT102>
        <IT104>12.0000</IT104>
      </ns0:IT1>
    </ns0:IT1Loop1>
  - <ns0:IT1Loop1>
    - <ns0:IT1>
        <IT101>2</IT101>
        <IT102>2</IT102>
        <IT104>10.0000</IT104>
      </ns0:IT1>
    </ns0:IT1Loop1>
  - <ns0:CTT>
      <CTT01>2</CTT01>
      <CTT02>44</CTT02>
    </ns0:CTT>
  </ns0:X12_00401_810>
```


Figure 3-21. *Test map output in XML*

7. With the output visually validated (i.e., matching what is expected by the developer to be output), the test map settings can be set to a higher level of validation. Right-click the map and select Properties. This time, set the Validate TestMap Output property to True.

8. Click OK, right-click the map again, and select Test Map. This time an error is thrown. There is invalid data in the N402 node. The sample data contains the string "State B," whereas the target schema indicates that the N402 node must contain a two-character code (state or province abbreviation). In this case, there are three options for solving this mapping issue:

   a. **Change the source data**: Instead of extracting the string from the database exactly as it is stored, logic could be implemented in the stored procedure to return the data in a two-character code.

   b. **Change the map**: Logic could be put into place in the map to convert the full string to a valid two-character string. This would most likely require either a lookup table in a database (string to state code characters) or a large case statement (case "California" then "CA").

c. **Change the target schema**: Depending on the requirements of the trading partner, it may be that the best place to change the requirement is in the target schema. Remove the restriction from the N402 element and save the schema. For this exercise, the approach that will be taken is to modify the target schema. In the case of the trading partner, Company X, the entire string denoting the state is required (i.e., the partner wants the full string, not just the two-character code). The steps for modifying the target schema are as follows:

i. Open the target schema (X12_00401_810_CompanyX.xsd) in Visual Studio.

ii. Expand the N1Loop1 node and click the N4 element N402. The properties should be displayed automatically. If they are not visible, right-click the element and select Properties. Change the Length property to nothing—remove the 2. Save the schema. This allows any length of string to be present in the element.

iii. Rebuild the solution (right-click the solution and select Rebuild Solution).

1. If the Clean Up Global Types window is open, click OK. There is no need to do anything with the information in this window.

2. If the X12 EDI Instance Properties window opens, skip it for now. It will be used later in this exercise.

3. If a dialog appears indicating that the destination schema for a map has changed, click OK.

9. Retest the map. Right-click the map and select Test Map. Two additional errors occur; this time on the IT104 node. The error indicates that the current value has too many decimal places and is not recognized as a valid value in the target schema. Again, there are three options in solving this issue:

a. **Change the source data**: The data is stored in SQL as a data type of Money and automatically sets four decimal places. The stored procedure could be modified to return two decimals or round to the nearest dollar. However, by fixing this in the stored procedure, the data will be extracted the same for all trading partners. Some partners may wish to have two decimals, while others may want it rounded to the nearest dollar (no decimal places). Changing this in the stored procedure would limit the result to one or the other.

b. **Change the target schema**: The target schema for the trading partner could have the restriction removed from the IT104 node. However, for this exercise, the trading partner requires that the restriction remain.

c. **Change the map**: The map can be updated with additional logic to ensure that the price is rounded and matches the target schema requirements. In this case, changing the map is the desired solution. See Figure 3-22 for a completed view of the modified map.

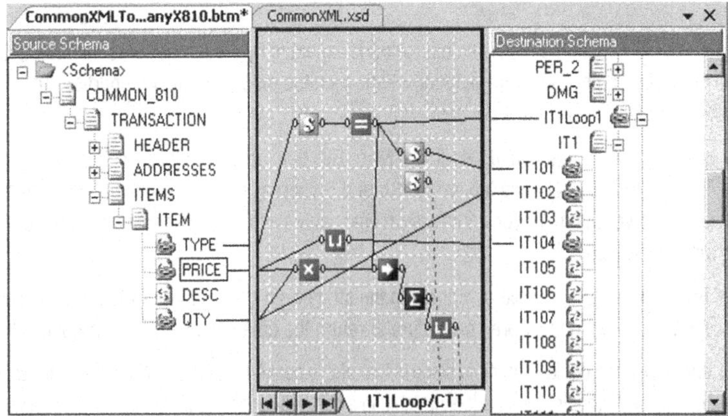

Figure 3-22. *Adding the round functoid to fix the IT1 and CTT rounding issue*

10. Open the map in Visual Studio. Remove the link between PRICE and IT104 by right-clicking it and selecting Delete.

11. Drop a Round functoid on the mapping surface.

12. Set the first input to this functoid as the PRICE element from the source schema. The second input should be a 2, which is the number of decimals to round the value to.
13. Drag the output of the Round functoid and drop it on the IT104 element in the target schema.
14. A similar approach can be taken for the Cumulative Sum functoid, which outputs to the CTT02 element. Drop a Round functoid to ensure that the value output from this functoid is rounded to two decimal places.
15. Save the map. Retest by right-clicking the map and selecting Test Map. This time the output will be validated.
16. The final step is to set the test map output to the Native EDI format. Right-click the map and select Properties. For the TestMap Output property, select Native. This time when the map is tested, the output will be generated in standard EDI format (instead of XML). Different trading partners require output in different formats, with different delimiters and trailing separators. All of this is configured for each trading partner in the EDI properties in the party settings. For testing the map, however, this is configured each time the map is tested in native format.
    a. Right-click the map and select Test Map.
    b. The X12 EDI Instance Properties dialog box will open; up to this point, this window has been ignored, as it has no impact on the XML output. However, in native format, the output of the document can be controlled. The most important setting to configure is the segment separator suffix. This value can be set to control whether each segment is on its own line, or whether the output is all on a single line. The only purpose for this during map testing is to allow a developer to more easily validate the output document, especially when checking against existing EDI documents. These settings have no impact on the map itself. Set the segment separator to CR LF and ensure that the Use Trailing Delimiters property is set to Yes. Continue to click OK until this value has been set (this dialog box may appear multiple times).
    c. The output box will again give a link to the generated output. Clicking the link will open the document shown in Figure 3-23. The output shown in Figure 3-23 matches the output shown earlier in the chapter in Listing 3-1.

```
ST*810*1000~
N1*ST*Company Y~
N4*City R*State B*23456~
IT1*1*2**12~
IT1*2*2**10~
CTT*2*44~
SE*7*1000~
```

Figure 3-23. *Test map output in native EDI format*

17. Save and rebuild the solution. The testing of the map is complete.

Final Discussion

This chapter covers many aspects of defining, retrieving, and mapping data. The mapping steps were specific to X12 EDI documents, but the principles of mapping are the same for all EDIFACT document types. Once the maps have been fully developed and tested, they must be deployed to BizTalk and added to the trading partner ports or incorporated into orchestrations. The steps for deploying, configuring, and adding the maps to trading partners is covered in detail in later chapters.

Additional topics that may be of use in EDI document mapping are the following:

- **Result sets as flat file feeds:** On occasion, it may be necessary to have the external data source process and deliver the data to BizTalk, rather than using BizTalk to poll it through a SQL Receive Adapter. Perhaps linked servers are not an option (the processing/network overhead is deemed to be too high or SQL Server is unable to connect), or perhaps it makes better business sense to process the data in large batches (on a daily or weekly schedule, rather than a single document at a time). In such cases other delivery methods must be implemented. An example of this would be using the SAP Adapter to retrieve IDOCS from an SAP system.
- In Figure 3-24, a high-level flow of publishing data to BizTalk server is shown. Whether that data is preformed in XML, or whether it is a flat file and requires a pipeline on the file adapter, the process of delivery is incumbent on the source application. BizTalk is a passive listener and waits for the data to be delivered.

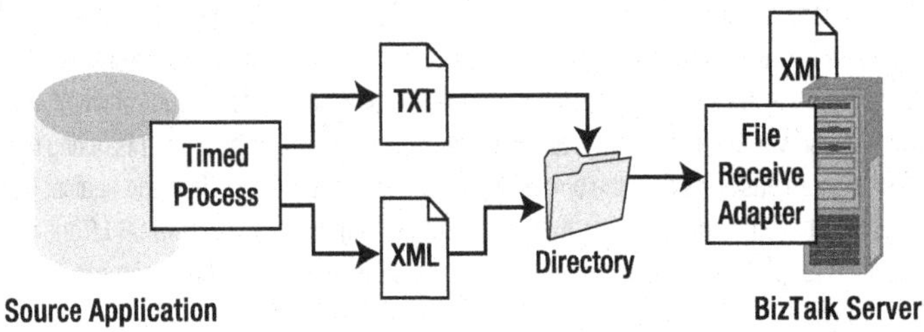

Figure 3-24. *Retrieving data as a file*

- **Data lookup tables:** Source data may require lookup tables in the map to properly convert the value to what the target party is expecting. In such situations, using some of the database functoids may be of use, or creating a custom functoid may be required.
- **XSLT and complex mapping:** For complex mapping situations, it may be necessary to use XSLT either in combination with, or as a substitute for, the graphical BizTalk mapping interface. XSLT documents provide a developer with complete flexibility in mapping data, provided that the developer understands XSLT and that it is a viable solution that can be supported once it has been developed.

CHAPTER 4

EDI and Orchestrations

Orchestrations enable complex handling of documents, either for processes that require multiple steps, or for processes that require extended exception handling capabilities or validation routines. This chapter outlines a number of scenarios in which orchestrations could be used in an EDI implementation, and it introduces a number of concepts that enable developers of BizTalk EDI solutions to support complex logic and flow, including the following:

- **Routing incoming EDI documents (and filtering)**: In most EDI environments, all EDI documents are received (and delivered) on the same location, often via FTP or VAN (value-added network). It is important to understand how to route different EDI document types to different objects within BizTalk (e.g., an 864 should be routed to one orchestration, whereas a document of a different type should be routed elsewhere).
- **Delivering EDI documents via orchestrations**: One of the top reasons to include document delivery within an orchestration (rather than to simply use send ports) is to ensure that a document passes EDI validation in the pipeline and, if it does not, to catch the exception and notify an administrator.
- **Exception handling**: One of the most important topics for any EDI solution (and integration projects in general) is exception handling. BizTalk Server 2006 provides for many ways to build robust exception handling, ensuring that the proper steps are taken when documents fail (such as notification of an administrator). This chapter outlines a generic exception handler that can be used for a variety of purposes.
- **Accessing schema data in orchestrations**: There is frequently the need to access values in messages that have arrived in an orchestration. When unique values exist and can be set as promoted properties or distinguished fields, this can be very straightforward. But when working with complex documents that may have undefined schemas (such as those using <ANY> nodes) or many recurring nodes (e.g., line items on an order) the use of XPath and/or BizTalk maps may be necessary.

Preparing the Solution Files

This chapter uses the sample files provided with the code that accompanies this book, which should be extracted to C:\Apress.Integration\Chapter 4. Exercise 4-1 prepares the sample code on the local machine.

■ Note The majority of exercises within this chapter write information to the Windows Event Viewer. This is simply to demonstrate that the orchestration is processing data and is primarily used to represent where actual orchestration steps would appear. One thing to note about logging data to the Event Viewer is that it has a maximum string length of 32K. It is acceptable to log information to the Event Viewer in a production orchestration, but it should be ensured that the data being logged does not exceed this length, or an exception will be thrown. Strings can be easily truncated prior to logging, if desired. The exercises in this chapter log very small snippets of information, and will not exceed the 32K restriction.

Exercise 4-1. Preparing the Solution Files

Use the following steps to prepare the environment on the local machine:

1. Make sure that the Chapter4 sample files have been extracted and placed on the C:\ drive.
2. The components can be deployed in a single package by importing the Chapter4.MSI file available in C:\Apress.Integration\Chapter 4\BizTalk Application. Open BizTalk Administration Console and right-click the Applications folder. Select Import ➤ MSI File. This will create the EDI.Demonstration.Chapter4 BizTalk application and all of the BizTalk artifacts used in this chapter.

   There are a total of two solutions included for this chapter:

   a. The first solution, the 864 Process, is contained in the solution called Apress.Integration.EDI864.Common.sln. This solution contains the following files:

      i. A copy of the standard X12 864 schema, X12_00401_864.xsd

      ii. An orchestration representing the "original" version of the solution (as outlined in Exercise 4-2, in the next section), named Process864_Original.odx

      iii. An orchestration representing the "extended" version of the solution, from Exercise 4-5, later in the chapter, named Process864_Extended.odx

   b. The second solution, the components needed for the exception handler, is contained in C:\Apress.Integration\Chapter4 and is called Apress.Integration.Generic.ExceptionHandler.sln. This solution contains the following:

      i. A schema representing a "custom exception" (CustomException.xsd)

      ii. An orchestration representing the "original" version of the solution (as outlined in Exercise 4-3, later in the "Exception Handling" section of this chapter), named ExceptionHandler_Original.odx

      iii. An orchestration representing the "extended" version of the solution, from Exercise 4-4, later in the chapter, named ExceptionHandler_Extended.odx

Additionally, there is a sample version of an 864 EDI document located in C:\Apress.Integration\Chapter 4\Test Documents (Sample864Instance.txt).

Routing Incoming EDI Documents (Filtering)

This section outlines how documents can be routed when multiple types of EDI documents are arriving on the same location. In the case of VANs, there is generally a single folder where all of the documents of all of the trading partners are routed; 810s, 404s, 864s, 997s, TAs, and any other document types all arrive on the same location. There are a variety of ways to use BizTalk to route these documents, but the most appropriate approach for many EDI solutions is to use filters on orchestrations and send ports. These filters allow a port or orchestration to receive only those documents they are interested in, ignoring all others, that arrive on a single incoming receive port.

For example, assuming that all documents come in on the same receive port, and that the EDI receive pipeline is being used, a message can be routed on a number of properties that have been automatically promoted. For X12 solutions, one of the most obvious fields is the ST01 element, as it contains an identifier telling the type of EDI document. Using this property (EDI.ST01), a document can be routed to the appropriate subscribers, as shown in Figure 4-1. Exercise 4-2 details the steps needed to create an orchestration that subscribes to 864 messages using this property.

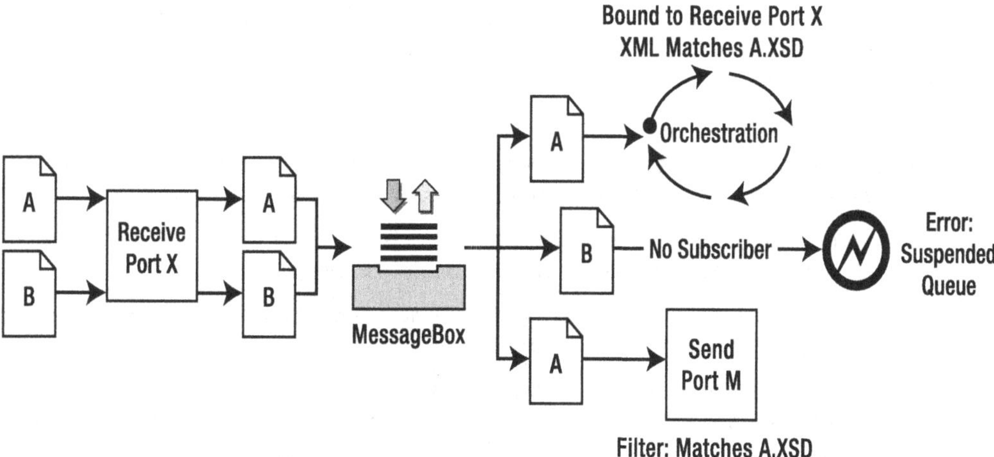

Figure 4-1. *Routing messages based on filters*

Exercise 4-2. Subscribing to EDI Documents with an Orchestration

This exercise outlines how to subscribe to specific types of EDI documents that arrive on a receive location. In actual EDI implementations, many types of EDI documents arrive on the same location, each of which is generally handled by a separate process. This exercise demonstrates how to create an orchestration that subscribes to only one type of document that arrives: the 864 (text message). This exercise uses the files contained in the solution C:\Apress.Integration\Chapter 4\Apress.Integration.EDI864.Common.sln, and uses the Process864_Original.odx orchestration file.

The orchestration developed in these steps is extended in a later exercise (Exercise 4-5) to demonstrate how to communicate exceptions and custom error messages. Figure 4-2 shows the flow of the components that are constructed in this exercise.

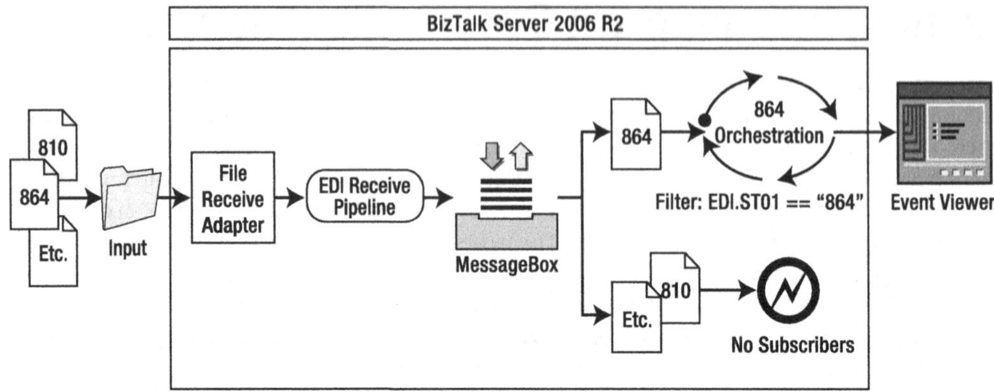

Figure 4-2. *864 process orchestration flow*

1. Create a new project in Visual Studio and do the following:

   a. Set a strong name key and reference it in the project properties. The creation of a strong name key can most easily be done by opening up a Visual Studio command prompt, relocating to the appropriate directory where the solution files are, and entering the following:

   ```
   sn -k [name of key].snk
   ```

   b. Ensure that the application name on the Deployment tab of the configuration properties in the project properties is set to an appropriate BizTalk application. For this solution, set it to EDI.Demonstration.Chapter4.

   c. Add a new orchestration by right-clicking the project and selecting Add ➤ New Item. Select a new orchestration and give it an appropriate name; this exercise uses Process864.odx. Click Add.

   d. With the orchestration open in Visual Studio, right-click the orchestration surface and select Properties Window. Set the Typename property to Process864Orch.

   e. Add a reference to Microsoft.BizTalk.Edi.BaseArtifacts.dll. This is located in Program Files\Microsoft BizTalk Server 2006. Adding this reference will allow the EDI properties to appear in the list available to the receive shape filter.

2. Using the following steps, create a new receive port and receive location, which are bound to a known file location. Different types of EDI documents are received on this file location, but only the 864 documents are routed to the orchestration:

   a. Right-click the port surface of the orchestration and select New Configured Port. Click Next to pass the first screen.

   b. Name the port Port_Receive864. Click Next.

   c. Leave the default values on the Select a Port Type page, except for the Port Type Name property, which can be set to PortType_Receive864. Click Next.

   d. Set the Port Direction property to I'll Always Be Receiving Messages on This Port, and the Port Binding property to Specify Now. Set the rest of the values as follows (shown in Figure 4-3):

      i. The Transport property should be set to FILE.

      ii. The URI should be an appropriate file directory where incoming EDI files will be dropped. For this exercise, it is set as C:\Apress.Integration\Chapter 4\Drops\Incoming - Subscribe 864 Only Demo*.*.

iii. Leave the receive pipeline set to the default. This value is set to the EDIReceive pipeline after the solution is deployed.

iv. Click Next and then Finish.

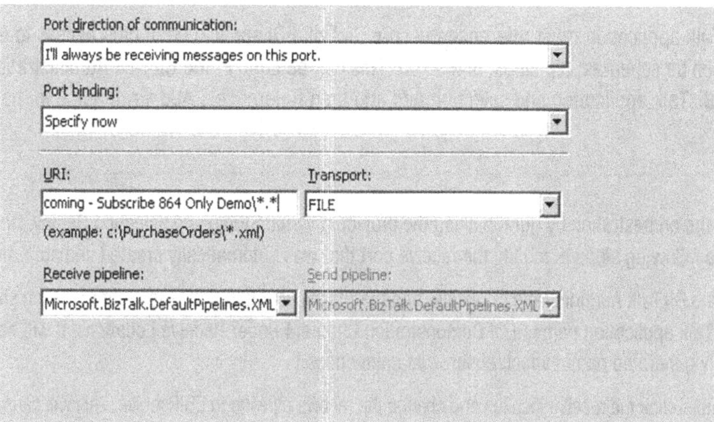

Figure 4-3. *Port binding for 864 orchestration*

3. Add the following items to the orchestration. The full orchestration is shown in Figure 4-7, at the end of this exercise.

   a. Create a new message on the Orchestration View tab. Right-click the Messages folder and select New Message. Set the message properties as follows:

      i. Name the message Msg_Incoming.

      ii. Set the Message Type property to System.Xml.XmlDocument.

   b. Drop a receive shape on the orchestration. Set the properties of this shape as follows:

      i. Name the shape Rec_864.

      ii. Set the Activate property to True.

      iii. Set the Message property to Msg_Incoming.

      iv. Set the Filter property as shown in Figure 4-4. This will ensure that even though the receive port allows for all XML documents to arrive, only those with the EDI ST01 property set to 864 will be allowed to instantiate the orchestration. This property, along with a number of others, is automatically promoted by the EDIReceive pipeline.

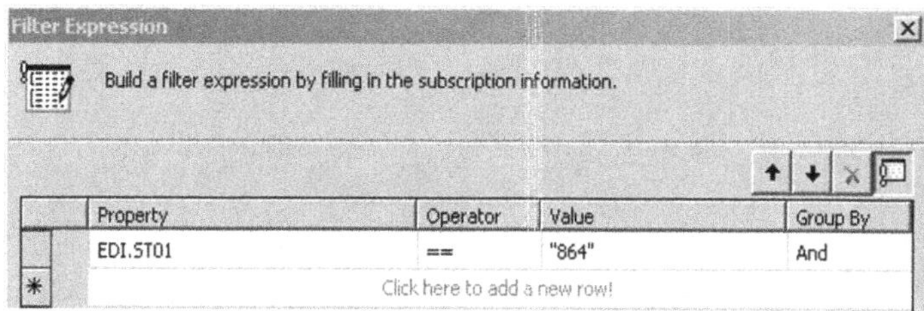

Figure 4-4. *Filter on receive shape*

c. Drop an expression shape on the orchestration after the receive shape that was just created. This will log an entry to the Windows Event Viewer by using the code shown here:

```
System.Diagnostics.EventLog.WriteEntry("864 Received","Demo");
```

■ **Note** A BizTalk application must reference the core BizTalk EDI application to gain access to the EDI-specific components, such as schemas, pipelines, and so on. This can be done in the BizTalk Administration Console by right-clicking a BizTalk application and selecting Add and then References. Add a reference to the BizTalk EDI application.

---

4. Deploy the orchestration by right-clicking the project in Visual Studio and selecting Deploy. Once it is deployed, take the following steps to modify the receive port that was automatically created and start the orchestration:

   a. In the BizTalk Administration Console, find the receive location that was created, which should be in the BizTalk application named EDI.Demonstration.Chapter4 under Receive Locations. It will have an automatically generated name, which ensures its uniqueness.

   b. Double-click the receive location and change the receive pipeline to EDIReceive. This will cause a number of the fields in the incoming EDI documents to be promoted and allow the filter created on the orchestration to retrieve documents with an 864 in the ST01 field. The EDI receive pipeline selection is shown in Figure 4-5.

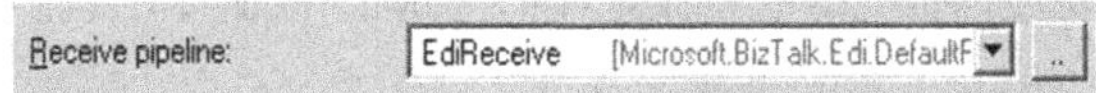

Figure 4-5. *Receive pipeline on receive location in BizTalk Administration Console*

■ **Note** Each time the orchestration is redeployed, the pipeline will be set back to the default pipeline, even if it has been set as EDIReceive in the BizTalk Administration Console. To make the EDI receive pipeline available in the orchestration development environment, a reference to the EDI pipeline assembly can be made. Right-click the Visual Studio project references, and add a new reference to Microsoft.BizTalk.Edi.EdiPipelines.dll, located in Program Files\Microsoft BizTalk Server 2006. Then when configuring the receive port on the port surface of the orchestration (or the Receive Port property in the properties window of the port), the option to select from a referenced assembly can be selected. This will pop up the window shown in Figure 4-6 and allow for the selection of the EDI receive port.

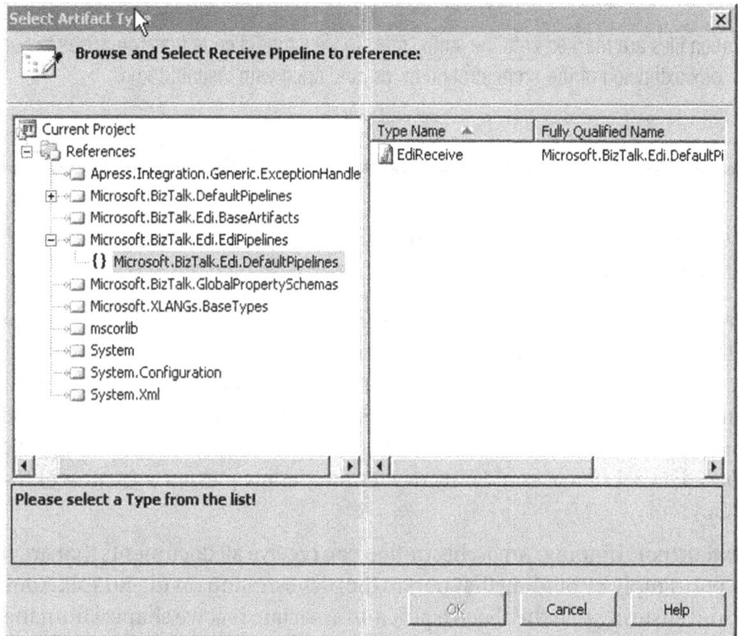

Figure 4-6. *Referencing EDI pipelines in the orchestration*

c. Click OK to save the settings in the Select Artifact Type window.

d. In the BizTalk Administration Console, click Platform Settings, click Host Instances, right-click the BizTalkServerApplication, and select Restart. This will ensure that the updated pipeline is used.

e. Start the orchestration by right-clicking it and selecting Start.

Test the solution by dropping a copy of the Sample864Instance.txt file, located in C:\Apress.Integration\Chapter 4\Test Documents, on the file directory where the receive location is listening (C:\Apress.Integration\Chapter 4\Drops\Incoming - Subscribe 864 Only Demo). When this document is dropped, an event will be logged to the Windows Event Viewer. Dropping a different type of document (that does not have an ST01 node equal to 864) will result in a "Subscriber not Found" exception being logged to the Event Viewer and a suspended message appearing on the BizTalk MessageBox.

Figure 4-7 shows the final outcome to the orchestration created in this exercise.

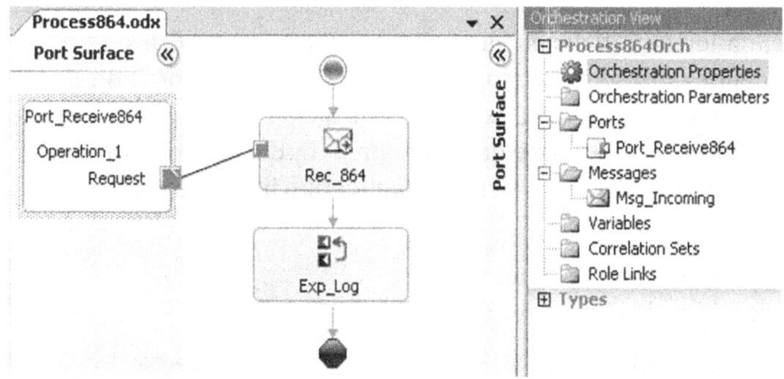

Figure 4-7. *864 orchestration*

Note Orchestration files are marked with the suffix .odx. To view the C# code that comprises the orchestration, simply change the .odx extension of the orchestration to .cs, and open with Visual Studio.

Aside from setting the filter shown in the preceding exercise, there are a variety of other ways to route messages, including the following:

- **Schema type**: Setting the schema type on the subscribing orchestration or send port to a known EDI document type will route documents that match that schema to the appropriate subscriber(s). The drawback to using schemas for routing EDI messages is that trading partners often have different schemas for the same message, meaning that even if both of them deliver an 864, there is no common schema shared by both, and therefore a subscriber listening for 864s based on a schema would only receive the trading partner's document that matches the schema.
- **Orchestration/port binding**: An orchestration can receive all documents that are received on a specific port simply by binding that port to the orchestration (in the BizTalk Administration Console) and ensuring that the receive port and associate receive shape within the orchestration indicate a generic document type (such as System.Xml.XmlDocument). For example, if a receive port is bound to an orchestration, and the orchestration is listening for all types of documents, all documents will instantiate the orchestration.
- **Other filter options**: There are a huge number of options in filtering, both for orchestrations and send ports. A send port, for example, can be bound directly to a receive port by defining the filter on the send port to listen to the receive port (this is defined by using the BTS.ReceivePortName property in the send port Filter properties).

Delivering Documents via Orchestrations

This section gives a short overview of the process of sending EDI documents out of an orchestration. The basic implementation differs little from the receiving of documents, as outlined in the previous section. Instead of stepping through an exercise on how to connect to a send port, a new concept will be introduced: the use of a *scope shape*, which wraps the send port to ensure that if any errors are thrown they will be caught and logged.

The majority of document validation on EDI documents occurs on the outgoing EDI send pipeline. When errors are thrown in pipelines and are not wrapped by scope shapes in an orchestration, the document is suspended on the MessageBox and the exception is logged to the Windows Event Viewer. The following message is what is available to external components by default, without further information from the MessageBox, when an EDI document fails validation in the EDI pipeline (regardless of the segment it failed on):

```
An unexpected failure occurred when processing a message.
The text associated with the exception is "Error in serialization".
```

An example of a full error, as logged to the Windows Event Viewer, indicating the exact validation issue, is as follows:

```
Error: 1 (Field level error)
```

```
SegmentID: N1
Position in TS: 4
Data Element ID: N104
Position in Segment: 4
Data Value:
1: Mandatory data element missing
```

To get the full error, an administrator must view the document in the BizTalk Administration Console—often a time-consuming process and frequently difficult to access (the BizTalk tools must be available on the local computer). Notifying administrators with the full description of the error is the ideal solution, but for this to work successfully, the full error message (such as "The value in N105 is invalid according to the schema; maximum length has been exceeded," rather than "The message failed") must be available. Figure 4-8 shows an orchestration that wraps a send shape and catches thrown exceptions, getting the full exception object and, therefore, the full error message.

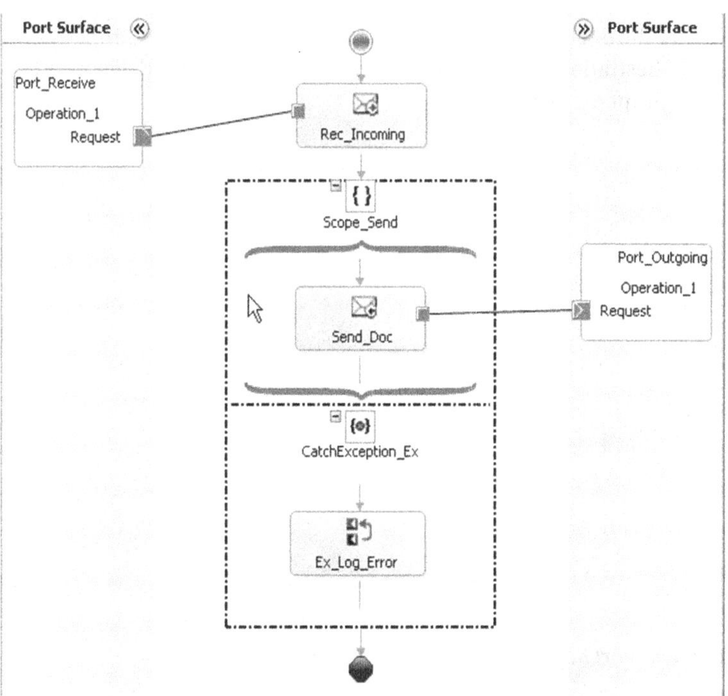

Figure 4-8. *Wrapping a send shape in a scope*

There are several key items to note when setting up a send port in an orchestration:

- **Setting the number of retries**: The number of times a port tries to deliver a document is defined in the port settings within BizTalk Administration Console. These settings differ based on the needs of the solution and what type of protocol is being used (e.g., FTP, HTTP, FILE, etc.).

■ **Note** The ports do not differentiate between pipeline errors and adapter errors. In other words, if a document fails validation, and the retry is set to 3, it will retry the serialization three times before raising the error. The ideal scenario is to fail the document immediately if it fails validation, and retry only if it cannot be delivered to the target recipient.

- **Setting the delivery notification property**: This is an extremely important field; it must be set to ensure that the status of the send port is sent back to the orchestration. If this property is set to None, the send port will operate asynchronously, not reporting success or failure back to the orchestration. Depending on the number of retries, a send port may take a long period of time before completing—either successfully or not. For example, if a send port tries to connect to an FTP site, but the FTP site is down, it may try to connect 100 times, once every ten minutes. During this time, if the send port Delivery Notification property is set to Transmitted, the orchestration will wait. On the other hand, if the property is set to None, it will move on to the next step, ignoring whether the document is sent without issue. To catch errors properly on the send port within an orchestration, this property must be set to Transmitted. Figure 4-9 shows this value set in the properties window.

Figure 4-9. *Orchestration send port delivery notification property*

- **Transaction types**: Scope shapes (and orchestrations themselves) have a Transaction Type property, which can be set to one of three values: None, Atomic, or Long Running. These values determine how the data is stored in BizTalk's databases and how memory is managed. When there are several steps that are not related to one another (e.g., steps that don't need to be "rolled back" if an error occurs), the None setting is appropriate. In cases where context must be preserved, and steps may need to be undone, either the Atomic or Long Running settings may be more appropriate.

- **Exception types:** When adding a catch block to a scope shape, it is necessary to define what type of exception will be caught. This can be somewhat tricky, as it is frequently necessary to define multiple catch blocks on a single scope. The first may be set to catch System.Exception, while the second may be set to catch Microsoft.XLANGs.BaseTypes.XLANGsException. There is no "master" type that will catch all exceptions, unlike standard .NET programming (where System.Exception is the class that all other exception types inherit from). The best way to determine what exception types are needed is to test the process and see what types of exceptions are thrown. (When an exception is thrown, it is always logged to the Windows Event Viewer by BizTalk Server, and the error message will indicate which exception type was thrown.)

Exception Handling

When subscribing to or delivering documents, it is important to look at how exceptions will be handled. BizTalk Server 2006, by default, will ensure that messages can be handled via the BizTalk Administration Console and Health and Activity Tracking (HAT) (as demonstrated in Chapter 6), but it is almost always necessary to notify an administrator (or other party) when an exception has occurred so that the issue can be treated immediately (BizTalk does not notify by default; it just logs the exception and suspends the messages and associated processes).

This section outlines how to implement an exception handler orchestration, and how to subscribe to *failed messages* (messages that would simply be suspended if this orchestration is not present). Once the basic concepts of error message routing are introduced, and the basic exception handler orchestration is created, the orchestration will be extended to subscribe to custom error messages created and published by orchestrations. Figure 4-10 illustrates the process of subscribing to failed messages, while Exercise 4-3 walks through the steps of implementing the necessary components.

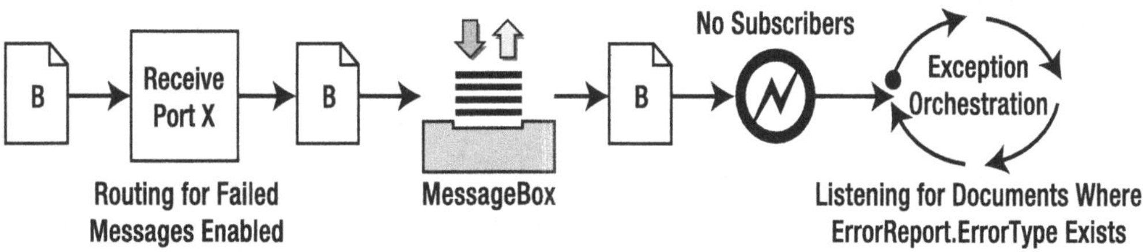

Figure 4-10. *Subscribing to failed messages*

Exercise 4-3. Subscribing to Failed Messages

This exercise demonstrates how to set up an orchestration and an associated receive port to subscribe to failed messages and log the information to the Windows Event Viewer. The result is a generic orchestration that subscribes to any message that fails. The completed solution can be found in C:\Apress.Integration\Chapter 4\Apress.Integration.Generic.ExceptionHandler.sln.

■ **Note** There are two versions of the exception handler orchestration in the solution files. This exercise uses the file named ExceptionHandler_Original.odx. If it is desired to work with the simplified version of the exception handler, add this file to the project and remove the ExceptionHandler_Extended.odx orchestration from the solution. Exercise 4-4 extends the functionality of this solution.

---

1. Create a new Visual Studio project that will contain one orchestration.

   a. Add a new orchestration to the project. Right-click the project and select Add ➤ New Item. Select a new orchestration and give it an appropriate name (this example uses ExceptionHandler_Original.odx). Click Add.

   b. In the project properties, reference a strong name key. This exercise references to the key at C:\Apress.Integration\Chapter 4\ Apress.Integration.Chapter4.snk.

   c. Ensure that the Application Name property points to the correct BizTalk application. For this exercise, it should read EDI.Demonstration.Chapter4, as shown in Figure 4-11.

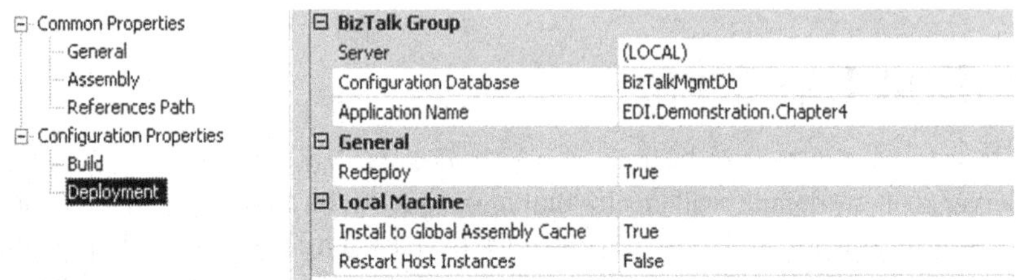

Figure 4-11. *Exception handler project properties*

   d. Once the orchestration is created, right-click the orchestration surface and select Properties Window. Set the Typename property to ExceptionHandlerOrch, as shown in Figure 4-12.

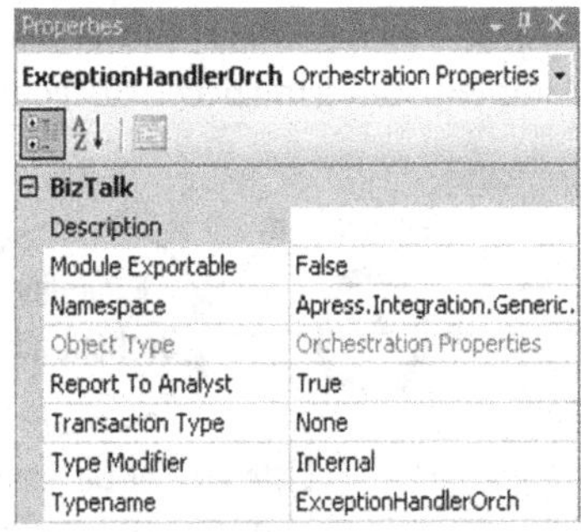

Figure 4-12. *Exception handler orchestration properties*

2. Add the following components to the orchestration (the final result is shown in Figure 4-13):

   a. Right-click the Port Surface and select New Configured Port. Click Next to pass the first screen of the wizard.

      i. Set the name of the port to Port_Rec_Failed_Msg. Click Next.

      ii. On the Select Port Type screen, set the following:

         1. Select Create New Port Type, and name it PortType_Rec_Failed_Msg.

         2. The Communication Pattern property should be set to One-Way.

         3. The Access Restrictions property can be left as Internal.

         4. Click Next.

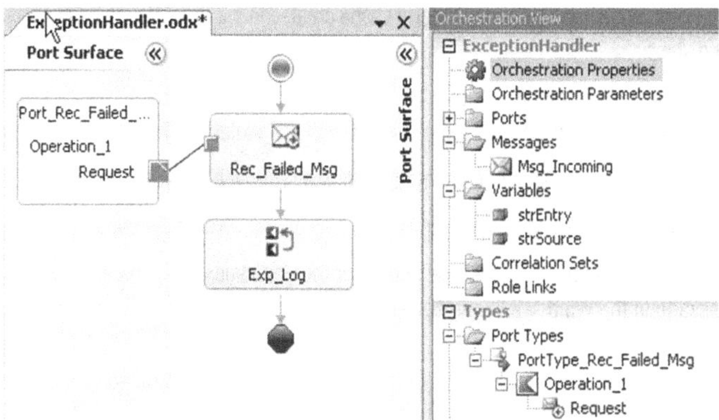

Figure 4-13. *Exception handler orchestration*

iii. On the Port Binding screen, set the following:

1. The Port Direction of Communication property should state "I'll always be receiving messages on this port."
2. Set Port Binding as Direct, and leave the default option selected to listen to the MessageBox.
3. Click Next and Finish.

iv. There is one more property to set on the port that was just created. Click the Request property on the port on the Port Surface and set the message type to System.Xml.XmlDocument. This is a generic specification and allows all messages, regardless of format, to arrive on this orchestration.

b. On the Orchestration View tab of the orchestration, right-click Messages and select New Message.

i. Name the message Msg_Incoming.

ii. Set the Message Type property as System.Xml.XmlDocument.

c. Drop a receive shape at the beginning of the orchestration, and set the properties of this shape as follows:

i. Rename the shape to Rec_Failed_Msg.

ii. Set the Message property to Msg_Incoming.

iii. Set the Operation property to Port_Rec_Failed_Msg.Operation_1.Request. Alternatively, drag the Port Request property and drop it on the receive shape. This will connect the receive shape with the incoming port.

iv. Set the Activate property to True.

v. On the Filter property, set the filter to only listen for messages that have the ErrorReport.ErrorType context property set to Exists. This is shown in Figure 4-14.

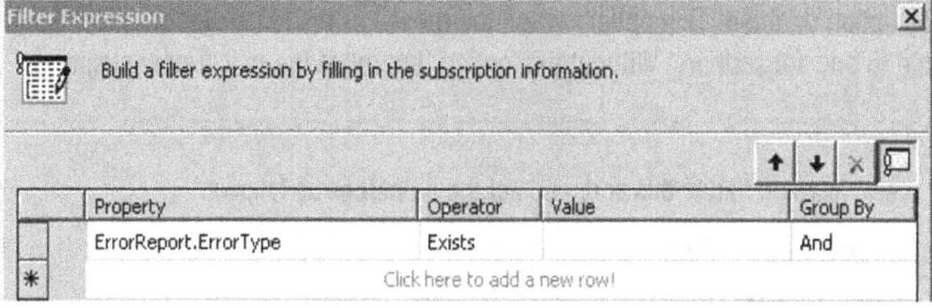

Figure 4-14. *Configuring the receive shape filter*

vi. Click OK to save the settings.

d. Drop an expression shape below the receive shape created in the previous step. Configure this shape using the following steps:

i. Create two orchestration variables on the Orchestration View tab (where the message was created in a previous step). Right-click Variables and select New Variable for each of the following variables:

1. The first variable should be named strSource. The type is System.String.

2. Name the second variable strEntry. It is also of type System.String.

ii. Double-click the expression shape and enter the code shown in Figure 4-15. This code will log a message to the Windows Event Viewer.

BizTalk Expression Editor

Enter an expression. Examples:
myInteger = 34;
myObject.method(param1, param2);
myPort(Microsoft.XLANGs.BaseTypes.Address) = "http://orders.myCompany";

```
strSource = "Demo Entry";
strEntry = "Failed Message Received.";
strEntry = strEntry + " Error Type is " + Msg_Incoming(ErrorReport.ErrorType);
System.Diagnostics.EventLog.WriteEntry(strSource,strEntry);
```

Figure 4-15. *Code in Expression Editor*

iii. Click OK to save the code in the expression shape.

3. Deploy the orchestration from Visual Studio by right-clicking the project or solution and selecting Deploy.

The next steps deal with creating a receive port and a receive location. These components will receive any type of document and publish it to the BizTalk MessageBox. However, no subscriber will exist, and the message will be routed to the exception handler orchestration as a failed message.

4. In the BizTalk Administration Console, create a new one-way receive port:

a. Give it an appropriate name. In this example, it is named EDI.Demonstration.Example.FailedMessage.FILE.Generic.

b. Make sure that the Enable Routing for Failed Messages property on the Generic tab is enabled, as shown in Figure 4-16.

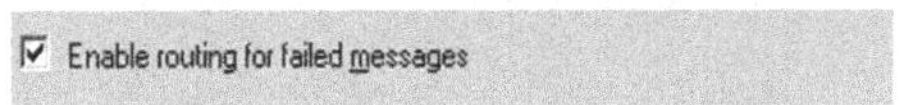

Figure 4-16. *Select the Enable Routing for Failed Messages option.*

■ **Note** When creating an orchestration to subscribe to all failed messages, all ports must have the Enable Routing for Failed Messages option enabled. This option wraps the message with ErrorReport information and makes this information available to any subscribers. Without this option, the message will simply suspend.

---

5. Create a receive location tied to this port, and set the properties as follows:

a. Name it FileReceiveFailedMessage.

b. Set the Type property to FILE.

c. Set the directory where the incoming files will be dropped. For this exercise, this directory is C:\Apress.Integration\Chapter 4\Drops\Incoming - Failed Message Demo.

   d. Enter *.* as the file mask.

   e. Set the receive pipeline to PassThruReceive.

   After saving the receive port and location settings, bind and start the components using the following steps:

6. In the BizTalk Administration Console, double-click the orchestration created earlier in this exercise and click the Bindings tab. Set the host to BizTalkServerApplication. Click OK.

7. Right-click the orchestration and select Start. The orchestration is now actively listening for failed messages to arrive on the MessageBox.

8. Enable the receive location.

   The remaining steps demonstrate the orchestration subscribing to a failed message:

9. Drop any file in the drop folder (C:\Apress.Integration\Chapter 4\Drops\Incoming - Failed Message Demo).

10. Monitor the Windows Event Viewer, as shown in Figure 4-17. It is accessible by clicking Start ➤ Control Panel ➤ Administrative Tools ➤ Event Viewer.

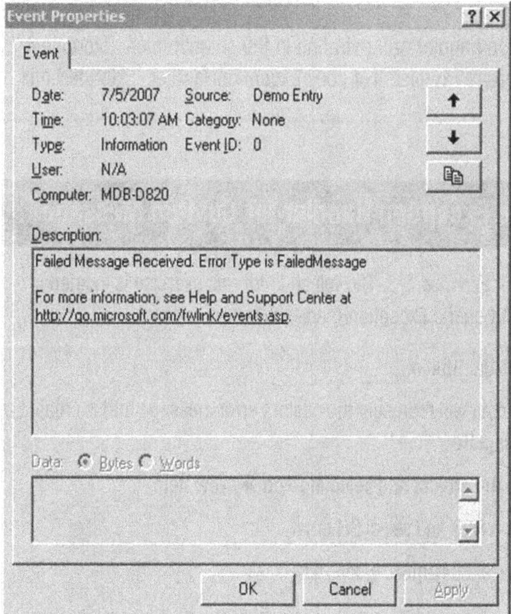

Figure 4-17. *Orchestration logging to event viewer*

The preceding exercise demonstrates how to subscribe to all failed messages on the MessageBox. The next step is to determine the solution to the following common scenarios:

- Handling messages that error in orchestrations (e.g., an exception is thrown and caught in a scope shape)
- Handling messages that a developer wants to mark as an error
- Handling all errors generically, reducing the overall number of components to as few as possible

With these goals in mind, the exception handler will be extended as outlined in Exercise 4-4. The architecture shown in Figure 4-18 is a combination of the results of both Exercise 4-4 and Exercise 4-5.

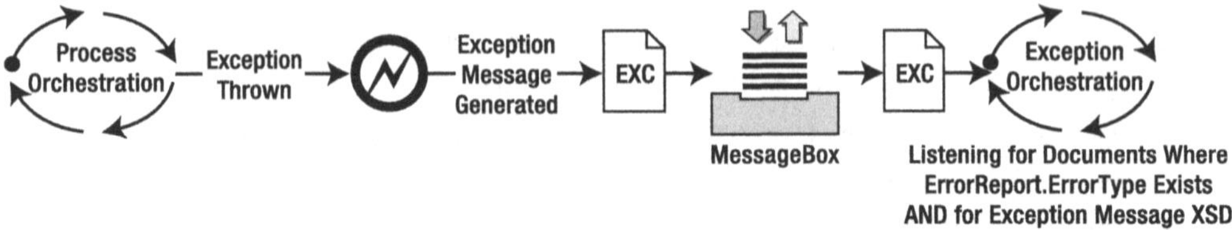

Figure 4-18. *Creating a custom error for the exception handler*

The exception handler is very versatile and easily extendible. Exercise 4-4 demonstrates how to extend it to support custom exception messages generated in orchestrations. Exercise 4-5 demonstrates how to create a message to instantiate the exception handler.

Note There are two versions of the exception handler orchestration in the solution files. Exercise 4-3 uses the file named ExceptionHandler_Original.odx, whereas Exercise 4-4 uses ExceptionHandler_Extended.odx.

Exercise 4-4. Extending the Exception Handler for Custom Messages

This exercise builds on the orchestration created in Exercise 4-3. The full code for this exercise is located in C:\Apress.Integration\Chapter 4\Apress.Integration.Generic.ExceptionHandler.sln.

1. Open the solution and orchestration in Visual Studio.
2. Begin by adding a new schema. This schema will represent the custom error message that is created by external orchestrations and dropped on the MessageBox:
   a. Add a new schema by right-clicking the project and selecting Add ➤ New Item.
   b. In the window that opens, click Schema Files and select Schema.
   c. Name the file appropriately—in this case, CustomException.xsd.
   d. Click Add.
3. Make the following modifications to the schema:
   a. Rename the root node to CustomException.
   b. Add a new element called MessageType by right-clicking the root node and selecting Insert Schema Node ➤ Child Field Element. This will contain information indicating the type of EDI message, such as 810, 404, and so on.
   c. Add a second element named ExceptionMessage. This will contain the custom error information.
   d. The third element should be called StackTrace. This will contain all of the available text in the caught exception.
   e. Set the Min Occurs and Max Occurs for each of the three elements to 1. This indicates that the nodes are unique, required elements.
   f. Set each of the fields as Distinguished Fields, so that their values are easily accessible within the orchestration that references the schema (this schema will be referenced by multiple orchestrations):

i. Right-click one of the nodes that is to be promoted and select Promote ➤ Show Promotions. The property promotion interface is shown in Figure 4-19.

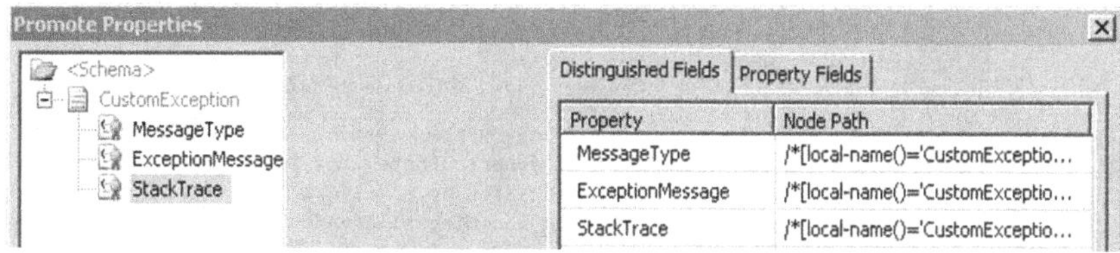

Figure 4-19. *Distinguished fields*

ii. Ensure that the Distinguished Fields tab is selected, and click the Add button to add each of the three nodes, one at a time.

iii. Click OK when complete.

g. Save the schema in Visual Studio.

The next steps involve making changes to the orchestration. The goal is to add logic to the exception handler so that it can determine whether the incoming message is a custom exception, or whether it is a standard failed message not created by an external orchestration.

4. On the Orchestration View tab, create a new message:

   a. Name the message Msg_Custom.

   b. Set the Message Type property to the schema created in the previous step, Apress.Integration.Generic.ExceptionHandler.CustomException.

5. Drop a decide shape immediately after the existing receive shape and expression shape, and set the following:

   a. Name the shape Decide_Exc_Type.

   b. Rename Rule_1 to Is_Custom?, and then double-click the shape and enter the expression shown in Figure 4-20. The value of ErrorReport.FailureCode will be set by the external orchestration in code and is a value that is never set automatically by BizTalk.

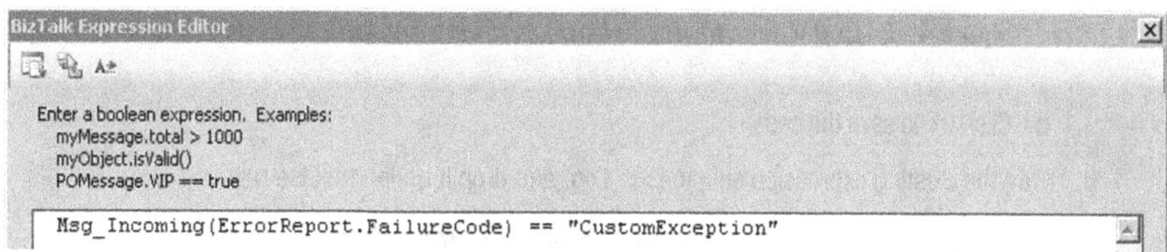

Figure 4-20. *Decide shape logic*

   c. Once the decide shape's expression is entered, click OK.

6. Drop a construct message shape under the Is_Custom? rule.

   a. Name the shape ConstructMessage_Custom.

   b. For the Messages Constructed property, select Msg_Custom.

   c. Drop a message assignment shape inside of the construct message shape. Double-click the shape and enter the code shown in Figure 4-21.

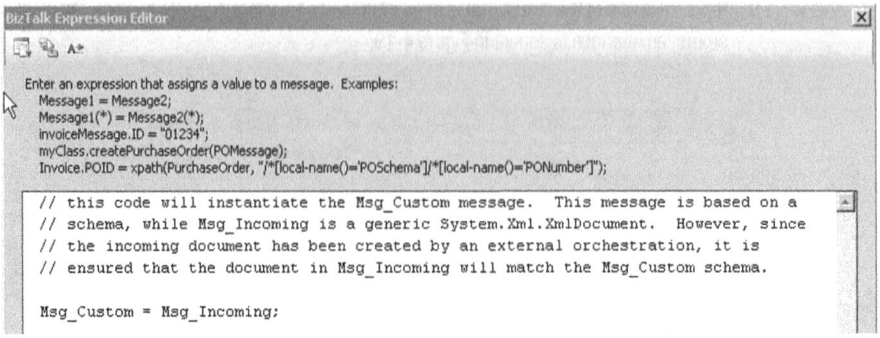

BizTalk Expression Editor

Enter an expression that assigns a value to a message. Examples:
Message1 = Message2;
Message1(*) = Message2(*);
invoiceMessage.ID = "01234";
myClass.createPurchaseOrder(POMessage);
Invoice.POID = xpath(PurchaseOrder, "/*[local-name()='POSchema']/*[local-name()='PONumber']");

```
// this code will instantiate the Msg_Custom message.  This message is based on a
// schema, while Msg_Incoming is a generic System.Xml.XmlDocument.  However, since
// the incoming document has been created by an external orchestration, it is
// ensured that the document in Msg_Incoming will match the Msg_Custom schema.

Msg_Custom = Msg_Incoming;
```

Figure 4-21. *Message assignment logic*

   d. Save the message assignment logic by clicking OK.

7. Drop an expression shape under the construct message shape.

   a. Rename the shape to Exp_Custom_Info.

   b. Enter in the expression shown in Figure 4-22.

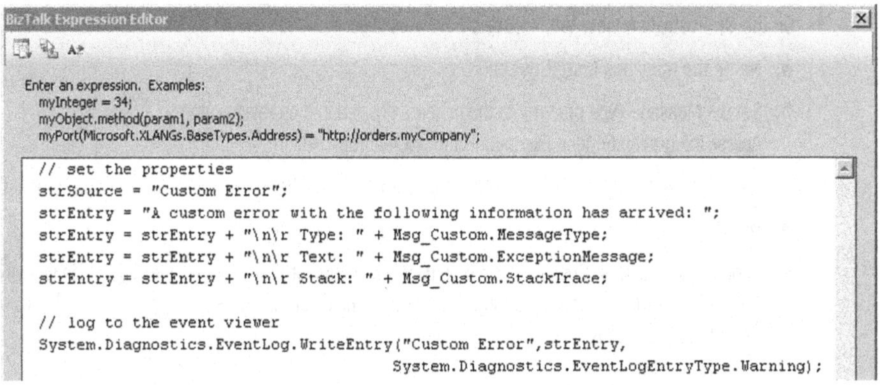

BizTalk Expression Editor

Enter an expression. Examples:
myInteger = 34;
myObject.method(param1, param2);
myPort(Microsoft.XLANGs.BaseTypes.Address) = "http://orders.myCompany";

```
// set the properties
strSource = "Custom Error";
strEntry = "A custom error with the following information has arrived: ";
strEntry = strEntry + "\n\r Type: " + Msg_Custom.MessageType;
strEntry = strEntry + "\n\r Text: " + Msg_Custom.ExceptionMessage;
strEntry = strEntry + "\n\r Stack: " + Msg_Custom.StackTrace;

// log to the event viewer
System.Diagnostics.EventLog.WriteEntry("Custom Error",strEntry,
                                       System.Diagnostics.EventLogEntryType.Warning);
```

Figure 4-22. *Exp_Custom_Info shape expression to log to event viewer*

   c. Click OK to save the code.

8. Drag the existing expression shape, Exp_Log, and drop it under the Else rule.

9. Build, deploy, and start the orchestration, using the following steps:

   a. Right-click the project in Visual Studio and select Deploy. If the orchestration has previously been deployed, it will first need to be unenlisted. Alternatively, setting the Redeploy property on the Deployment tab in the project properties to True will allow the orchestration to be deployed over an existing instance.

   b. Start the orchestration by right-clicking it in the BizTalk Administration Console and selecting Start.

   c. Stop and start the BizTalk Server application to ensure that the most current version of the code is used. In the BizTalk Administration Console, expand Platform Settings, click Host Instances, and right-click BizTalkServerApplication. Select Restart.

10. Validate that the orchestration picks up failed messages, using the same process as in Exercise 4-3, as follows:
    a. Drop any file in the drop folder (C:\Apress.Integration\Chapter 4\Drops\Incoming - Failed Message Demo).
    b. Monitor the Windows Event Viewer. It is accessible by clicking Start ➤ Control Panel ➤ Administrative Tools ➤ Event Viewer.

A custom exception message will be created in Exercise 4-5 that will instantiate the exception handler and run the code added in this exercise. The complete orchestration created in this exercise is shown in Figure 4-23.

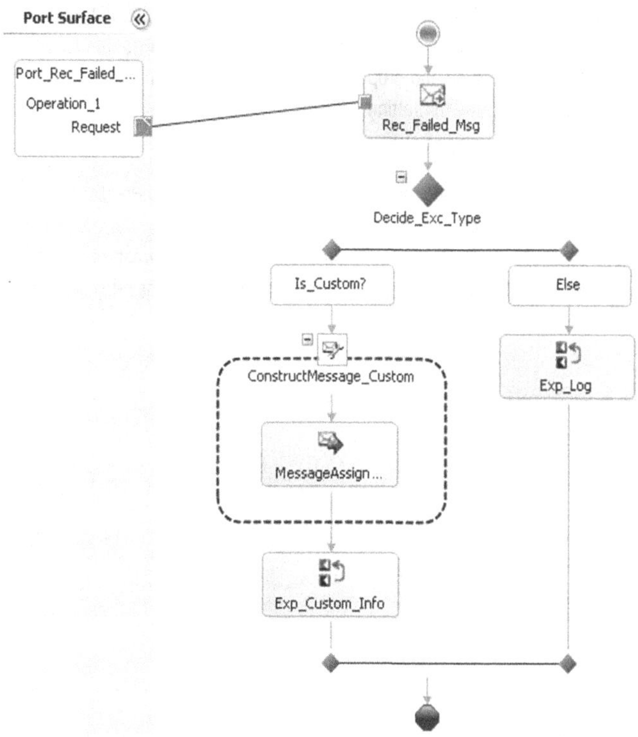

Figure 4-23. *Extended exception handler orchestration*

With the exception handler fully extended and subscribing both to failed messages and custom messages that arrive on the MessageBox, it is necessary to demonstrate how to create a custom message that will instantiate the exception handler. Exercise 4-5 outlines the necessary steps.

Exercise 4-5. Publishing a Custom Error to the Exception Handler

In Exercise 4-4, the exception handler orchestration was extended to listen for custom error messages published to the BizTalk MessageBox. In this exercise, the steps to publish a custom error message to the MessageBox are outlined. The steps that deal specifically with publishing the custom message are generic and can be incorporated into any orchestration.

This example builds upon the orchestration built in Exercise 4-2, which subscribes to 864 EDI documents. In this exercise, the 864 is mapped to a custom error message, and this message is sent to the exception handler.

■ **Note** There are two versions of the 864 process orchestration in the solution files. The original exercise uses the file named Process864_Original.odx, whereas this solution uses Process864_Extended.odx.

---

1. Open the solution and orchestration in Visual Studio. It is also available in a completed format at C:\Apress.Integration\Chapter 4\ Apress.Integration.EDI864.Common.sln.

   Begin by adding a reference to the exception handler solution. This reference needs to be created so that the custom exception schema is available and the properties are promoted. It is not a requirement that a reference be made—it just simplifies the creation and population of the document. If the reference is not made, the document could be manually created in the orchestration and dropped on the MessageBox. In this exercise, a reference is made, and the distinguished fields are used for setting values:

   a. Right-click the References folder in the Visual Studio project and select Add Reference.

   b. Browse to the location of the exception handler assembly (Apress.Integration.Generic.ExceptionHandler.dll), most likely found at C:\Apress.Integration\Chapter 4\Apress.Integration.Generic.ExceptionHandler\bin\Deployment. If the assembly does not exist, build the exception handler solution (this will create the DLL). Alternatively, a project reference could be made; this would require adding the project to the Visual Studio solution. The reference to this assembly is shown in Figure 4-24.

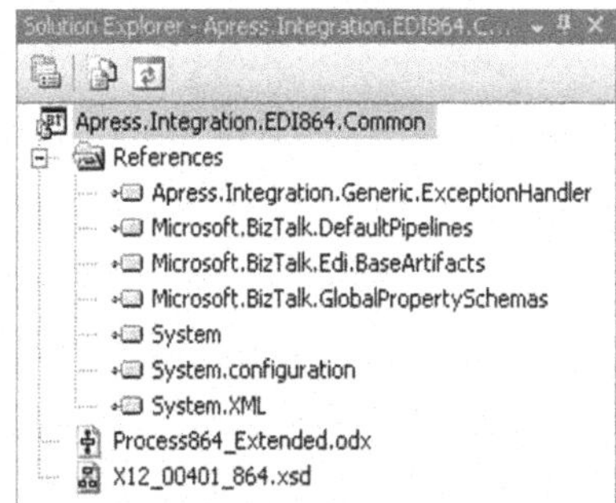

Figure 4-24. *Referencing the exception handler assembly*

2. Create a new correlation set. This ensures that documents that are dropped have the appropriate message context properties set so that the subscribing orchestrations (in this case the exception handler) see them as valid published documents. On the Orchestration View tab, right-click Correlation Sets and select New Correlation Set. Set the remaining properties as follows:

   a. Give the correlation set an appropriate name (using the Identifier property); in this exercise it is Correlation_CustomError.

   b. Set the Correlation Type as follows:

      i. Select Create New Correlation Type from the drop-down menu.

      ii. Set the Identifier property on the newly created correlation type to an appropriate name, such as CorrelationType_ErrorReport.

      iii. Set the Correlation Properties value to ErrorReport.ErrorType (as shown in Figure 4-25) and click OK.

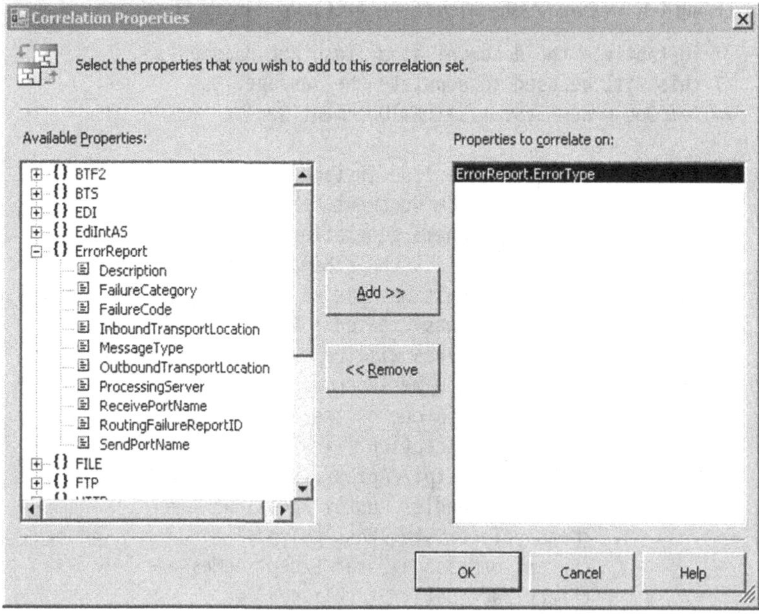

Figure 4-25. *Setting correlation properties*

3. Drop an expression shape below the first receive shape. This expression shape contains an XPath expression that will extract the value of MSG01 and place it into a string variable, as shown here:

   a. Create a new orchestration variable on the Orchestration View tab called str864TextMessage and make it of type System.String.

   b. Enter the code shown here into the Expression Editor:

   ```
   str864TextMessage = xpath(Msg_Incoming,"string(//MSG01)");
   ```

   c. Click OK to save the code in the expression shape.

4. There is an existing expression shape called Exp_Log. This can remain in the orchestration but will be updated to show the value that is in str864TextMessage by modifying the code as shown here:

```
System.Diagnostics.EventLog.WriteEntry("864 Received"
                                        ,"Demonstration: "
                                        + str864TextMessage);
```

5. Drop a message assignment shape after the expression shape. This will automatically add a construct message shape:

   a. Name the two shapes appropriately.

   b. Create the following objects on the Orchestration View tab:

      i. A message called Msg_CustomError, which is of the type Apress.Integration.Generic.ExceptionHandler.CustomError. This is accessed by selecting the schema from the referenced assemblies.

      ii. A variable called strXMLDoc, of type System.String.

      iii. A variable called xmlTempDoc, of type System.Xml.XmlDocument.

   c. Set the Messages Constructed property on the construct message shape to Msg_CustomError.

   d. In the message assignment shape, the code that will create the custom error message will be added. Listing 4-1 shows the code to be entered, with comments describing each line. Once this is fully entered, click OK.

Listing 4-1. *Message Assignment Code for Custom Error Message*

```
// instantiate the document as a fresh XML document.
// this will be used to populate the message.
xmlTempDoc = new System.Xml.XmlDocument();

// set a string equal to a true instance of the
// CustomError schema.  The document here was
// generated using the schema generation tool in
// Visual Studio (right click the schema and generate
// an instance).  The result was pasted here, to ensure
// that a valid instance was created.  Once this is added
// to the message, the values will be overridden.  There
// are other ways to create messages, such as through the
// use of maps, but this is one of the simplest ways to do so.
strXMLDoc = "<ns0:CustomException " +
            "xmlns:ns0='http://Apress.Integration.Generic" +
            ".ExceptionHandler.CustomException'>" +
            "<MessageType>Data</MessageType>" +
            "<ExceptionMessage>Data</ExceptionMessage>" +
            "<StackTrace>Data</StackTrace>" +
            "</ns0:CustomException>";

// populate the doc with the contents of the string
// A message is XML, but cannot be instantiated from a
// string (through LoadXML).  It can only be created by
// referencing a populated XML doc.
xmlTempDoc.LoadXml(strXMLDoc);

// now instantiate the actual Message
Msg_CustomError = xmlTempDoc;

// reset the values using the distinguished fields (if
// the fields were set with the correct values in the
// string above, this step would not be necessary.  It
// simply demonstrates how to use the schema.
// Additionally, there would be no need to reference the
// Exception Handler Assembly.
Msg_CustomError.ExceptionMessage = str864TextMessage;
Msg_CustomError.MessageType = "864";

// in the case of a true exception, this could be set to
// the System.Exception Stack Trace (or anything else).
Msg_CustomError.StackTrace = "N/A";

// Set the ErrorReport Properties. These are promoted
// properties on all messages, and are only set to
// force the message to be seen as a "FailedMessage"
// when it is sent to the MessageBox so that the
// Exception Handling orchestration will subscribe to it.
Msg_CustomError(ErrorReport.ErrorType) = "FailedMessage";
Msg_CustomError(ErrorReport.FailureCode) = "CustomException";
```

6. Next, create the send port and send shape that will drop the newly created custom exception message on the MessageBox:
   a. Right-click the Port Surface and create a new configured port, setting the properties as follows:
      i. Name the send port appropriately—in this case Send_CustomError.
      ii. Give the new port type a name such as PortType_SendCustomError.
      iii. The port direction of communication should be set to I'll Always Be Sending Messages on This Port.
      iv. Set the Port Binding property to Direct, and leave the default to publish to the MessageBox.
      v. Click Finish to save the settings.
   b. Click the Request property of the newly created send port, and set the message type to System.Xml.XmlDocument (or to the CustomError.xsd schema; either will work).
   c. Drop a send shape at the end of the orchestration, and configure it as follows:
      i. Name it Send_CustomErr.
      ii. Set the Message property to Msg_CustomError.
      iii. Set the Initializing Correlation Sets property to Correlation_CustomError.
      iv. Connect the send shape to the send port.
7. Build and deploy the orchestration, using the following steps:
   a. Check that all orchestrations for this exercise and the exception handler are started and that all receive locations are enabled.
   b. It is always a good idea to restart the BizTalkApplicationServer in the Platform Settings of the BizTalk Administration Console to ensure that the most current versions of all components are loaded.

Figure 4-26 shows the final outcome to the orchestration changes made in this exercise.

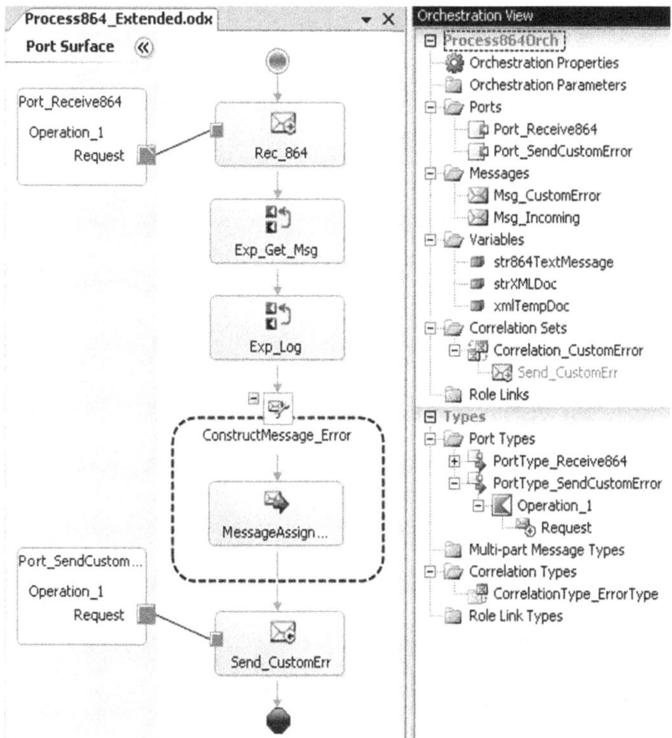

Figure 4-26. *Extended 864 orchestration*

Test the process by dropping the 864 instance on the receive location. There should be an event logged to the Event Viewer from two orchestrations: the 864 process and the exception handler (see Figure 4-27).

Application 15,215 event(s)

Type	Date	Time	Source
Warning	7/7/2007	11:48:02 ...	Custom Error
Information	7/7/2007	11:48:00 ...	864 Received
Information	7/7/2007	11:47:50 ...	BizTalk Server 2006
Information	7/7/2007	11:47:47 ...	BizTalk Server 2006

Figure 4-27. *Event Viewer results*

With both the 864 process orchestration and the exception handler extended to interact with each other, it is now appropriate to refer back to the discussion on delivering documents and see how the send orchestration can be updated (refer to Figure 4-8). Originally, the flow ended with catching the exception and publishing information to the Windows Event Viewer. Using the same steps outlined in Figure 4-5, which are directly related to publishing a custom message, the send orchestration can be extended (as shown in Figure 4-28). By creating a message, populating it with the exception information, setting up a correlation type, and publishing the message to the MessageBox, the exception handler will be able to receive the custom error message. The code within the message assignment shape shown in Listing 4-1 would only need to be modified as shown here to access the exception data caught in the catch block:

```
Msg_CustomError.ExceptionMessage = Ex.Message;
Msg_CustomError.MessageType = "810";
Msg_CustomError.StackTrace = Ex.StackTrace;
```

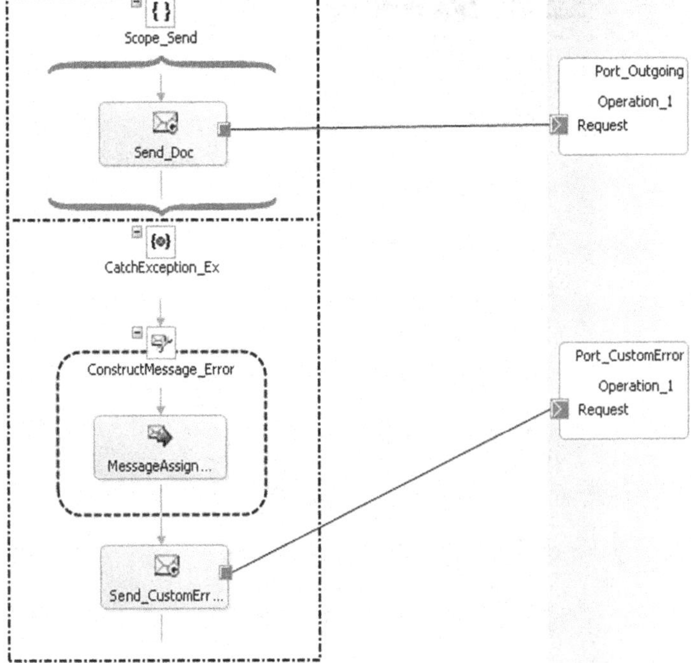

Figure 4-28. *Extending the document delivery orchestration*

Accessing Schema Data in Orchestrations

Promoted properties and distinguished fields (introduced in Chapter 1) are the primary way in which to access element values in expression and message assignment shapes. However, these are limited to unique, known, nonrepeating elements. In many cases, messages will have repeating nodes (such as numerous line items on an order) that have repeating elements. In other cases, schemas may be defined with ANY elements, the contents of which are unknown to the schema (though frequently known to the developer). This section looks at using XPath and BizTalk maps for accessing and setting field values in schemas within orchestrations.

Recall that an EDI document arrives in text format and is transformed into XML in the receive pipeline before being delivered to the orchestration. Both XPath and maps work with documents in XML, not in the original EDI text format. The flow of an EDI document is outlined in Figure 4-29.

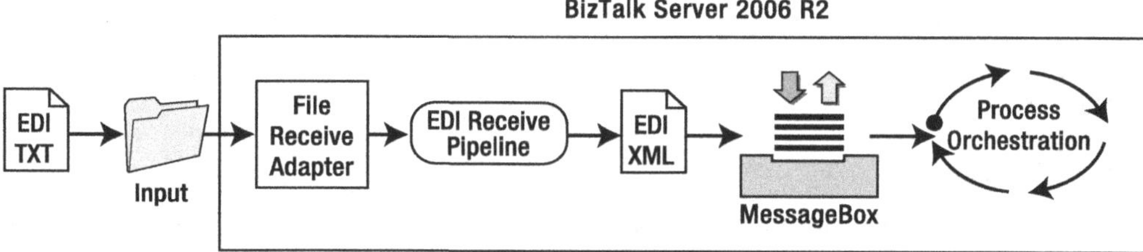

Figure 4-29. *Diagram showing EDI text transformed to EDI XML in pipeline*

An ANY element in a schema simply allows for any document structure to be contained within the node. For example, if the node <WrappedDocument> in an XSD is marked as type ANY, it can contain any XML structure within it and it will not have any validation. If the value of an element within the undefined XML document is to be retrieved, it will be necessary for the developer to know ahead of time what that structure is, even if it cannot be defined in the schema (e.g., it is known that a node called ID will always be present, but it is not known where it will occur or what the root node is), and to know the XPath expression to be used to retrieve the value.

Using XPath

XPath is an extremely useful tool, allowing access to elements within an XML document (or BizTalk message). In Exercise 4-5, a string was populated by using XPath within a message assignment shape, as follows:

```
str864TextMessage = xpath(Msg Incoming,"string(//MSG01)");
```

This statement indicates that the string str864TextMessage will be equal to the string value of the content of the first occurrence of the MSG01 element in the XML document contained in Msg_Incoming. In Exercise 4-5, the incoming 864 only has a single MSG element. However, in the majority of cases with 864 documents, there are multiple MSG nodes. For purposes of illustration, assume that the incoming 864 document looks like that shown in Listing 4-2.

Listing 4-2. *864 EDI Document with Multiple MSG Nodes (EDI Text Version)*

```
ISA*00*00000ISA02*00*11111ISA04*01*2222222222ISA06*01*3333333333ISA08*670123*
0123*U*00200*111111891*0*I*:~
GS*AA*GS02*GS03*45670123*01234567*892*X*00401~
ST*864*ST02~
BMG*00~
DTM*001~
N1*001~
N2*N201~
N3*N301~
N4*N401~
REF*01***01:C04002~
PER*1A~
MIT*MIT01~
MSG*Line one of text message.~
MSG*This is line #2.~
MSG*The third line of the text message.~
SE*14*ST02~
GE*3*892~
IEA*1*111111891~
```

When the EDI document arrives on BizTalk, it is passed through the EDI receive pipeline (removing the header and footer nodes: ISA, GS, GE, and IEA) prior to arriving on the orchestration. The document is validated and translated from the EDI text format into the equivalent XML format, as shown in Listing 4-3.

Listing 4-3. *864 EDI Document with Multiple MSG Nodes (EDI XML Version)*

```
<ns0:X12_00401_864 xmlns:ns0="http://schemas.microsoft.com/BizTalk/EDI/X12/2006">
 <ST>
  <ST01>864</ST01>
  <ST02>ST02</ST02>
 </ST>
 <ns0:BMG>
  <BMG01>00</BMG01>
 </ns0:BMG>
 <ns0:DTM>
  <DTM01>001</DTM01>
 </ns0:DTM>
 <ns0:N1Loop1>
  <ns0:N1>
   <N101>001</N101>
  </ns0:N1>
  <ns0:N2>
   <N201>N201</N201>
  </ns0:N2>
  <ns0:N3>
   <N301>N301</N301>
  </ns0:N3>
  <ns0:N4>
   <N401>N401</N401>
  </ns0:N4>
  <ns0:REF>
   <REF01>01</REF01>
```

```
    <ns0:C040>
      <C04001>01</C04001>
      <C04002>C04002</C04002>
    </ns0:C040>
  </ns0:REF>
  <ns0:PER>
    <PER01>1A</PER01>
  </ns0:PER>
 </ns0:N1Loop1>
 <ns0:MITLoop1>
  <ns0:MIT>
    <MIT01>MIT01</MIT01>
  </ns0:MIT>
  <ns0:MSG>
    <MSG01>Line one of text message.</MSG01>
  </ns0:MSG>
  <ns0:MSG>
    <MSG01>This is line #2.</MSG01>
  </ns0:MSG>
  <ns0:MSG>
    <MSG01>The third line of the text message.</MSG01>
  </ns0:MSG>
 </ns0:MITLoop1>
 <SE>
  <SE01>14</SE01>
  <SE02>ST02</SE02>
 </SE>
</ns0:X12_00401_864>
```

Now that there are three MSG nodes, each with the MSG01 element populated within them, the XPath becomes more complex. To get the entire text message (all three nodes) placed within a single string variable, the code in Listing 4-4 would need to be written and placed within the expression shape.

Listing 4-4. *Populating a String Variable with All Three MSG Nodes*

```
// first, get the value for each node.  Note that the local-name()
// function must be used, since the MSG node is prefixed with ns0
// (i.e. ns0:MSG).

strA = xpath(Msg_Incoming,"string(//*[local-name()='MSG'][1]/MSG01)");
strB = xpath(Msg_Incoming,"string(//*[local-name()='MSG'][2]/MSG01)");
strC = xpath(Msg_Incoming,"string(//*[local-name()='MSG'][3]/MSG01)");

// now populate the final variable with all three
str864TextMessage = strA + "," + strB + "," + strC;
```

There are a number of issues with using XPath when there are multiple nodes—the most common of which is that the number of nodes is not always known. In the previous sample, assuming that there are always going to be three MSG nodes, the XPath expressions used to access those values will always work. But if there are only two nodes that come in, and the code remains the same, an exception will be thrown when trying to access the third node. In the case of 864 documents, the number of incoming MSG nodes can never be known in advance, and so it makes more sense to work with a BizTalk map.

Using BizTalk Maps

The key difference between an XPath expression and a BizTalk map, when using the same sample messages as those shown previously, is that the map requires a schema to be declared for both the source and the target. In the case of XPath, the source document is the incoming 864 document, while the "target document" is the string variable, str864TextMessage. Using a map instead of XPath requires that a small schema (in this case named ErrorNotify) be created that represents the string variable, as shown in Figure 4-30.

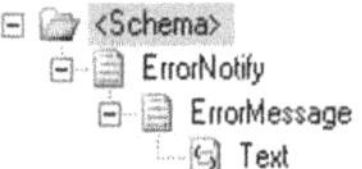

Figure 4-30. *Simple schema (ErrorNotify) with a single element*

Once the schema is created, a map can be developed and added to the orchestration (using a transform shape). The map that represents the same logic as that shown for the XPath expression in Listing 4-4 is shown in Figure 4-31.

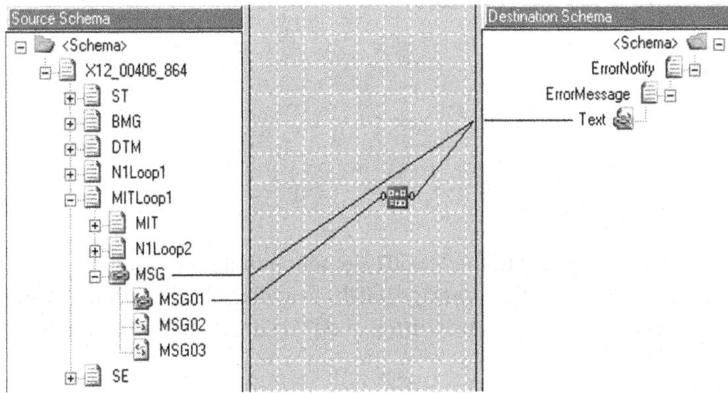

Figure 4-31. *Mapping the 864 MSG nodes*

There are now a variety of ways to get the string value from the Text node of the ErrorNotify document. One of the ways is to use an XPath expression. Another way is to grab the InnerText of the XML document, as shown in Listing 4-5.

Listing 4-5. *Accessing the InnerText Value of the XML Document*

```
// first instantiate an XML doc (this must be created as an
// orchestration variable of type System.Xml.XmlDocument.
xmlDoc = new System.Xml.XmlDocument();

// now populate with the output of the map.  Assume that the
// message created was named Msg_ErrorNotify (this is specified in the
// Contruct Message shape that contains the transform shape and the
// Map.
xmlDoc = Msg_ErrorNotify;

// the InnerText can be placed into the original string variable now
str864TextMessage = xmlDoc.InnerText;
```

Final Discussion

Orchestrations provide a great deal of leverage in how EDI solutions are architected. This chapter outlined some of the most important concepts, including options around delivering or receiving documents and working with exception handling. To simplify the process of architecting and building orchestrations, note the following pointers:

- **Logging errors**: All of the exercises in this chapter that log information of any kind log it to the Windows Event Viewer; this is intended to be a place holder for a more robust logging application. In a true implementation, this is not the ideal approach. One option is to use the Trace class. There are a number of tools available to listen to events that are written out, and it provides for a much more scalable way to monitor orchestrations. Listing 4-6 shows a sample use of this class in an expression shape.

  Listing 4-6. *Using the Trace Class*

  ```
  // set the trace flag based on a setting in the BizTalk configuration file
  System.Configuration.ConfigurationSettings.AppSettings.Get("DBugFlag");

  strOrchName = "sampleorch.odx";

  if (DebugTrace) {
  TraceSB = new System.Text.StringBuilder();
  TraceSB.Append(System.DateTime.Now.ToString());
  TraceSB.Append(System.Environment.NewLine);
  TraceSB.Append("Orchestration Started: " + strOrchName);
  System.Diagnostics.Trace.WriteLine(TraceSB.ToString());
  }
  ```

- **Notification**: The exception handling orchestration developed in Exercise 4-3 (and extended in Exercise 4-4) logs information to the Windows Event Viewer; in a true implementation, this would likely be code that sends an email to a distribution list. There are a number of ways in which to send email from BizTalk Server, and it is an extremely useful architectural design to implement, especially if it is configurable. Ways to do this include the following:
  - **SQL DBMail and/or .NET assembly**: The capabilities of DBMail are extensive and can be easily incorporated into a stored procedure called from an orchestration using a .NET assembly. This type of architecture allows for the ability to look up different configurable recipients from database tables, format the email in HTML or text, and ensure that the email is sent. Any errors that occur can be easily traced through the SQL mail database tables.
  - **BizTalk SMTP adapter**: The SMTP adapter can be helpful when needing to send attachments or catching errors in sending email and handling them within BizTalk. It can be somewhat complex to customize the format of an email using this adapter (though there are techniques that can be used, such as the idea of the "raw string"), but for basic notifications to administrators it may be an adequate solution.

- **Printing orchestrations for review:** Often orchestrations are made up of a series of steps defined by non-BizTalk developers. These include business logic, business rules, loops, decision shapes, and so on. In traditional coding projects, there is generally a code review, which places the developed code in front of an independent coder who can validate that the code is well-formed and matches requirements. With BizTalk there are frequently only a small handful of people within an organization who can review the code—and, generally, the visual portion of the "code" consists of orchestrations. One of the best ways to get the orchestrations in front of non-BizTalk people for review is to print the full orchestration on plotter paper (if available) or on traditional 8 1/2-by-11-inch paper and post it on a wall. The logic can be reviewed and changes can be penciled in as appropriate. One item that can help in preparing a view of the orchestration that will aid in printing is the concept of *zooming*. All orchestrations can be zoomed in on or out on. Simply right-click the orchestration surface and select Zoom. It may be necessary to use screen capture tools to get it in a format that will print appropriately.
- **Commenting orchestrations:** It is often helpful to comment orchestrations, just as traditional code is commented; however, there is no "annotation" option to place text on the orchestration where needed. The best solution to this dilemma is to use the *group shape*. Group shapes can be added at almost any place within an orchestration (the initial receive shape being one exception) and can contain text that describes what is occurring in the shapes contained within it. An example of using the group shape is shown in Figure 4-32.

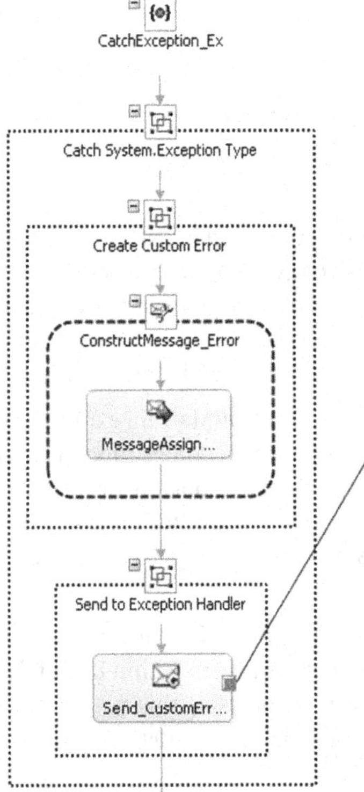

Figure 4-32. *Using group shapes for commenting orchestration logic*

CHAPTER 5

Transporting Documents

EDI documents can be routed between trading partners in virtually any way that the partners mutually agree, including (but not limited to) file transmissions, email attachments, and FTP. The most common approaches today are to use a value added network (VAN) using standard or secure FTP, or to communicate directly between partners using AS2. BizTalk Server R2 provides a number of options around transporting documents, and this chapter covers them in detail:

- **VAN architecture**: The discussion covers how a VAN routes messages and how to interact with a VAN to send and receive messages.
- **AS2 architecture**: AS2 is EDI using S/MIME over HTTP(S), and there are several options when working with this in BizTalk Server R2. When trading partners do not need the overhead of a VAN, and wish to communicate in a secure fashion directly with one another, AS2 is an increasingly popular solution.
- **Batching EDI documents**: The ability to group numerous individual EDI documents into a single batch file and deliver it on a timed or triggered basis to a trading partner is frequently a requirement, especially when dealing with companies that send large volumes of documents.

Preparing the Solution Files

In the majority of exercises in this book, the processes can be fully implemented without difficulty on a development machine. However, when working with secure FTP and AS2, it is much more complex to set up a working environment. To demonstrate the secure FTP adapter, the exercises in this chapter use a standard FTP site, with information on how to configure SSL when connecting to a secure FTP site. To demonstrate AS2, an AS2 server is necessary. Unfortunately, there is no simple way to create one on the local machine. An AS2 server that can be used for testing purposes is necessary.

Note There are a number of test AS2 servers on the Internet that can be used in a development environment. If an AS2 server is not available during the development or test cycles, or one is needed to work through these exercises, do a search on the Internet for **test AS2 servers**.

Exercise 5-1 walks through setting up the solutions and related components that are used in this chapter.

Exercise 5-1. Preparing the Solution Files

This chapter uses the files located in C:\Apress.Integration\Chapter 5. Use the following steps to prepare the environment on the local machine:

1. Make sure that the Chapter 5 sample files have been extracted and placed on the C:\ drive.
2. This chapter makes use of /n software BizTalk adapters, which can be downloaded at /n software's website at `http://www.nsoftware.com:80/download/biztalk.aspx`. Installation is very straightforward and is outlined in the installation documents. A free version of the adapters can be used for a trial period. Both the secure FTP and AS2 adapters are used in this chapter. Once the adapters are successfully installed, they will appear in the adapter list, as shown in Figure 5-1.

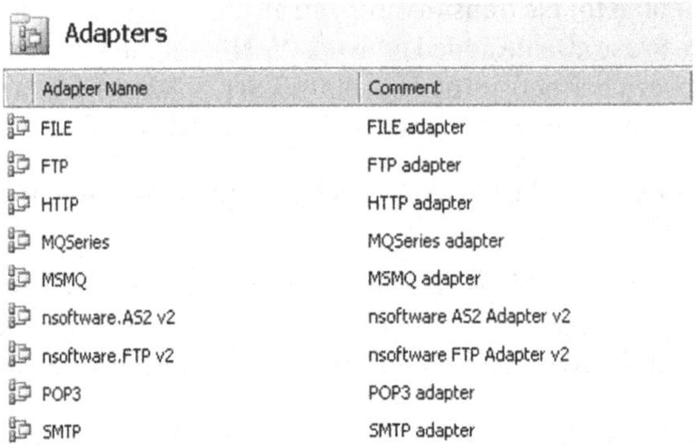

Adapters

Adapter Name	Comment
FILE	FILE adapter
FTP	FTP adapter
HTTP	HTTP adapter
MQSeries	MQSeries adapter
MSMQ	MSMQ adapter
nsoftware.AS2 v2	nsoftware AS2 Adapter v2
nsoftware.FTP v2	nsoftware FTP Adapter v2
POP3	POP3 adapter
SMTP	SMTP adapter

Figure 5-1. *Adapter list in BizTalk Administration Console*

3. The components can be deployed in a single package by importing the Chapter5.MSI file available in C:\Apress.Integration\Chapter 5\BizTalk Application. Alternatively, the binding file (Chapter5Bindings.xml) can be used to create the ports.
4. There is a sample EDI document (Input EDI Doc.txt) in the Test Documents folder that is used for demonstration. Set this file aside, as it will be used to kick off a process.
5. To demonstrate the FTP functionality, it is necessary to either have access to a test FTP server or to set one up on the development machine. Take the following steps to set up an FTP site on Windows Server 2003. You will likely need to insert the original Windows installation CD:
   a. Click Start ➤ Control Panel ➤ Add or Remove Programs.
   b. Click Add or Remove ➤ Components.
   c. Select Application Server and click Details.
   d. Select Internet Information Services (IIS) and click Details.
   e. Select File Transfer Protocol (FTP) Service, as shown in Figure 5-2.
   f. Click OK to save each of the open windows, and on the main Windows Component window click Next. The FTP components will begin to install.

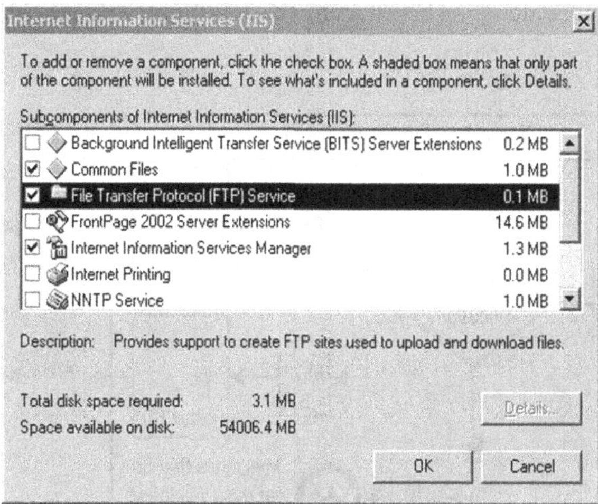

Figure 5-2. *Installing FTP components (for testing purposes)*

6. Create a new FTP folder for the exercises in this book:
   a. Create a folder called EDI.Demonstration in C:\inetpub\ftproot (or wherever the root FTP directory is located).
      i. Create one subfolder called VAN - Outbox.
      ii. Create a second subfolder named VAN - Inbox.
   b. Ensure that the folder has the proper permissions set so that files can be written to it:
      i. In Windows Explorer, right-click C:\Inetpub\ftproot\EDI.Demonstration and check that the Read Only setting is not turned on for the folder.
      ii. Open the FTP site in an FTP client (such as Internet Explorer) and make sure that a file can be copied to the FTP site without errors.

VAN Architecture

VANs provide a number of services, the most important of which is the validation and routing of documents between trading partners. All documents routed through a VAN are tracked, and a full history of all transactions is retained, acting as a receipt that two trading partners did business. Trading partners send EDI documents to a VAN and the VAN routes them to the appropriate recipient based on the contents of the header information. If a trading partner cannot be determined, or the data within the document is found to be invalid, the VAN will flag the message as having an error and processing will stop.

Regarding document delivery, the VAN can be envisioned as an FTP server, with basic folder hierarchy consisting of one MailBox for each trading partner. Generally, trading partners are given a *MailBox ID* (which is essentially a username). When logging in with this ID through an FTP client, the user is routed to the trading partner MailBox, where two folders exist: the inbox and the outbox. These folders contain all of the document that are being received from trading partners (the inbox) or being delivered to trading partners (the outbox).

Documents remain in the inbox until requested by the trading partner. When a message arrives in the outbox, the VAN will automatically try and deliver it to the appropriate trading partner. An outline of a typical VAN architecture, denoting how documents flow through this environment, is shown in Figure 5-3.

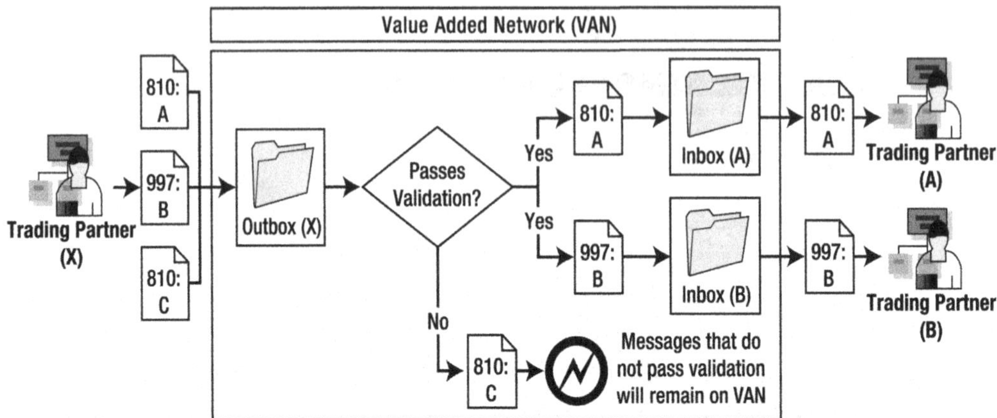

Figure 5-3. *Processing EDI documents on a VAN*

Generally speaking, VANs have user interfaces that allow trading partners to log in and view the status of transmitted documents, including details about when the transaction occurred, whether it arrived successfully, and any relevant error information. Figure 5-4 is an example of a view within a trading partner outbox on the VAN. The content of each message can be viewed, the status is shown, and the number of documents within a batch is displayed (in this case, all of the documents have a single interchange, and no batched documents were delivered).

Document Tracking - Outbox Summary View

Mailslot: DEMOSLOT Password: ●●●●●●●●●●● Refresh

From Date/Time: 071407 1223 To Date/Time: 071707 1223 (MMDDYY HHMM) Eastern Time

Record 1 - 16 of 80

View Detail	Transmitted▼	Processed	Batch #	Status	# of Interchanges	
☐	07/16 21:09	07/16 21:09	1488823	Complete	000001	View Data
☐	07/16 21:08	07/16 21:08	1488819	Complete	000001	View Data
☐	07/16 21:01	07/16 21:01	1488656	Complete	000001	View Data
☐	07/16 20:55	07/16 20:55	1488283	Complete	000001	View Data
☐	07/16 20:55	07/16 20:55	1488281	Complete	000001	View Data
☐	07/16 20:54	07/16 20:54	1488277	Complete	000001	View Data

Figure 5-4. *Example of a VAN outbox, with EDI documents delivered to partners*

In most cases, documents are delivered to VANs using FTP. BizTalk determines success or failure of the delivery of those documents by a successful FTP transfer—no different than any standard FTP transmission. What happens after the document has arrived on the VAN, whether the document is validated or not, and whether it can be routed to the specified trading partner, does not get communicated back to BizTalk. The only piece that will indicate full delivery to the trading partner is the reception of an acknowledgement; the acknowledgement is generated by the trading partner and is delivered back to the original sender of the document via the VAN and is routed like any other document. If an acknowledgement is not received, an administrator will need to log on to the VAN and find out what the issue is. The full document delivery process is outlined in Figure 5-5.

■ **Note** It is good practice for an administrator to periodically log in to the VAN to make sure that documents are being processed as expected, especially if acknowledgements are not configured.

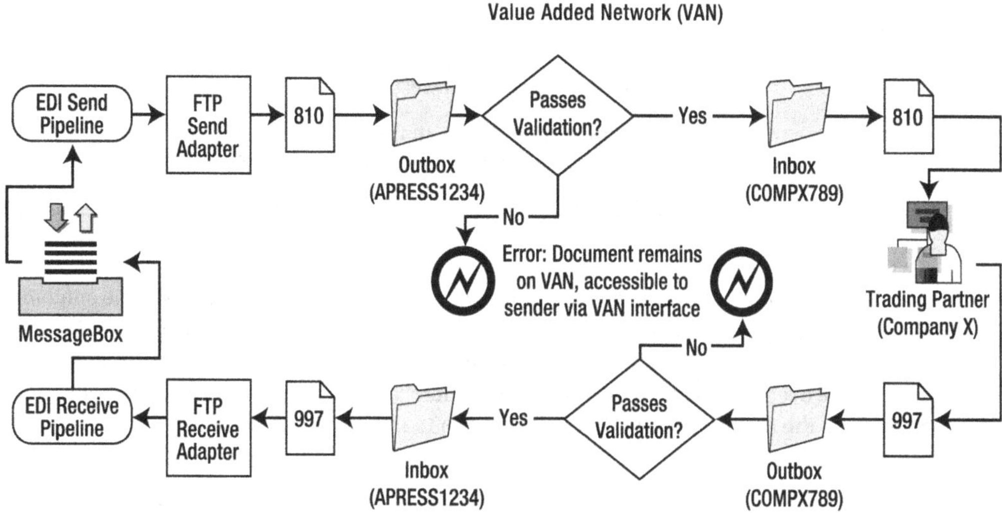

Figure 5-5. *Document flow from BizTalk through VAN*

Sending Documents to the VAN

This section outlines the process of sending documents to the VAN using the secure FTP adapter for BizTalk Server 2006. The secure FTP adapter allows for the handling of certificates, which the standard FTP adapter does not. Exercise 5-2 demonstrates all of the steps needed to configure and send a document using the secure adapter. In addition to this exercise, two concepts are introduced that will be of use in document delivery.

- **Naming files with macros**: When a document is delivered, it must have a filename. BizTalk provides a number of macros that allow for the creation of descriptive and unique filenames. The macros shown in Table 5-1 are the most common that are used in conjunction with EDI implementations. There are a number of additional macros that may be of use, all of which can be found in the BizTalk Server Documentation (via the index, under Macros). Macros can be entered in alone, combined, or entered in association with constant strings (as demonstrated in the exercises in this chapter).

Table 5-1. *Common EDI BizTalk Filename Macros (Used in FTP File Delivery)*

Macro	Description
%datetime%	Current date and time, in the UTC format, as shown: [YYYY]-[MM]-[DD]T[hh][mm][ss]. Note that if multiple files are written out at the same time, such as in the case of large batches, this may not ensure uniqueness of name.
%MessageId%	Name of the GUID of the BizTalk message. This is guaranteed to be a unique filename.

Table 5-1. *Common EDI BizTalk Filename Macros (Used in FTP File Delivery) (Continued)*

Macro	Description
%DestinationParty%	Name of the target party. This is best used in conjunction with a unique macro, such as %DestinationParty%%MessageId%.
%SourceParty%	Name of the source party. Again, this should be used in combination with another macro to ensure uniqueness (e.g., %SourceParty%_%MessageId%).
%time%	Simple time stamp, in the UTC format [hh][mm][ss]. This does not ensure uniqueness, unless combined with the %MessageId% macro.

- **Adding maps to send ports**: When sending documents, it is possible to transform the outgoing document using a map. If a document transformation needs to occur, it can be performed either in an orchestration or in a receive or send port. For outgoing processes that do not require the overhead of an orchestration (e.g., there is no business logic beyond the need to perform the transformation), adding the map to the send port is a simple and effective alternative.

Exercise 5-2 walks through creating a solution that delivers an XML document to an FTP site (representing a VAN) using the secure FTP adapter. Once this is completed, Exercise 5-3 shows the steps needed for adding a map to the outgoing FTP send port.

Exercise 5-2. Sending Documents Using Secure FTP (FTPS)

Depending on the requirements of the trading partner or the VAN, it may be necessary to deliver documents via secure FTP to ensure data is encrypted properly. BizTalk Server 2006 R2 comes with only one FTP adapter—the "standard" FTP adapter. This exercise demonstrates how to configure the /n software secure FTP adapter to send an EDI document. The installation of this adapter is covered in Exercise 5-1.

1. Begin by creating a receive port and receive location in BizTalk Administration Console that will pick up a document and deliver it to the MessageBox. This port will be subscribed to by the secure FTP send port that will be created in this exercise. The receive port is used to facilitate the illustration in this exercise through the file delivery method—in a true implementation, the send port may subscribe directly to the MessageBox, be called from an orchestration, or be configured in a variety of other ways to deliver a document.
   a. In an appropriate BizTalk Application (this exercise uses EDI.Demonstration.Chapter5), right-click Receive Ports and create a new receive port called EDI.Demonstration.Example.SecureFTP.FILE.
   b. On the Receive Locations tab of the receive port, create a new receive location that listens for a file to be dropped on a file directory (at C:\Apress.Integration\Chapter 5\Drops\Incoming - Secure FTP Demo). This pipeline can be left as PassThruReceive, as no validation or transformation will be done on the test document.

2. Right-click Send Ports and create a new static one-way send port:
   a. Set the Name property (in this case, EDI.Demonstration.Example.SecureFTP.FTP).
   b. Set the Type property to the Secure FTP Adapter (nsoftware.FTP v[x]).
   c. Click the Configure button next to Type and set the following properties on the adapter (these are the most common properties to set. Additional settings can be made but are not covered in this exercise; see the /n software documentation for more details).
      i. Set Remote File to EDIDemo_%MessageId%.txt.
      ii. Set the Remote Path to /EDI.Demonstration/VAN - Outbox. This exercise assumes that the FTP site being delivered to is the one configured in Exercise 5-1.
      iii. Set the Temp Dir to a path on the local machine where the data can be stored while being transmitted. This is not a required field but can help ensure that data has been fully transferred and is recoverable in the case of a partial or lost FTP transaction. In this exercise, it is set to C:\Temp.
      iv. Set Transfer Mode to ASCII. All EDI transmissions via VANs (and therefore FTP) are ASCII; binary will be delivered, but will not be understood by the target environment, and will fail validation on the VAN.
      v. Leave FTP Port at 21 for this demonstration. On secure FTP sites, this is generally set to a secure port.
      vi. Set FTP Server to the target FTP server. This exercise uses the FTP site configured in Exercise 5-1, therefore it can be set to localhost. In general, this will either be an IP address or a fully named FTP site. It does not include the subfolder that is to be the actual location of delivery (this property is set in the Remote Path field).
      vii. Set Passive to Yes. This will depend on the configuration of the target FTP site, but it is generally set to this value.
      viii. Enter the username into the User property. A local administrator or user account can be used if running the FTP site locally.
      ix. Enter the password of the target site in the Password property.
      x. If the FTP site that is being connected to is a secure FTP site, set the following:
         1. SSL Accept Server Cert is the key property that is not available on the standard FTP adapter. This allows the adapter to interact with the server to authenticate the certificate. The easiest thing to do with this property is set it to ANY, which will allow any certificate on the FTP server to be automatically accepted by the adapter. This ensures that processes will continue to run even if the target FTP server (VAN or otherwise) changes the certificate.
         2. SSL Start Mode is a property that indicates how the adapter interacts with the server to negotiate the certificate. Set this property to Explicit.
      xi. If the site is not a secure FTP site (which will be the case with a local FTP site set up on Windows Server, as shown in this exercise), set the properties as follows:
         1. Leave SSL Accept Server Cert blank.
         2. Set SSL Start Mode to None.
      xii. Setting Trace Mode to Debug is useful during development, as everything that occurs in the adapter is logged to the Windows Event Viewer. Once the adapter has been configured and tested, it can be set to Error, which only logs information if an error is encountered in the adapter. The fully configured properties should look similar to what is shown in Figure 5-6.

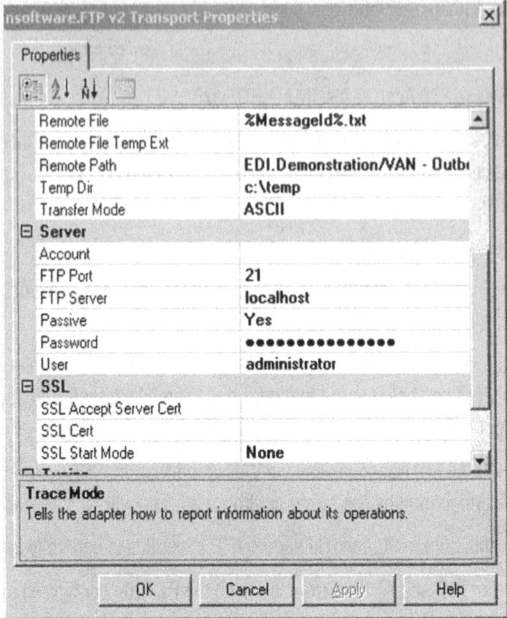

Figure 5-6. */n software FTP adapter settings*

d. Click OK once the settings have been entered to configure the FTP properties.

e. Set the Send Pipeline property to PassThruTransmit.

3. Click the Transport Advanced Options tab of the send port, and configure the properties as follows (and as illustrated in Figure 5-7).

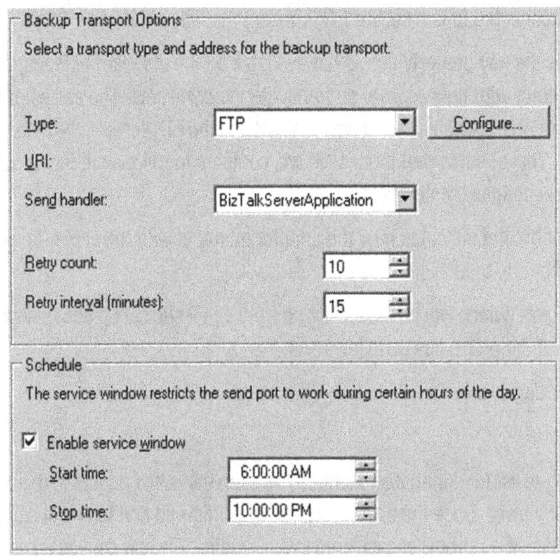

Figure 5-7. *Backup transport settings*

a. Set the Retry Count and Retry Interval to appropriate values. This indicates how the adapter handles exceptions that are thrown. For instance, if an FTP site cannot be accessed, this tells the adapter to wait a specified amount of time and try again. There are numerous occasions with FTP where retries are invaluable. For instance, if an FTP site is being rebooted and cannot be connected to, the adapter will sleep and try again. The next time it tries, the site will likely be restarted, and therefore it will be able to connect without issue.

■ **Note** When a send port is bound to an orchestration, the orchestration will wait until the adapter has successfully delivered a document, regardless of the number of retries, as long as the Delivery Notification property on the send port has been set to Transmitted (this is set on the send port properties within the orchestration). If this is not set, the orchestration will continue to move forward, regardless of the success or failure of the document transmission.

---

b. The Ordered Delivery flag ensures that messages are processed in the order in which they arrive on the MessageBox, and that if a message does suspend, messages that come after it through the same port will be queued and not delivered.

c. The Enable Routing for Failed Messages property must be turned on if complex exception handling has been implemented (see Chapter 4).

d. Leave the Service Window settings as they are; this exercise uses the default values. The scheduling properties are valuable when documents should only be processed within a certain window. Occasionally trading partners will only want documents delivered during "business hours," and these properties ensure this is easily accommodated.

4. Click the Backup Transport tab of the send adapter. When delivering documents via FTP, it is frequently useful to set the properties on this tab, as shown in the steps that follow:

   a. Often there will be a secondary (alternative) FTP site that can be delivered to if the primary one is not available or cannot be connected to. For example, if delivering to a VAN, the VAN may provide two FTP sites: a primary and a secondary. Configuring the secondary on the Backup Transport page, exactly as the primary is configured (except for the FTP server property) allows BizTalk to work with both of the servers in case one of them is inaccessible.

   b. If there is no alternative site, it can be helpful to deliver failed documents to an internal location—such as a file drop—where an administrator can monitor progress. This is a simple alternative to a robust exception handling model (taking only a moment to configure).

5. The final tab to be discussed is the Filters tab. It must be configured to subscribe to the receive port set up in the first step, so that the adapter can be tested. Click the Filters tab and then the filter as shown in Figure 5-8.

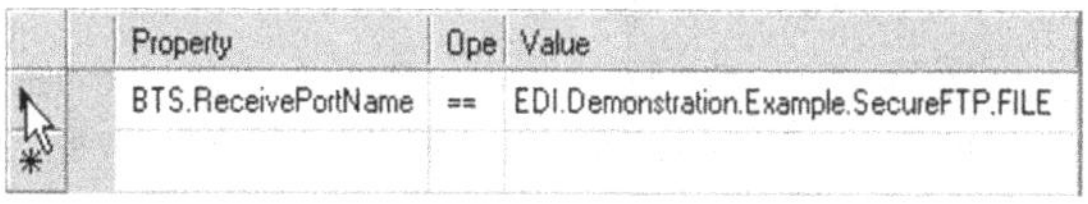

	Property	Ope	Value
	BTS.ReceivePortName	==	EDI.Demonstration.Example.SecureFTP.FILE
*			

Figure 5-8. *Setting the filter*

6. Finish this exercise by testing that a file can be successfully delivered to the FTP site:

   a. Start the receive location and the send port via the BizTalk Administration Console.

   b. Drop a file on the input folder (in this case C:\Apress.Integration\Chapter 5\Drops\Incoming - Secure FTP Demo) and ensure that it has been delivered to the FTP site.

   c. Monitor the Windows Event Viewer to validate that no errors were thrown.

■ **Note** When sending files over FTP, regardless of what adapter is being used, it is important to understand that files are transmitted in chunks, and that the connection can be interrupted at any time. Always test FTP solutions to ensure that if a file is only partially transmitted, and the connection is lost, no issues will arise. One common issue that occurs is that once the FTP adapter is able to connect again, there is a partially written file already on the FTP site. If the filename is not unique, and the adapter is not set to overwrite, there will be an error thrown. The best way to test how a solution will handle FTP transmissions is to transfer a massive file (e.g., 100MB), which will give the tester time to interrupt the transmission (such as by pulling the network cable) before it is complete. The next step would be to connect the solution back up and test that the file is delivered successfully the second time.

With the secure FTP solution completed, which delivers an XML document to an FTP site, Exercise 5-3 works through the steps needed to add a map to this solution.

Exercise 5-3. Mapping on a Send Port

This exercise builds on the secure FTP adapter configured in Exercise 5-2. It demonstrates how to add a map to the send port to deliver a validated EDI document. The map that is used was developed in Chapter 3.

1. Begin by deploying the schemas and map that were developed in Chapter 3:
   a. Open the solution at C:\Apress.Integration\Chapter 3 in Visual Studio and deploy it. It contains two projects, both of which must be deployed.
      i. Add the two files to the Company X project and deploy the schema and map found in C:\Apress.Integration\Chapter 3\Company X Final Schema and Map.
      ii. Make a reference to a strong name key in both projects if necessary. There is one in the root folder for Chapter 3 files.
   b. After the solution has been deployed, add a reference to the Chapter 3 BizTalk application:
      i. Right-click EDI.Demonstration.Chapter5 and select Add References.
      ii. In the window that opens, select EDI.Demonstration.Chapter3 and click OK. This will make all maps and schemas available to components in the Chapter 5 BizTalk application.
2. In the EDI.Demonstration.Chapter5 BizTalk application, open the FTP send port that was created in Exercise 5-2. To ensure that the maps are available, the application may need to be refreshed (right-click the BizTalk application and select Refresh).
   a. On the General tab set the Send Pipeline property to EdiSend.
   b. Click the Outbound Maps tab. Under the Map property; click the drop-down. There should be one map available. Select it; both the Source Document and Target Document properties will be automatically set (as shown in Figure 5-9).

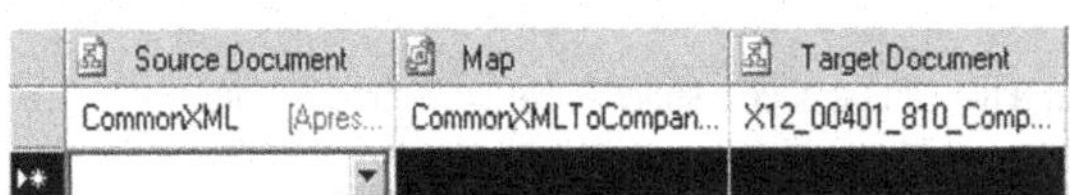

Figure 5-9. *Referencing a map in a send port*

   c. Click OK to save the updates.

■ **Note** Multiple maps can be added to a port. If an incoming document does not match the source document in the first map, it will move on to the next map in the list until it finds a schema that it matches. If no match is found, the document will be suspended. This approach can be useful when delivering different documents via the same port.

---

3. Change the Receive Pipeline property on the receive location created in Exercise 5-2 to XMLReceive.
4. Validate that the receive location and send port are started. Restart the BizTalkApplicationHost (in BizTalk Administration Console, Host Instances) to ensure that the most current configurations are present.
5. Drop an EDI 810 instance on the receive location to test that the solution is working:
   a. Copy the file Source 810 XML.xml from C:\Apress.Integration\Chapter 3\Test Documents. This is the document that matches the Source Document property of the map.
   b. Drop the file in C:\Apress.Integration\Chapter 5\Drops\Incoming - Secure FTP Demo.
   c. Check that the file is mapped and arrives on the FTP site in EDI format.

Receiving Files from the VAN

In the same way that documents going from BizTalk to the VAN are sent to trading partners via the outbox, trading partners delivering documents to the home party via the VAN deliver documents to the inbox, and BizTalk monitors this folder and processes them accordingly. Generally speaking, all EDI document types will arrive in the same inbox, including acknowledgements. This section describes how to configure the secure FTP adapter to subscribe to documents on the VAN.

Though VANs are set up to handle FTP transfers, they are far more complex than a simple FTP site. Frequently, their configurations are atypical for FTP settings. For example, it is common to find VANs do not support the SYST command. Unfortunately, the standard BizTalk FTP adapter that ships with BizTalk Server does not support transmissions when the FTP server does not support the SYST command; files are seen, a warning is logged (see Figure 5-10), but the transmission never occurs. There is no error, but there is also no success. The SYST command is required. Because of this, it is necessary to use the secure FTP adapter to receive files.

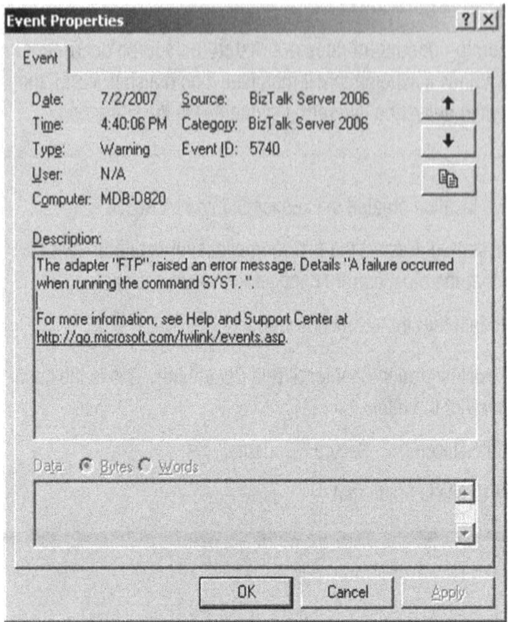

Figure 5-10. *Standard FTP terminates when SYST is not supported*

Exercise 5-4 outlines how to work with the secure FTP adapter to retrieve files from an FTP site.

Exercise 5-4. Receiving Documents Using Secure FTP

This exercise outlines the steps needed to configure the /n software secure FTP adapter to subscribe to an FTP site and deliver the documents to a local file directory:

1. Begin with creating a new one-way receive port. This receive port will be named EDI.Demonstration.Example.SecureFTP.FTP for this exercise.
2. Add a receive location to this port, and configure it as follows:
    a. Name this location ReceiveSecureFTP.
    b. Set the Type property to nsoftware.FTP v2.
    c. The Receive Pipeline property can remain as PassThruReceive.
    d. Click the Configure button. Set the following fields as directed (where a field is not indicated, leave it set to the default value). A fully configured version of this screen is shown in Figure 5-11.
        i. Set the Delete Mode to Always or On Success.

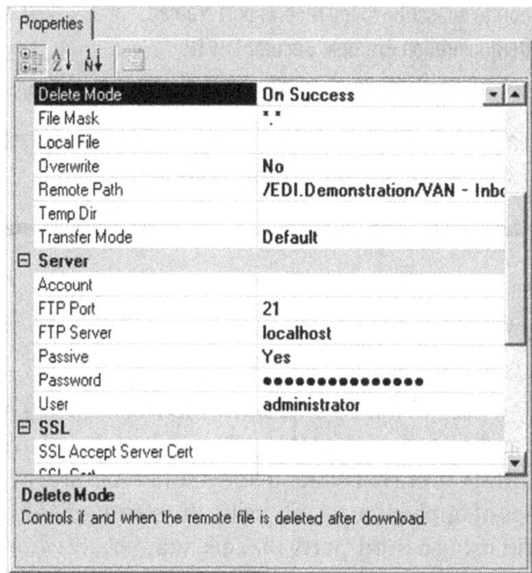

Figure 5-11. */n software secure FTP adapter settings*

Note Different VAN architectures will handle files differently. Some will require that the files be deleted by the trading partner to ensure that they are not picked up twice, while others (such as GXS) will automatically manage access to files (i.e., in this case, once a file has been successfully received, the VAN will mark the file as processed and make it unavailable for future requests).

---

ii. Set the File Mask to *.*. This will pick up all files on the site.

Note Typical file masks in BizTalk are *.txt, *.xml, or *.*. In the case of VANs, file extensions are rarely used. Setting the file mask to *.* will frequently not return any results, even if multiple files are available. To remedy this, always set the file mask to a single asterisk (*) to pick up all files, which is a necessity for many EDI solutions polling a VAN.

---

iii. Using the FTP site setup in Exercise 5-1, this adapter will listen for files on the inbox. Set the Remote Folder to /EDI.Demonstration/VAN - Inbox/.

iv. Set the Transfer Mode to ASCII.

v. Set the FTP Server property to localhost.

vi. Set the User and Password properties to appropriate values (a local administrator always works for testing purposes).

vii. If the FTP site is not secure (which it will not be if it is a local FTP site), set the SSL Start Mode to None.

e. Click OK to save the configuration settings.

3. Click OK again to save the port settings.

4. Create a new send port that has a Type property set to File and writes to a local file directory (this exercise uses C:\Apress.Integration\Chapter 5\Drops\Outgoing - Secure FTP Demo).

5. Set the Filter property on the send port to subscribe to the receive port created. For this exercise, the filter would be BTS.ReceivePortName == EDI.Demonstration.Example.SecureFTP.FTP.
6. Start both the receive location and the send port, and restart the BizTalk Server Host instance.
7. Test the solution by dropping a file on the FTP site, in the appropriate directory. Check that the file was picked up and delivered to the file output folder, and that it was deleted from the FTP server.

AS2 Architecture

In many B2B environments, there is no need to have a VAN sitting between trading partners. To eliminate the unnecessary overhead and cost of using a VAN, AS2 was introduced. AS2 is the secure transmission of documents using S/MIME over HTTP(S). To understand AS2 architecture, the best approach is to work through two types of implementations: using the standard AS2 functionality that ships with BizTalk Server R2, and using a third-party BizTalk adapter. By working through Exercise 5-5 and Exercise 5-6, both of which implement a full end-to-end transmission of an EDI document over AS2, this architecture will be understood.

■ **Note** Additional information regarding AS2 and how party properties are configured is covered in Chapter 2.

Exercise 5-5. Using Standard AS2 Functionality

The standard AS2 functionality that ships with R2 relies on a combination of the HTTP adapter, the AS2 pipelines, party settings, and the Windows certificate store. The configuration of these components for an operational AS2 transmission is outlined in this exercise. The components used in this exercise are outlined in Figure 5-12.

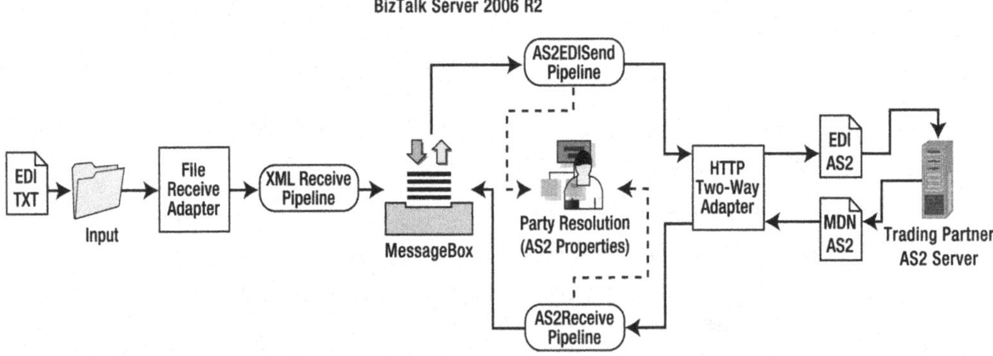

Figure 5-12. *Exercise component flow*

1. Begin by creating a party that can be configured to handle AS2 documents:
   a. Right-click Parties in BizTalk Administration Console and select New ➤ Party.
      i. Name the party AS2StandardDemo. Set up the Aliases properties as shown in Figure 5-13.

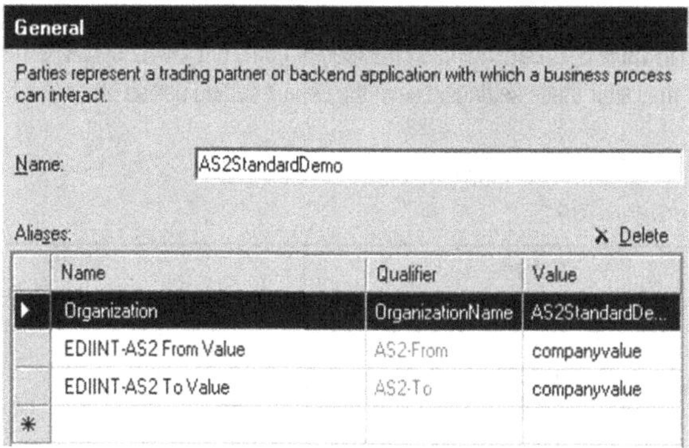

Figure 5-13. *Aliases for the AS2 party*

Note The standard AS2 functionality resolves the party based on the AS2-From and AS2-To values in the Aliases tab. Standard EDI (non-AS2) implementations generally ignore the fields in the Aliases pane.

- ii. Click OK.

b. Right-click Parties again and select EDI Properties. The EDI settings should be set up as described in previous chapters, based on whether the party is acting as a sender or a receiver. The ISA and GS segments should be set based on the EDI implementation guide. For this exercise, use the following settings. Note that the EDI settings have nothing to do with the AS2 functionality, but only the EDI document that is wrapped in the AS2 transmission:

- i. Click the ISA Segment Definition tab. Leave the default value for any field that is not listed:
  1. Set ISA05 to 01.
  2. Set ISA06 to APRESS1234.
  3. Set ISA07 to ZZ.
  4. Set ISA08 to AS2Standard.
  5. Set the Suffix to CR LF.
- ii. Click the GS and ST Segment Definition tab. Leave the default for any field not listed:
  1. Set the value for ST01 to 810 – Invoice.
  2. Set the Version/Release to 04010.
  3. Set the Target Namespace to `http://schemas.microsoft.com/BizTalk/EDI/X12/2006`.
  4. Set GS1 to IN – Invoice Information.
  5. Set GS2 to APRESS1234.
  6. Set GS3 to AS2Standard.
  7. Select any value for GS4 and GS5.
  8. Set GS7 to X – Accredited Standard.
  9. Set GS8 to 04010.
- iii. Click OK to save the EDI properties.

c. Right-click Parties again and select AS2 Properties. Click the Party As AS2 Message Receiver tab. These values are based on what is shown in Table 5-2. Depending on the requirements of the AS2 server, especially in the way encryption is handled, it may alter these settings. Leave the default setting unless otherwise indicated.

Table 5-2. *AS2 Configuration Information*

Field/Information	Value
URL	`http://as2.sampleserver.com:8080/HttpReceiver`
Encryption	3DES
MDN	sync
Sender AS2 ID	AS2StandardDemo
Sender Private Key	Key1.pfx (password: test)
Receiver AS2 ID	companyvalue
Receiver Certificate / Public Key	Key2.cer

i. Place a check mark next to Sign Message.

ii. Set a check mark next to Encrypt Message and select DES3.

iii. Set the AS2-From value to AS2StandardDemo.

iv. Set the AS2-To value (which should be equal to what is in all of the values on the Party Alias tab) to companyvalue.

v. Enable Request MDN and set a check mark next to Request Signed MDN.

■ **Note** The Signed-Receipt-MICalg field is by default set to MD5. If an error is generated when receiving the MDN, such as "The AS2 Decoder failed processing when validating the MIC value returned in the MDN," try setting this value to **SHA1**. This setting can generally be found on the Thumbprint Algorithm property of the certificate, via the Certificate Console.

---

vi. Click OK to save the settings.

d. Click OK to save all of the party settings.

2. Add the public and private keys to the Windows certificate store. There are numerous different certificate combinations; this example uses a public key (.cer) and a private key (.pfx) to demonstrate how to work with certificates:

a. Click Start ➤ Run and type **mmc**.

■ **Note** Certificates must be installed by a user who has the appropriate permissions. Since BizTalk will be referencing the certificates, they must be installed using the same user as BizTalk runs under. To run mmc under a different user than the one currently logged in, open a command prompt and start mmc using the format **runas /u:[*username*] mmc**.

---

b. In the mmc console that opens, click the File menu option and select Add/Remove Snap In.

c. In the Add/Remove window that opens, click Add.

d. Select Certificates and click Add.

e. Select My User Account and click Finish. Close the Add/Remove window.

f. Expand the certificate directory and locate the Personal ➤ Certificates folder, as shown in Figure 5-14.

Figure 5-14. *Certificate Console*

g. Import both the .cer and .pfx certificates using the following steps:

   i. Right-click the Certificates folder and select All Tasks ➤ Import.

   ii. In the Certificate Import Wizard that opens, click Next on the first page.

   iii. On the second page, click the Browse button and select the certificate file. Click Open once the certificate has been selected.

   iv. Click Next. The certificate can remain in the Personal folder, though depending on permissions and how certificates are organized, a different folder may be more appropriate for a given solution.

   v. Click Next and then Finish the Wizard.

h. The certificates need to be copied to two other certificate locations to ensure that the AS2 BizTalk components have access to them. Again, depending on how the certificates have been created, these steps will likely be different:

   i. Begin by copying and pasting both of the certificates that were imported into the Personal folder into the Trusted Root Certificate folder. To copy the certificates, right-click them and select from the menu.

   ii. Now add them to the Other People folder on the local computer:

      1. In the Console, click the File menu option and select Add/Remove Snap In.

      2. In the Add/Remove window that opens, click Add.

      3. Select Certificates and click Add.

      4. Select Computer Account and click Next.

      5. Select the Local Computer option and click Next, then Finish.

      6. Return to the main Console window, and the new folder will be available. Expand this folder and locate the Other People folder. Copy the public certificate that was added to the Personal folder (right-click and select Copy) and paste it into the Other People folder (alternatively, these certificates can be imported again, overwriting the loaded versions).

i. The certificates have all been added successfully at this point. This can be validated by double-clicking the certificate and checking that there are no errors on the General tab. A public key will look like that shown in Figure 5-15 if it is a trusted certificate and if the private key is available.

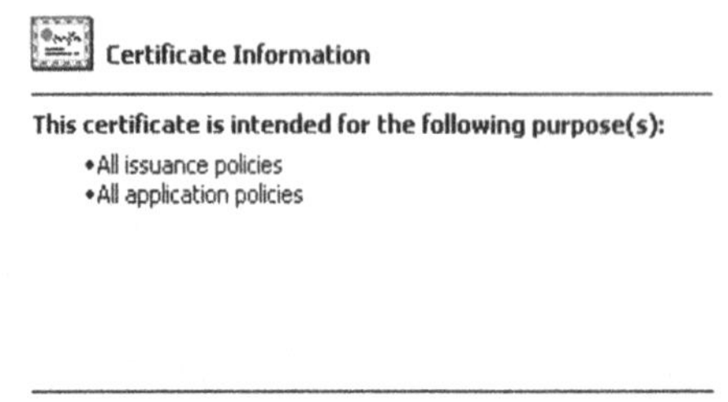

Certificate Information
This certificate is intended for the following purpose(s):
•All issuance policies
•All application policies
Valid from 12/1/2005 to 8/10/2019
You have a private key that corresponds to this certificate.

Figure 5-15. *Valid public key sample*

3. Create a new send port by right-clicking Send Ports in the BizTalk Administration Console and selecting New ➤ Static Solicit-Response Send Port. This is a two-way port that receives the MDN:

   a. On the General tab, set the following:

      i. Set the Name property of the port to EDI.Demonstration.Example.AS2Standard.HTTP.810.

      ii. The Type field should be HTTP.

      iii. Set the Send Pipeline property to AS2EDISend.

      iv. Set the Receive Pipeline property to AS2Receive.

      v. Click the Configure button.

         1. Uncheck the Enable Chunked Encoding option.

         2. Set the Destination URL to `http://as2.sampleserver.com:8080/HttpReceiver`.

   b. On the Outbound Maps folder, set the map to the same map used in Exercise 5-3, which is Apress.Integration.EDI810.CompanyX.CommonXMLToCompanyX810.

   c. Click the Filters tab, and set the filter to subscribe to the same receive port created in Exercise 5-2: BTS.ReceivePortName == EDI.Demonstration.Example.SecureFTP.FILE.

   d. Click the Certificates tab. The public key will now be added to this send port.

      i. It is required that the thumbprint of the certificate be entered. Access this by double-clicking the public certificate in the Certificate Console (from the previous step).

         1. Click the Details tab.

         2. Scroll down to the Thumbprint property. Copy this value.

      ii. Paste the value that was copied into the Thumbprint property of the send port Certificate tab, as shown in Figure 5-16. There is no need to type in a common name; this will be automatically set after the window is closed, based on the properties within the certificate.

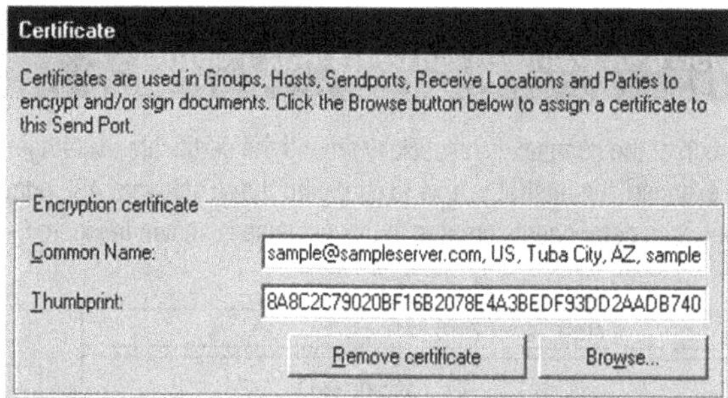

Figure 5-16. *Certificate tab on send port with public certificate thumbprint*

   e. Click OK to save the send port properties.

4. The next step is to add the private key certificate to the BizTalk Group:
   a. Right-click the BizTalk Group and select Properties.
   b. Click the Certificate tab. Using the same technique shown in step 3, paste the value of the private key's thumbprint into the Thumbprint value on this tab.
   c. Click OK to save the certificate reference.

5. Now test the solution by taking the following steps:
   a. Since the send port subscribes to the same receive port used by other send ports in other exercises in this chapter, make sure that all of the send ports are unenlisted.
   b. Enlist and start the send port created in this exercise.
   c. Enlist and start the receive port that the send port is subscribing to.
   d. Click Host Instances in the BizTalk Administration Console and restart the BizTalkServerApplication.
   e. Drop an EDI 810 instance on the receive location to test that the solution is working.
      i. Copy the file Source 810 XML.xml from C:\Apress.Integration\Chapter 3\Test Documents. This is the document that matches the Source Document property of the map.
      ii. Drop the file in C:\Apress.Integration\Chapter 5\Drops\Incoming - Secure FTP Demo.
      iii. Monitor the Windows Event Viewer to ensure that no errors were thrown.

Note Monitoring the AS2 process and looking at the EDI reports is fully explained in Chapter 6.

The standard AS2 functionality relies on the use of the certificate store to work through security layers and works with settings on the party to manage document delivery. The /n software AS2 adapter ignores both of these components, functioning like a traditional adapter, where all configurations are handled on the adapter itself. There is no need to configure AS2 properties, and no need to load certificates into the certificate store.

The drawback to the standard method of working with AS2 transactions is that it can be difficult to understand how to manage certificates and set the AS2 properties. The drawback to the /n software AS2 adapter is that much of the AS2 reporting provided in the BizTalk EDI AS2 report is lost. However, purely from the point of view of document delivery, the overall configuration of the AS2 adapter is fairly straightforward, as shown in Exercise 5-6.

Exercise 5-6. Using /n software AS2 Adapter

The /n software adapter eliminates much of the complexity (especially around the certificate exchange) that the standard BizTalk AS2 solution introduces. This exercise demonstrates how to configure the /n software AS2 adapter and interact with an AS2 server. The interaction between components created in this exercise is shown in Figure 5-17.

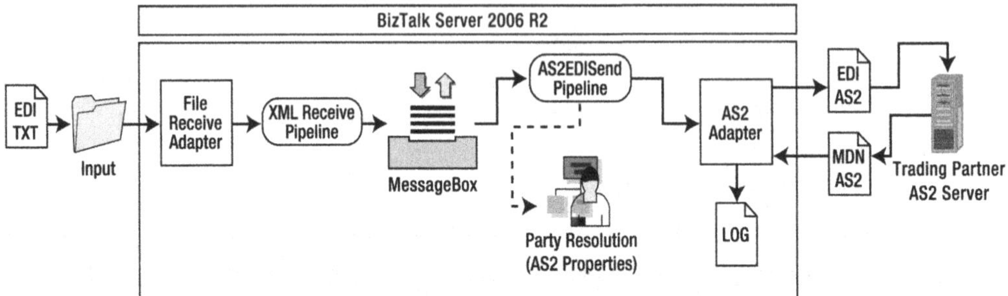

Figure 5-17. *Exercise component flow*

1. Create a new BizTalk party set to work with this AS2 configuration:
   a. Right-click Parties in BizTalk Administration Console and select New ➤ Party.
   b. Name the party HomePartyDemoAS2. Set up the aliases properties as shown in Figure 5-18.

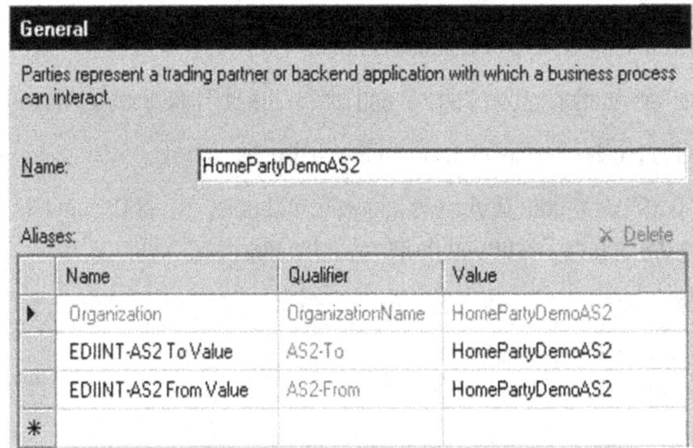

Figure 5-18. *Aliases for the AS2 party*

   c. Right-click the newly created party and select AS2 Properties.
      i. Click the Party As AS2 Message Receiver tab.
      ii. Set the AS2-From property to HomePartyDemoAS2.
      iii. Set the AS2-To property to TradingPartnerDemoAS2.

■ Note With the /n software AS2 adapter, there is no need to set any of the AS2 properties on the party. These properties are only used with the standard BizTalk 2006 R2 AS2 functionality.

---

2. Table 5-3 shows the settings for communicating with a mock AS2 server. Substitute the appropriate values for the AS2 server available in the development environment.

Table 5-3. *AS2 Configuration Information*

Field/Information	Value
URL	`http://as2.sampleserver.com:8080/HttpReceiver`
Encryption	3DES
MDN	sync
Sender AS2 ID	HomePartyDemoAS2
Sender Private Key	Key1.pfx (password: test)
Receiver AS2 ID	TradingPartnerDemoAS2
Receiver Certificate / Public Key	Key2.cer

3. This exercise uses the same receive port and receive location created in step 1 of Exercise 5-2. If Exercise 5-2 has been deployed, the FTP send port is subscribing to the File receive port. To simplify the current exercise, right-click the FTP send port and unenlist it. This will prevent it from executing when the steps in this exercise are demonstrated. To create and configure the /n software AS2 port, open BizTalk Administration Console, right-click Send Ports, select New, and create a static one-way send port. Then set the properties as shown in the steps that follow (illustrated in Figure 5-19):

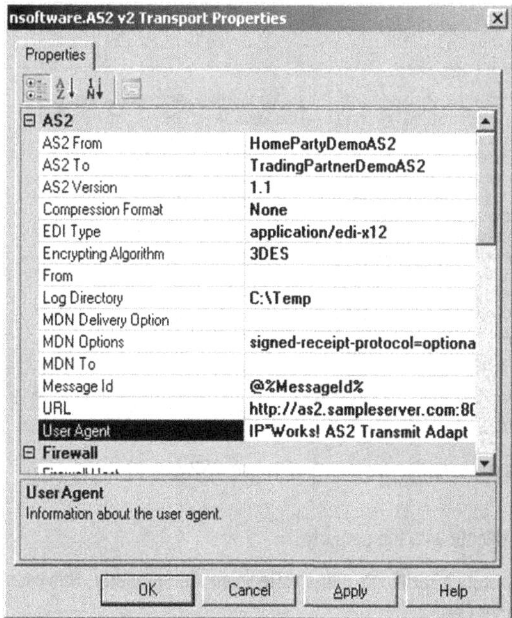

Figure 5-19. */n software adapter settings*

a. Name this port appropriately. For this exercise, it will be called EDI.Demonstration.Example.nSoftwareAS2.AS2.810.

b. Set the Type property to nsoftware.AS2 v2.

c. Set the Send Pipeline property to AS2EDISend. By using the EDI version of the AS2 pipeline, the EDI document will be validated.

d. Click the Configure button and set the following parameters (values not listed should remain at their default value):

   i. Set AS2-From to an appropriate value. For this exercise, use HomePartyDemoAS2.

   ii. Set AS2-To to an appropriate value. This exercise uses TradingPartnerDemoAS2.

   iii. Set the Log Directory to a path on the local computer where the adapter can write details out to a file. This will aid in troubleshooting. For this exercise, it is set to C:\Temp.

   iv. The URL should be set to `http://as2.sampleserver.com:8080/HttpReceiver`.

   v. The next step is to load the certificates. The AS2 adapter allows the certificates to be loaded without having to work through a separate mmc console (but if certificates are already loaded, they can be referenced), as directed in these steps:

      1. Click the ellipsis (...) next to the Receipt Signer Cert property.

      2. Click the Certificate File tab and click Browse.

      3. Find the directory that contains the .cer file, select it, and click Open. The certificate will be displayed, as shown in Figure 5-20.

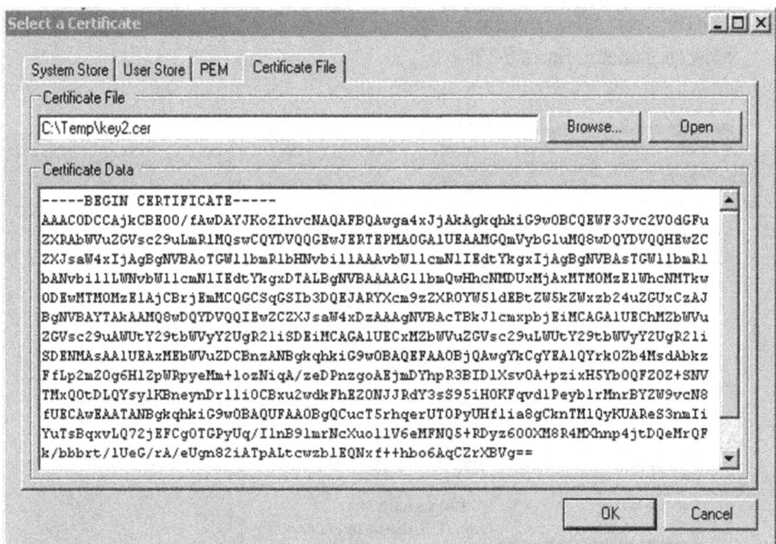

Figure 5-20. *Accessing certificate file from n Software AS2 adapter*

      4. Click OK to associate the certificate with the property.

      5. Follow the same steps to associate a certificate with the Recipient Cert property. This uses the same certificate as the Receipt Signer Cert.

      6. Click the ellipsis (...) next to the Signing Cert and click the PFX Store tab.

      7. Click Browse and find the .pfx file (private key). Select it and click Open, as shown in Figure 5-21.

8. Enter the password for the key, if applicable.

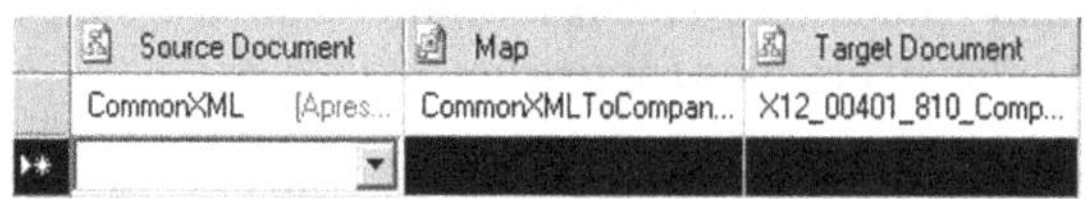

Figure 5-21. *Adding the private key*

9. Click the Open button and the certificate will be available in a list. Click it and select OK.

vi. Click OK on the Transport Properties window to save the fully configured properties.

e. On the main Send Port Properties window, continue with configuring the send port by clicking the Outbound Maps tab. Under the Map property, click the drop-down. There should be one map available. This is the same map used for the FTP send adapter in Exercise 5-3. For reference, the map configuration is shown in Figure 5-22.

Source Document		Map	Target Document
CommonXML	[Apres...	CommonXMLToCompan...	X12_00401_810_Comp...

Figure 5-22. *Referencing a map in a send port*

f. Click the Filter tab and set the filter to BTSReceivePortName == EDI.Demonstration.Example.SecureFTP.FILE.

g. Click OK to save the /n software AS2 port settings.

4. Start the send and receive ports and restart the BizTalk host application.

5. Test the solution by taking these steps:

a. Copy the file Source 810 XML.xml from C:\Apress.Integration\Chapter 3\Test Documents. This is the document that matches the Source Document property of the map.

b. Drop the file in C:\Apress.Integration\Chapter 5\Drops\Incoming - Secure FTP Demo.

c. Check the log file configured for the /n software AS2 adapter. It will contain all of the information about the document that was sent (including full EDI document with header and footer), encryption information, and information about the success or failure of the document transmission. A portion of the log file, indicating that the document was successfully received and an MDN was returned, is shown in Figure 5-23.

```
AS2 message received.
-------=_Part_160_1982244.1184685841064
Content-type: message/disposition-notification
Content-Transfer-Encoding: 7bit

Reporting-UA: sample AS2 Server
Original-Recipient: rfc822; TradingPartnerDemoAS2
Final-Recipient: rfc822; HomePartyDemoAS2
Original-Message-ID:
<b5912afe-606c-4bbe-a7ff-c7ec71d0cb61@593465c5-90e1-42b0-84be-e528032d26a6>
Disposition: automatic-action/MDN-sent-automatically; processed
Received-Content-MIC: fh8ODbmc1FpviH6/O2aKV2UcwUk=, sha1

-------=_Part_160_1982244.1184685841064--

---END RESPONSE---

Transmission was successful.
```

Figure 5-23. *AS2 adapter log file*

■ **Note** Using the AS2 adapter as outlined allows the MDN to be received, but the MDN information is only accessible through the log file. It is possible to use the AS2 adapter as a two-way solicit-response port and receive the MDN and do something with it. In such a case, the port is called from an orchestration, and the MDN comes back on the response. There are context properties on the message that allow the values in the MDN to be accessed.

Message Batching

Frequently, trading partners want to send many documents at once within a single batched delivery. Batch files contain one or more individual EDI documents, all wrapped by a single header and footer segment. For trading partners with a high volume of EDI documents coming in or being delivered out of systems, batching can drastically reduce the overall bandwidth required to support these deliveries. BizTalk supports several different batching approaches, as follows:

- **Scheduled:** Batches can be set to be delivered to trading partners on a timed interval.
- **Number of documents:** Batches can be triggered based on the number of documents queued and ready for delivery. For example, the batch can be set to be delivered whenever there are a total of 50 documents ready to be sent.
- **Number of characters in the batch:** The trigger can be set to execute when a certain number of characters have been received.
- **External trigger:** If either the number of documents to be delivered, or the time interval needed, are dynamic or set by a system other than BizTalk, a control message can be delivered to BizTalk indicating the batch properties. This process uses a combination of the following components:
  - **Batch control schema:** This is the control document that specifies how the batch is supposed to be handled. The document structure is shown in Figure 5-24.

```
- <ControlMessage xmlns="http://SQLControlMessage.IssueSelect">
  - <PAM_Control>
      <DestinationParty>6</DestinationParty>
      <ActionType>EdiBatchActivate</ActionType>
      <ActionSource />
      <ActionDateTime>2007-07-15T12:00:00.000</ActionDateTime>
      <ToBeBatched>true</ToBeBatched>
    </PAM_Control>
  </ControlMessage>
```

Figure 5-24. *Sample batch control message*

  - **BatchControlMessageRecvPipeline:** This is a pipeline component that can interpret the document that matches the batch control schema and cause the appropriate processes to listen and batch the incoming files.

The flow of a standard batched process is outlined in Figure 5-25. The process begins with creating a receive port and location with a pipeline that contains the batch marker component. This component is available on the EDI receive pipeline, or can be added to a custom pipeline (as shown in Figure 5-26). When a document is picked up on the receive location, the batch marker component will evaluate it against the batching filter criteria for all parties.

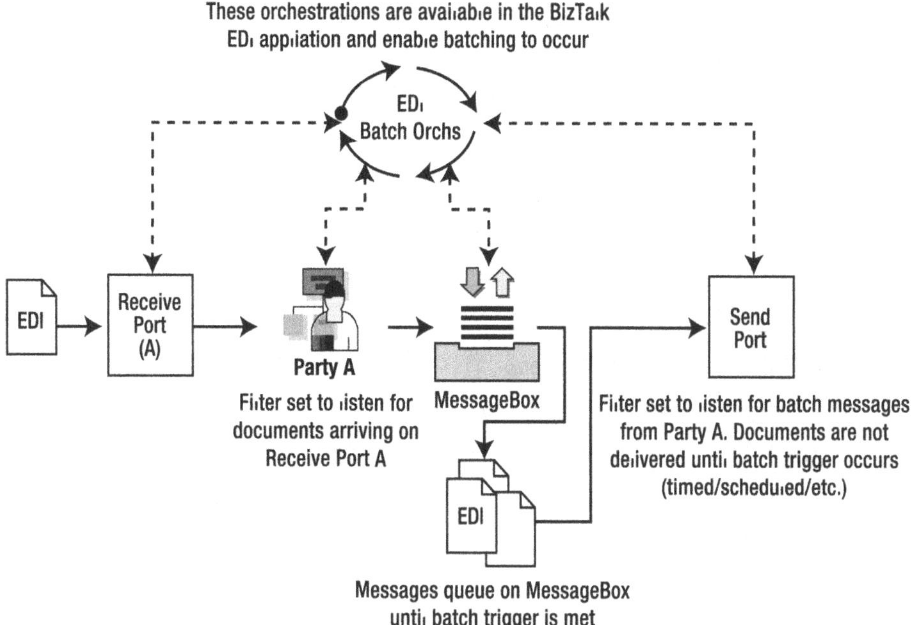

Figure 5-25. *Batching flow*

If the document matches the criteria for a single party, it will be stamped with the appropriate properties that will enable the MessageBox to route it to the EDI batching orchestration instance for that party. The orchestration determines whether the batch trigger has been met, and determines when and how to release a batch of documents (all documents are queued in the orchestration until it is time to deliver).

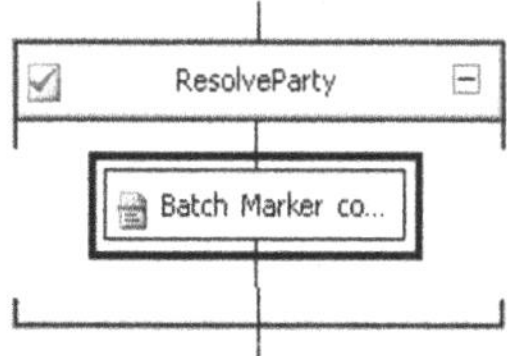

Figure 5-26. *Batch marker pipeline component on a custom pipeline*

In the case where the document matches the criteria for multiple parties, it will be stamped with properties that route it to the EDI batch routing orchestration, which in turn creates the corresponding number of copies (one for each party), stamping each message with the appropriate properties that will then enable them to be routed to the specific party's EDI batching orchestration instance.

Exercise 5-7 introduces basic batching functionality.

Exercise 5-7. Delivering Batched EDI Documents

1. Begin by creating a new receive port and receive location. Set the following:
   a. The Name property of the receive port is EDI.Demonstration.Example.BatchDemo.FILE.
   b. Set the Type property of the receive location to FILE.

c. The file directory where the receive location listens for incoming files is C:\Apress.Integration\Chapter 5\Drops\Incoming - Batch Demo.

d. Set the Receive Pipeline property to EDIReceive.

■ **Note** For batching to work, the incoming pipeline must have the batch marker component added to the ResolveParty stage. The EDI receive pipeline contains this component and supports batching.

---

2. Create a new party:

   a. Set the Name of the party to BatchingDemo.

   b. In the EDI properties of the party, set the following:

      i. Click the ISA Segment Definition tab. Leave the default value for any field that is not listed:

         1. Set ISA05 to 01.
         2. Set ISA06 to AAA.
         3. Set ISA07 to ZZ.
         4. Set ISA08 to BBB.
         5. Set the Suffix to CR LF.

      ii. Click the GS and ST Segment Definition tab. Leave the default for any field not listed:

         1. Set the Value property for ST01 to 810 – Invoice.
         2. Set the Version/Release property to 04010.
         3. Set the Target Namespace property to `http://schemas.microsoft.com/BizTalk/EDI/X12/2006`.
         4. Set GS1 to IN – Invoice Information.
         5. Set GS2 to AAA.
         6. Set GS3 to BBB.
         7. Select any value for GS4 and GS5.
         8. GS7 can be set to X – Accredited Standard.
         9. Set GS8 to 04010.

      iii. Click the Interchange Batch Creation Settings tab.

         1. Click the Filter button and set the filter to listen for documents coming in on the receive port created earlier in this exercise, as shown in Figure 5-27. Click OK to save the filter setting.

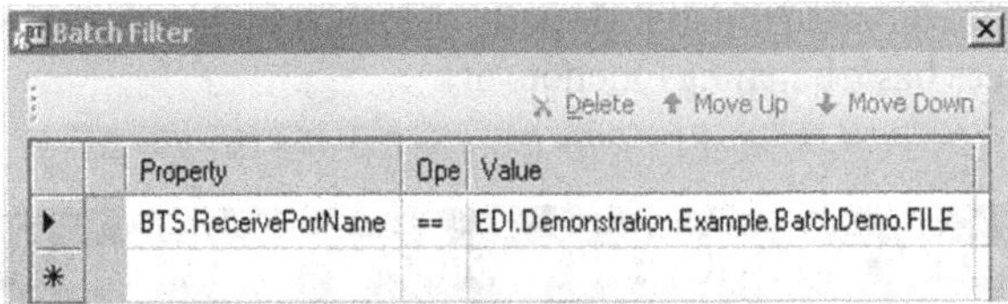

Figure 5-27. *Party batch filter*

        2. Select the Maximum Number of Transaction Sets property and set the Interchange property to 2. This means that a batch file will be sent out whenever two documents are ready to be sent to the trading partner. The batching orchestration will hold a reference to each message on the MessageBox until the messages are ready to be released as a batch.
        3. Click the Start button to begin the batching orchestration for the party. Ignore any pop-up boxes warning about start dates.
        4. Take note of the filter settings shown in Figure 5-28. These values must be set in the send port (created in the next step) that is associated with this party.

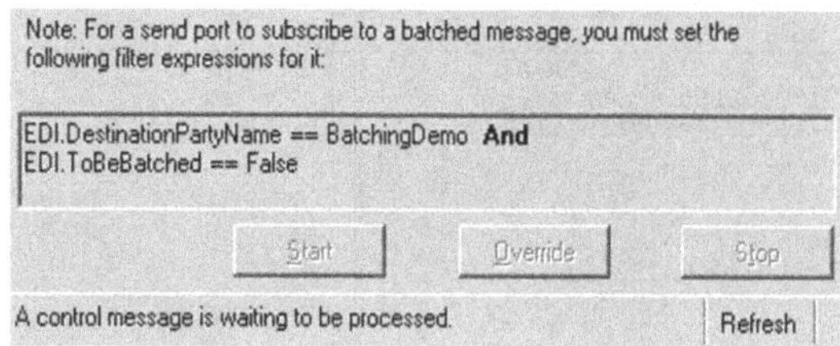

Figure 5-28. *Batch settings*

    c. Click OK to save all of the EDI properties.

3. Create a new send port:
    a. Name the send port EDI.Demonstration.Example.BatchDemo.FILE.
    b. Set the Type property to FILE, and the output file directory to C:\Apress.Integration\Chapter 5\Drops\Outgoing - Batch Demo.
    c. Set the Send Pipeline property to EDISend.
    d. Click the Filters tab and set the send port filter as shown in Figure 5-28.
    e. Click OK to save the send port settings.
4. Associate the send port with the party by double-clicking the party and clicking the Send Port tab. Select the send port created in the previous step.
5. Start the batching orchestrations:
    a. Click the BizTalk EDI application, and select the Orchestrations folder.
    b. Start all three of the batching orchestrations (shown in Figure 5-29).

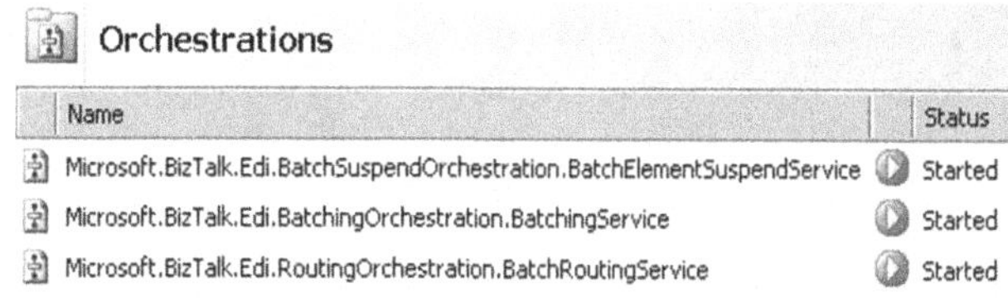

Figure 5-29. *Batching orchestrations*

6. Enlist and start the receive location and send port created in this exercise.
7. Restart the BizTalk host application to ensure all of the current settings are updated.

8. Test the solution as follows:

   a. Copy the file Input EDI Doc.txt from C:\Apress.Integration\Chapter 5\Test Documents.

   b. Paste the file in the receive location folder at C:\Apress.Integration\Chapter 5\Drops\Incoming - Batch Demo.

   c. Paste the file a second time in the same folder.

   d. Check the output folder at C:\Apress.Integration\Chapter 5\Drops\Outgoing - Batch Demo. The two files will appear in a single batched file, as shown in Figure 5-30.

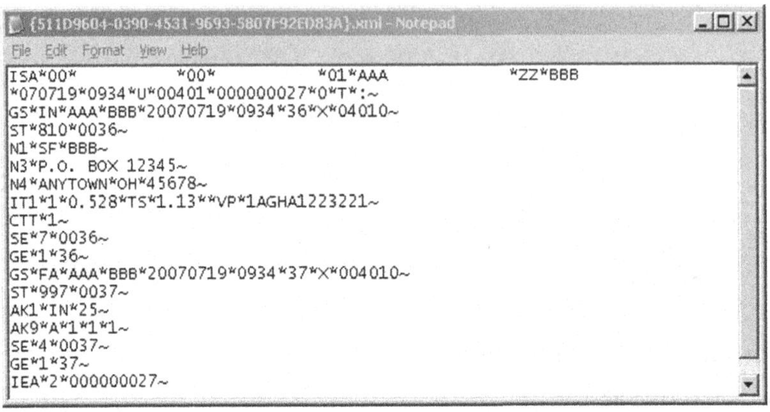

{511D9604-0390-4531-9693-5807F92ED83A}.xml - Notepad

File Edit Format View Help

```
ISA*00*          *00*          *01*AAA            *ZZ*BBB
*070719*0934*U*00401*000000027*0*T*:~
GS*IN*AAA*BBB*20070719*0934*36*X*04010~
ST*810*0036~
N1*SF*BBB~
N3*P.O. BOX 12345~
N4*ANYTOWN*OH*45678~
IT1*1*0.528*TS*1.13**VP*1AGHA1223221~
CTT*1~
SE*7*0036~
GE*1*36~
GS*FA*AAA*BBB*20070719*0934*37*X*004010~
ST*997*0037~
AK1*IN*25~
AK9*A*1*1*1~
SE*4*0037~
GE*1*37~
IEA*2*000000027~
```

Figure 5-30. *Final batched file*

Final Discussion

This chapter outlined some of the more complex processes associated with EDI: delivering documents over secure FTP, working with AS2 transmissions, and implementing document batching. Used in conjunction with the exercises provided in the BizTalk Server Documentation that ships with the product, there should be ample material to fully understand and implement these concepts.

CHAPTER 6

Trading Partner Testing

There are two basic phases to trading partner testing. The first is validating that the content of the EDI documents is correct; the second is ensuring that the processes that create and deliver or receive those documents function as expected. This chapter works through a number of exercises that introduce the core tracking tools and basic approaches that are necessary for successful trading partner testing. The following topics are discussed:

- **Basic test plans**: The process of working with trading partners during the test phase can be greatly aided with the proper use of test documentation. This section illustrates some very basic approaches to minimal documenting of test cases and introduces how trading partners outline their testing requirements.
- **Validating document content**: EDI implementations generally require that interactions with the partner occur to ensure the accuracy of the document; in most cases, trading partners require that the documents are first validated by someone on their staff before any EDI documents can be delivered in a production setting. This section contains an exercise that outlines a detailed approach to EDI document content validation.
- **Tracking documents**: There are a number of options available for effective tracking of EDI transmissions in BizTalk Server. This section introduces the most appropriate tools and reports to use for EDI solutions: standard document tracking and EDI reporting.

Note The exercises in this chapter rely on solutions that have been developed in previous chapters. There are no code files specific for this chapter—only configurations of existing solutions as outlined in the exercises.

Basic Test Plans

Before moving into the specifics of how to validate content and track EDI documents, it is important to first look at a basic approach to writing documentation and working through the trading partner's testing requirements. Because the test process generally involves interacting with the trading partner (to validate that the received files fit their format), it is essential that the test cycle be approached in a systematic way and that the results of the tests are documented.

In many cases, the trading partner will have outlined a number of steps for testing; it is necessary to get approval from the partner that testing has been completed to their satisfaction. The following list outlines an example of trading partner test requirements. It shows the level of manual testing that must occur for acceptance in a typical implementation:

1. Begin by contacting the EDI coordinator to initiate the testing.
2. Send a test transaction of an 810 document with the STO2 segment equal to the testing value of 1.
3. If a negative 997 acknowledgment is received, contact the EDI coordinator.
4. Send a hard copy of the invoice. This invoice will be compared to the EDI transmission and the hard copy of the invoice to make sure that all of the data matches the expected format.
5. Repeat steps 2–4 until two invoices have completely passed all of the requirements.
6. With step 5 complete, parallel testing can begin. This is a combination of hard copy invoices and EDI transactions that are manually compared to each other to validate accuracy. Contact the EDI coordinator for more information.
7. Repeat step 6 until two 810 EDI documents have been approved.
8. Once step 7 is completed, approval for production EDI transmissions will be granted. Hard copies of the invoice will no longer be required.

■ **Note** Every trading partner has different testing requirements. It is absolutely necessary to know what these requirements are as early in the development phase as possible. Often there are numerous steps that can take a great deal of time to work through.

The trading partner may have outlined the requirements that must be met to get approval that the documents are accurate, but there also must be requirements on the side of the EDI BizTalk implementer to track what has been tested and what the result of the test is. With as much data as there is within any given EDI document and the number of BizTalk components and configurations used to generate and process those documents, it is necessary to put together some level of documentation. For developers who are creating EDI solutions without the involvement of a structured testing environment (such as a full test project team and enterprise-level test phases and documentation), it may be helpful to point out a very basic and simple approach to documenting test cases.

Table 6-1 shows an example of a test document that has two test cases in it. Each one describes the test case, the expected result, information about the outcome, and a status. By using even this simple form of documenting tests, trading partner testing will be greatly improved and simplified. Any time there are requirements set by multiple parties, it is good practice to keep a paper trail of what has occurred.

Table 6-1. *Sample Test Case Document*

Text Case	Expected Result	Verification Method	Status	Notes
Drop an XML instance on a file receive port and validate that the document is delivered to the expected FTP site.	A file will be delivered to the target FTP site.	Monitor the FTP site to ensure the document arrives. Check the event log for errors	Pass	This was validated on a standard FTP site only. It should be tested on a secure FTP site.
Validate that the document on the output site has been mapped correctly (i.e., transformed from XML to EDI format).	The document will be in EDI format.	Check the file on the FTP site.	Fail	The document arrived in XML. The EDI send pipeline was not configured on the send port.

As tests are performed, the results of the tests are added to the document. When questions are raised by trading partners as to why data is in a certain format, the test case document can be referred to. The complexity of business rules around mapping EDI content often results in some level of misunderstanding or difficulty in interpretation, and the notes and status to outcomes, when documented, can be easily referred to at a later date. Once a basic approach to documenting test cases has been put into place, the process of validating the content of the data being received and/or delivered can be started.

Validating EDI Content

EDI content validation refers to the process of ensuring that all of the maps, ports, orchestrations, and pipelines that have processed an EDI document result in the creation of a valid document. There are two types of EDI BizTalk solutions: those that are completely new solutions, built from the ground up; and those that are replacements (or upgrades) of existing systems. The approach to content validation is the same with either type of implementation, but the overhead of communicating with the trading partner may be substantially different, for the following reasons:

- **Replacing or upgrading an EDI implementation:** In an environment where there is an existing EDI implementation that is being replaced, existing documents that have been delivered to trading partners by the legacy system can be used for data content comparison. For example, if the legacy system delivers an 810 document to Company X, that document could be used as a known valid instance to be compared against. In the BizTalk solution that is developed as the replacement, the source data that is used to create a document could be set to the same source data that created the original known source instance, with the expectation that (unless mapping requirements have changed) the two instances should result in identical output.
- **Creating a new EDI implementation:** Conversely, in an environment where the BizTalk implementation is the first EDI solution, there will likely be no existing documents and no history of trading partner interactions. Because of this, there will be no way to test that content is truly valid without some amount of interaction with the partner. At a minimum, this means that EDI instances must be requested from the partner, and if possible, the source database. In reality, the process of validation usually means sending an instance to the partner via email, having them review it manually, and receiving their feedback so that any changes required can be implemented. Obviously, this can turn into a lengthy process with multiple interactions and revisions before the content can be fully validated.

The easiest approach to content validation is to get a copy of a known valid instance of a document and compare a newly generated instance against it. The steps in Exercise 6-1 outline an approach to EDI document validation with the assumption that a valid instance can be procured. If no documents can be obtained, it will be necessary to work closely with someone on the trading partner's staff who can manually validate the content of documents.

■ **Note** There are a number of free content validation applications available via the Internet. These applications allow the comparison of documents side-by-side, highlighting the differences between the documents. Several of these also allow for entire directories of documents to be compared against each other. Exercise 6-1 refers to using a content validation tool as a core need to validating EDI documents.

Exercise 6-1. EDI Content Validation

The steps in this exercise outline one approach to document validation. This exercise demonstrates how to compare a document generated by BizTalk with a known instance of a document from a trading partner and how to interpret the difference between expected and unexpected differences in the two documents. This exercise assumes that there is a valid instance of an 810 EDI document, and it also assumes that the source data that formed this document is also available. The valid instance from the trading partner is shown in Figure 6-1.

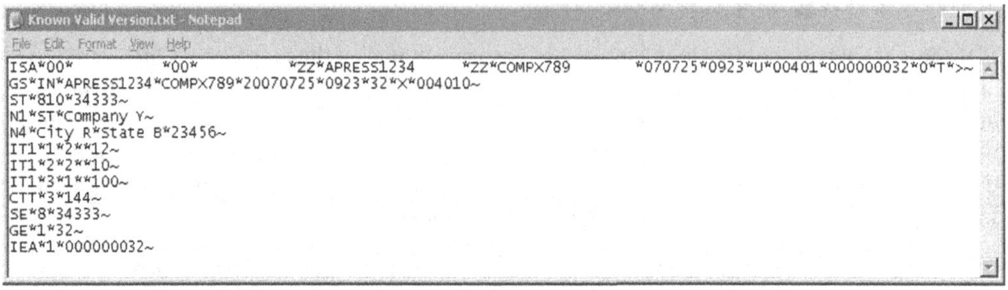

Known Valid Version.txt - Notepad

File Edit Format View Help

```
ISA*00*          *00*          *ZZ*APRESS1234     *ZZ*COMPX789       *070725*0923*U*00401*000000032*0*T*>~
GS*IN*APRESS1234*COMPX789*20070725*0923*32*X*004010~
ST*810*34333~
N1*ST*Company Y~
N4*City R*State B*23456~
IT1*1*2**12~
IT1*2*2**10~
IT1*3*1**100~
CTT*3*144~
SE*8*34333~
GE*1*32~
IEA*1*000000032~
```

Figure 6-1. *Known valid version of EDI document provided by trading partner*

1. The first step is to create an EDI document in BizTalk that is based on the same data as that which created the valid instance. For example, assume that the data shown in Listing 6-1 represents the data as it was originally retrieved from the database. This data is the same data that was used to create the valid instance at some point in a legacy environment and will be used to create the new instance in the BizTalk EDI solution.

Listing 6-1. *Input Instance*

```
<COMMON_810 xmlns="http://schemas.Apress.com/Common/810/v1">
<TRANSACTION>
  <HEADER>
    <GUID>8F97D20B-687F-4B82-A231-13BB30944E47</GUID>
    <DOCID>1000</DOCID>
    <DESC>Sample Invoice #1 for Company Y</DESC>
    <PARTNER>Company Y</PARTNER>
  </HEADER>
  <ADDRESSES>
    <ADDRESS>
      <TYPE>Billing</TYPE>
      <STREET>99 Highway R</STREET>
      <CITY>City R</CITY>
      <STATE>State B</STATE>
      <ZIP>23456</ZIP>
    </ADDRESS>
  </ADDRESSES>
  <ITEMS>
```

```
    <ITEM>
      <TYPE>Standard</TYPE>
      <PRICE>12.0000</PRICE>
      <DESC>Item K</DESC>
      <QTY>2</QTY>
    </ITEM>
    <ITEM>
      <TYPE>Standard</TYPE>
      <PRICE>10.0000</PRICE>
      <DESC>Item K</DESC>
      <QTY>2</QTY>
    </ITEM>
    <ITEM>
      <TYPE>Hidden</TYPE>
      <PRICE>100.0000</PRICE>
      <DESC>Item J</DESC>
      <QTY>1</QTY>
    </ITEM>
  </ITEMS>
</TRANSACTION>
</COMMON_810>
```

2. Now create an instance of the document in BizTalk Server. In this case, the document can be run through any port that contains a copy of the map created in Chapter 3. This exercise assumes that the output of the mapping of the source data is that which is shown in Figure 6-2. This will be referred to as the *BizTalk Instance* for the rest of this exercise.

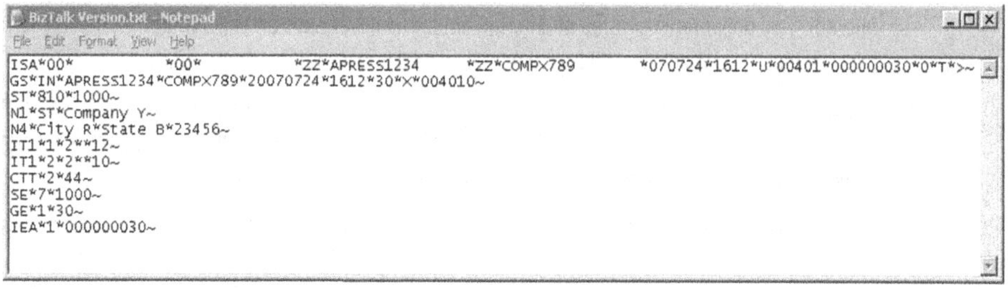

```
BizTalk Version.txt - Notepad
File Edit Format View Help
ISA*00*          *00*          *ZZ*APRESS1234     *ZZ*COMPX789       *070724*1612*U*00401*000000030*0*T*>~
GS*IN*APRESS1234*COMPX789*20070724*1612*30*X*004010~
ST*810*1000~
N1*ST*Company Y~
N4*City R*State B*23456~
IT1*1*2**12~
IT1*2*2**10~
CTT*2*44~
SE*7*1000~
GE*1*30~
IEA*1*000000030~
```

Figure 6-2. *Version of EDI document created in BizTalk solution (BizTalk instance)*

3. Using a document comparison tool, open both the known valid instance and the BizTalk instance and compare them side-by-side. Figure 6-3 illustrates how such a tool would look if it were comparing the known valid instance in Figure 6-1 with the BizTalk instance in Figure 6-2.

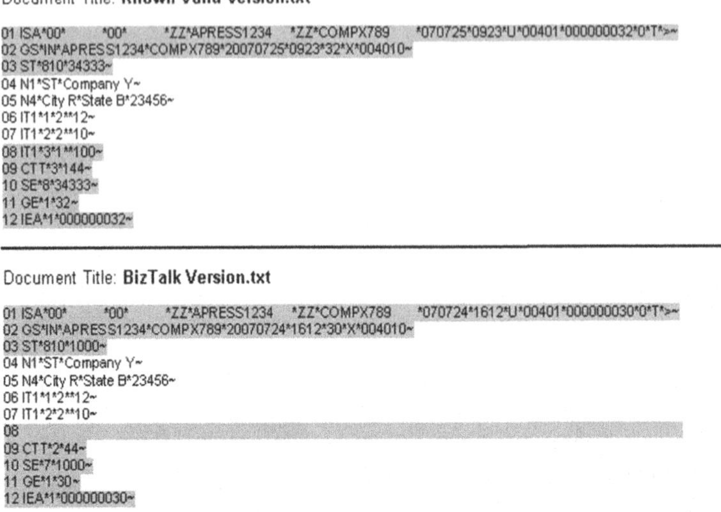

Document Title: **Known Valid Version.txt**

```
01 ISA*00*          *00*          *ZZ*APRESS1234     *ZZ*COMPX789       *070725*0923*U*00401*000000032*0*T*>~
02 GS*IN*APRESS1234*COMPX789*20070725*0923*32*X*004010~
03 ST*810*34333~
04 N1*ST*Company Y~
05 N4*City R*State B*23456~
06 IT1*1*2**12~
07 IT1*2*2**10~
08 IT1*3*1**100~
09 CTT*3*144~
10 SE*8*34333~
11 GE*1*32~
12 IEA*1*000000032~
```

Document Title: **BizTalk Version.txt**

```
01 ISA*00*          *00*          *ZZ*APRESS1234     *ZZ*COMPX789       *070724*1612*U*00401*000000030*0*T*>~
02 GS*IN*APRESS1234*COMPX789*20070724*1612*30*X*004010~
03 ST*810*1000~
04 N1*ST*Company Y~
05 N4*City R*State B*23456~
06 IT1*1*2**12~
07 IT1*2*2**10~
08
09 CTT*2*44~
10 SE*7*1000~
11 GE*1*30~
12 IEA*1*000000030~
```

Figure 6-3. *Comparing the documents side-by-side*

4. This step looks at the results in Figure 6-3 and describes what is shown and how to interpret the differences. A highlighted line indicates that there is a difference between the two documents. The lines can be interpreted as follows:

   a. Start with Line 01. The difference in this line is with the variable header/context fields, such as the date (ISA09) and the time (ISA10). By looking at the other fields, such as the company identifiers in ISA05–ISA08, it is possible to validate that this line is in the correct format, since it is understood that these values will be different. Two documents created at different times will never have an exact match on the ISA segment; this does not mean, however, that the document is invalid because it does not match.

   b. On Line 02, the only differences are in date and time (GS04 and GS05) and ID (GS06). Again, looking at these differences, and understanding they are due to expected time changes, indicates that the document is being created correctly and that the differences are expected and do not invalidate the content.

   c. Line 03 has one difference, which is ST02, the transaction set control number. This should be a unique number for every document, or at least very rarely duplicated. In this case, it is different in both documents, yet the content is completely valid.

   d. Lines 04–07 show that the two documents are identical. This means that all of the mapping for the N1 loop is correct, and that the IT1 segment mappings are occurring correctly, at least as far as this instance shows.

   e. On Line 08, there is a difference. In the BizTalk instance, the IT1 node that is showing on the known valid version is missing. To understand what is causing the difference, follow these steps:

      i. To begin with, look at the map that is creating the document to find out what the logic is for mapping the IT1 segment. The map used to create the current document is shown in Figure 6-4.

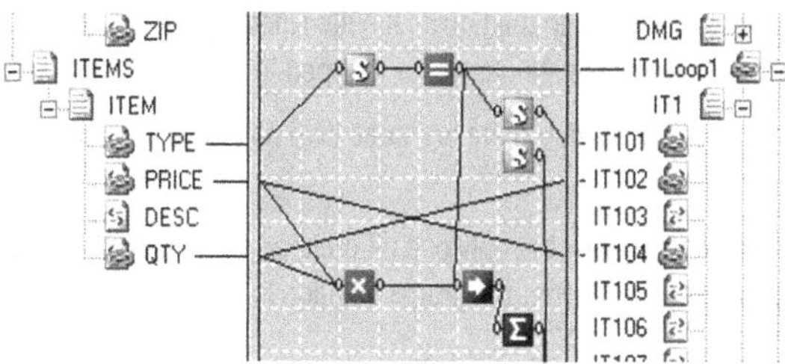

Figure 6-4. *Mapping the IT1 loop*

ii. Within the map, the IT1 loop is made up of logic that uses a combination of a Scripting functoid and an Equals functoid. Opening the Scripting functoid shows the code in Listing 6-2, while the Equals functoid is shown in Figure 6-5.

Listing 6-2. *Contents of Script Shape*

```
// if ITEM is hidden, it will not be mapped or counted in the
// iteration total.
public string strItemType (string strTYPE) {
 string strRetVal = string.Empty;
 switch (strTYPE) {
  case "Hidden": strRetVal = string.Empty; break;
  default: strRetVal = "Map"; break;
 }
 return strRetVal;
}
```

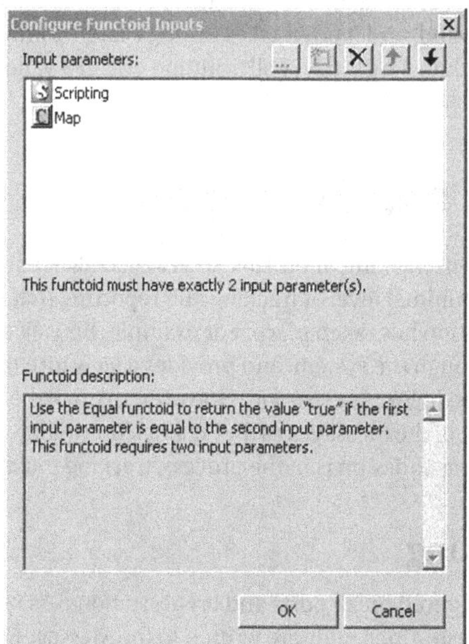

Figure 6-5. *Configuring the Equals functoid*

iii. The logic of the Scripting functoid combined with the Equals functoid indicates that if the incoming value in the TYPE field is equal to HIDDEN, the value should not be mapped.

iv. The original document, in Listing 6-1, shows that there are three item nodes. One of the item nodes has a TYPE that is equal to HIDDEN.

5. The documents are different on a number of segments, but only one difference causes the content to be invalid, that is the IT1 loop. It is now necessary to determine what the proper solution to this discrepancy is.

Exercise 6-1 ends with the result that the two EDI instances are different in several ways, and that the content is invalid. To understand how to solve this problem, the following questions must be asked:

- **Is the mapping valid?** Where did the mapping requirement come from? Is this something that the trading partner requested, or was it accidentally copied from another trading partner map?
- **Are there new requirements?** Is this new business logic, something that has been added since the known valid instance was created? It is common that business logic is added, especially during a new implementation. Occasionally, the EDI implementation guide used to create the map is outdated, and the known valid instance is a more accurate representation of how data is to be displayed.
- **Is there bad data in the source data?** Where did the source document come from, and can its data be trusted?

The solution to this problem lies in what the answer is to each of these questions. If the mapping is wrong, the map must be updated. If the known valid instance is found to be invalid, the trading partner must be contacted and the rules of the mapping must be verified (there will likely be additional business rules that have changed). It often takes several rounds of testing and updates to ensure that the content of a document is valid, and it often takes testing a large number of instances to ensure that all documents that are produced by the BizTalk solution end in a valid document in every case.

Tracking Documents and EDI Reporting

BizTalk provides for two levels of document tracking in BizTalk Server 2006 R2: standard tracking and EDI reporting. By default, there is a minimal level of tracking and reporting that is always available, regardless of whether any configuration has taken place. For example, BizTalk always allows a user to see what messages have flown through the system, and provides a view into the information about these messages and whether processing was successful. However, to track the full flow of the document, to get access to the full content of the messages as they change throughout the processes, and to get a full picture of where an EDI transmission is in the process, tracking must be configured.

Standard Document Tracking

Standard document tracking can be configured on all ports and orchestrations. As messages pass through ports, maps, pipelines, and orchestrations, they are written to the MessageBox. Depending on how tracking has been configured, the changing state of these messages will be saved and can be queried for retrieval, even after the successful processing of the messages. Figure 6-6 shows a high-level view of when a message is stored to the MessageBox, and what standard reporting tools are available to view these documents.

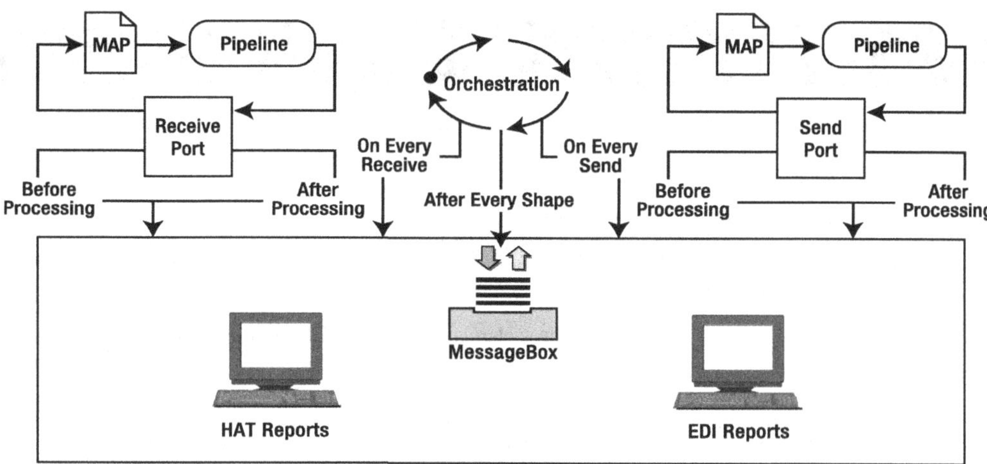

Figure 6-6. *How messages are saved to the MessageBox when tracking is configured*

Standard tracking increases the overall load on the BizTalk Server tracking database. Performance will not necessarily be affected, but database growth will be. As a message flows through ports and orchestrations and is tracked at different stages, the data is saved to the MessageBox. The following formula gives an estimate as to what can be expected for growth:

```
[#Messages * #MessagesTracked * (MessageSize)] / 1024 = Size in MB.
```

The parameters for this formula can be described as follows:

- **#Messages**: Total number of messages coming into the system.
- **#MessagesTracked**: Total number of times that the message is stored based on how tracking has been configured. For example, if a receive port is set to track the message before and after port processing, the #MessagesTracked parameter would be equal to 2.
- **MessageSize**: This is the size of the message (in KB) at the time it is saved to the MessageBox. A message can change size during processing. For example, if the incoming message is in XML and is mapped to a second XML format and is output in EDI format, there are three different message sizes; each XML format has a different number of elements, and the EDI document is a flat file.

Configuring Tracking on Send and Receive Ports

Tracking can be set on receive and send ports to track the message before and after processing. If any pipeline other than a pass-through is used, the document will be different before processing than after. Similarly, if a map is used on the port, the document will be different after port processing. Tracking is very easy to configure on ports, as shown in Exercise 6-2.

Exercise 6-2. Configuring Tracking on Ports

This exercise demonstrates how to enable tracking on a send or receive port, using the BizTalk Administration Console:

1. Right-click the port and select Tracking.
2. Set the tracking as needed (as shown in Figure 6-7):
   a. Track Message Bodies stores the actual content of the messages, either before port processing or after port processing.
   v. Track Message Properties makes the context information about the message available.

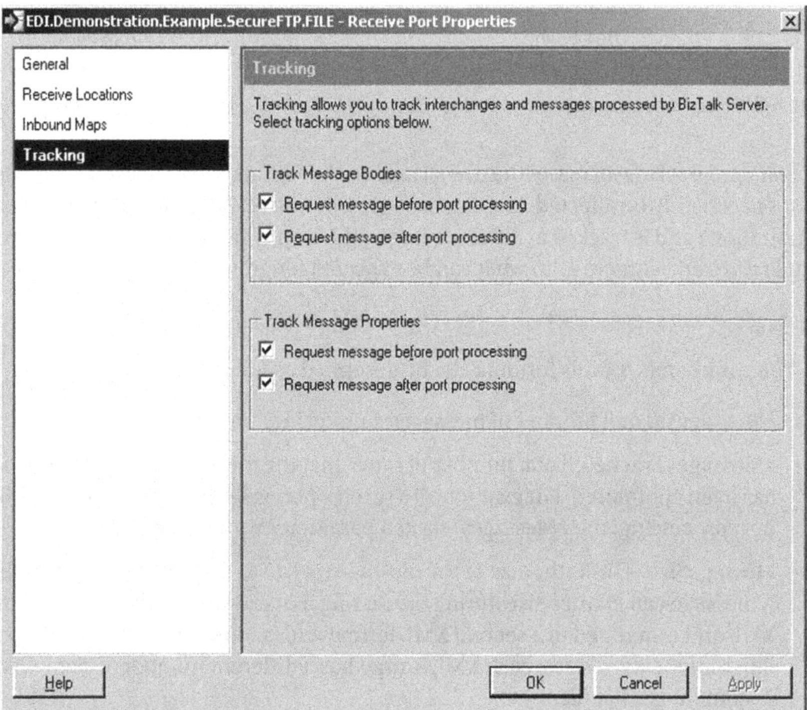

Figure 6-7. *Port tracking settings*

3. Click OK to save the settings and restart the BizTalk host application to ensure that the settings take effect.

Configuring Tracking on Orchestrations

Like ports, tracking can be set on orchestrations to track the message before and after orchestration processing. This provides for a view into the data of all messages as they are received and as they are sent, even when there are multiple ports associated with the orchestration flow. Unlike ports, the events within the orchestration that modify the content of a message can be tracked (there are usually multiple steps within an orchestration, and the document can be tracked before and after each step). This level of tracking allows for easier debugging of orchestrations and a better view into how a document changes over the course of the orchestration (there will be more context to where a message is in the process). To set up tracking on orchestrations, follow the steps outlined in Exercise 6-3.

Exercise 6-3. Configuring Tracking on an Orchestration

This exercise demonstrates how to enable tracking on an orchestration:

1. In BizTalk Administration Console, expand a BizTalk application that contains an orchestration.
2. Right-click the orchestration and select Tracking. Set the appropriate tracking options as shown in Figure 6-8.

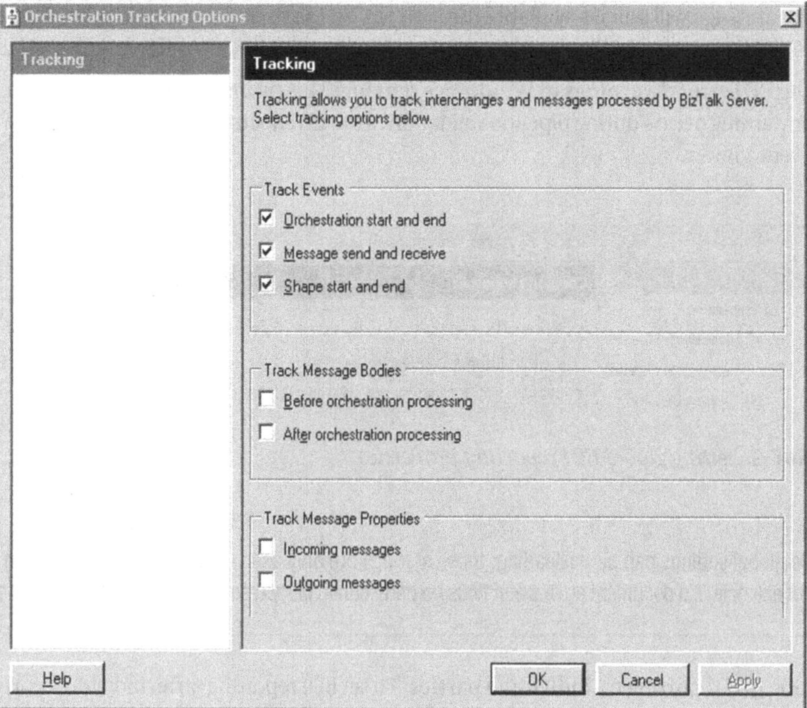

Figure 6-8. *Orchestration tracking settings*

3. Click OK to save the settings and restart the BizTalk host application to ensure the settings take effect.

EDI Reporting and the Group Hub Page

EDI reporting is set on the properties of a BizTalk party and is made available through a number of EDI reports available in the Group Hub page of the BizTalk Administration Console. EDI reporting and AS2 reporting are both configured on the individual parties. Remember that an AS2 document is a wrapper around an EDI document, and both are tracked separately from one another. An acknowledgment for an AS2 transmission may be required as well as a functional acknowledgment for the EDI document contained within the AS2 envelope. Several items to note when configuring reporting are outlined in the list that follows:

- **Setting global EDI reporting**: In BizTalk Administration Console, right-click Parties and select EDI Global Properties. There are three properties that can be set (shown in Figure 6-9), as outlined here:
  - **Activate EDI reporting**: This allows the EDI documents to be tracked in the EDI reports, available in the BizTalk Group Hub page.
  - **Store transaction set/payload for reporting**: This ensures that the content of the EDI document is available within the reports. The payload is the data between the ST and SE segments (or the UNH and UNT with EDIFACT) for individual transactions. The content of the message will still be available through HAT (Health and Activity Tracking), even if this setting is not enabled (as long as standard tracking has been configured properly).
  - **Log EDI errors/warnings to Windows event log**: This property ensures that when an error or warning occurs during pipeline validation of the EDI document, it is logged to the Windows Event Viewer.

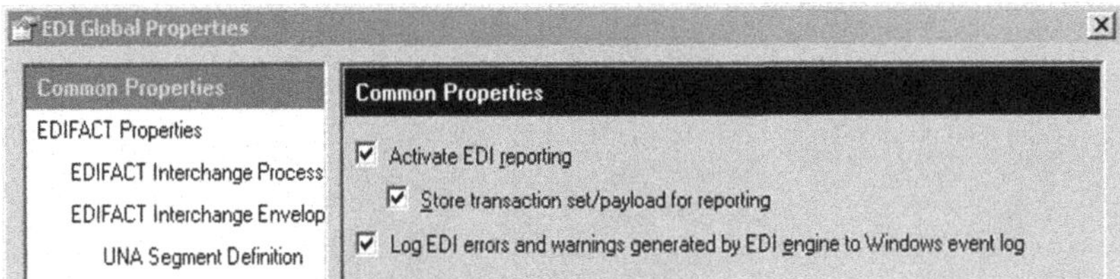

Figure 6-9. *Setting global EDI reporting properties*

■ **Note** The global settings can be misleading; these settings are only used when no party is found during party resolution. For example, if a document arrives and finds no party during party resolution, it will use the global settings.

- **Setting EDI reporting on individual parties**: To set EDI reporting on an individual party, simply right-click the party and select EDI Properties. The EDI reporting properties can be set on the General tab, as shown in Figure 6-10.

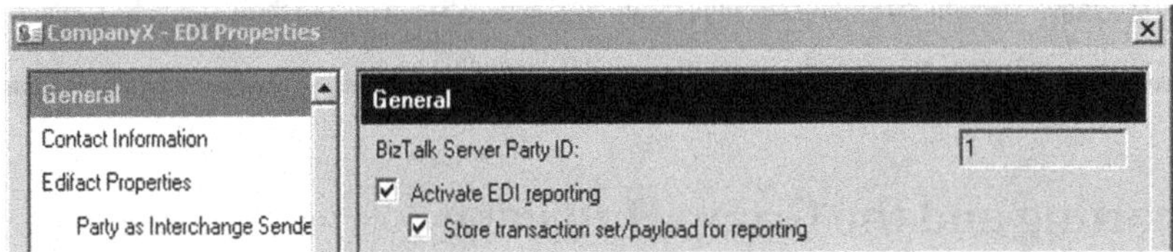

Figure 6-10. *Setting EDI reporting on an individual party*

- **Setting AS2 reporting**: AS2 reporting can be set in addition to standard EDI reporting and is configured by right-clicking the party and selecting AS2 Properties. Enable the Activate AS2 Reporting property shown on the General tab (see Figure 6-11).

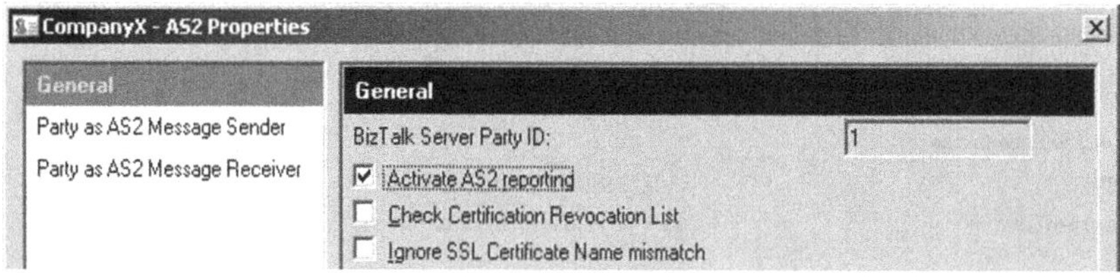

Figure 6-11. *Enabling AS2 reporting*

Note The AS2 reports may only work when using the standard AS2 functionality that ships with BizTalk Server R2. Third-party AS2 adapters do not necessarily interact with the EDI engine in the same way and therefore are not tracked in the same way.

The EDI and AS2 reports are available via the BizTalk Group Hub, and are accessible only through the BizTalk Administration Console, as described in the next section.

Tracking Tools

There are two basic tools used for document tracking and EDI reporting in BizTalk. The first is the BizTalk Administration Console (which provides access to the EDI reports through the Group Hub page), and the second is the HAT application. The majority of information about EDI documents needed on a day-to-day basis is available through the Group Hub page, and this is generally the place to start tracking documents. HAT provides for a more granular approach to querying data and is especially useful when troubleshooting documents that have terminated unexpectedly. This section gives an overview of how to use both of these tools.

Using BizTalk Administration Console for EDI Reporting and Tracking

All of the EDI reports and tracking capabilities are accessed through the BizTalk Group Hub, which can be opened by right-clicking the main BizTalk Group (or any BizTalk application) and selecting View ➤ Group Hub Page. This will bring up the screen shown in Figure 6-12.

Work in Progress

Running service instances --

- Dehydrated orchestrations --
- Retrying and idle ports --
- Ready service instances --
- Scheduled service instances --

Suspended Items

Suspended service instances

- Resumable
- Non-resumable

Suspended MSMQT messages

Grouped Suspended Service Instances

Grouped by Application

No information has been collected.

Grouped by Service Name

No information has been collected.

Grouped by Error Code

No information has been collected.

Grouped by URI

No information has been collected.

EDI Status Reports

EDI Interchange and Correlated ACK Status

Batch Status

Interchange Aggregation Report

Transaction Set Aggregation Report

EDIINT Status Reports

AS2 Message and Correlated MDN Status

Figure 6-12. *The BizTalk Group Hub page*

The reports that are available fall into three main categories: Work in Progress, Suspended Items, and EDI Status Reports. Each of these reports is comprised of queries that search the various BizTalk databases for data. To understand how the reports function, Exercise 6-4 gives a brief overview of creating a custom query. Following this, Exercise 6-5 outlines the use of the EDI reports and how to track the status of documents using them.

Exercise 6-4. Creating a Custom Query in the Group Hub

This exercise outlines how to create a custom query in the BizTalk Group Hub:

1. Click the New Query tab in the BizTalk Group Hub window.
2. Set the value for the Search For row. Depending on what value is selected, different subquery values will be made available. In this exercise, the Batch Status is being searched on. There are five subquery options available for Batch Status, one of which is the Activation Date Time. For illustration, the values are set as shown in Figure 6-13.

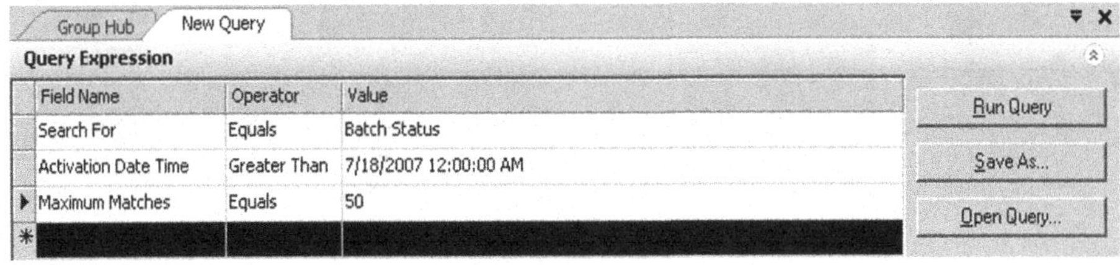

Figure 6-13. *Setting values in the Query Expression*

3. Click the Run Query button to return the result set shown in Figure 6-14.

Query results (11 items were found):

Batch Status	Destination party	Activation Time	Batch Occurren...	EDI encoding t...	Batch Type	Batch Target
Active	BatchingDemo	7/19/2007 8:40 ...	1	X12	Messages count...	2
Completed	BatchingDemo	7/19/2007 9:20 ...	1	X12	Messages count...	2
Completed	BatchingDemo	7/19/2007 9:20 ...	2	X12	Messages count...	2

Figure 6-14. *Subset of query results*

4. Click the Save As button to save the query; click the Open Query button to open and run previously saved queries.

Using Health and Activity Tracking (HAT)

HAT is generally not used in EDI solutions except when messages are suspended unexpectedly or data needs to be queried in a more complex manner than what is available through the Administration Console. Exercise 6-5 demonstrates how to use HAT specifically to track an EDI document and save out the messages. Before beginning the exercise, this section attempts to give a brief sketch of the more generic uses of HAT and how to configure components to ensure that document data can be accessed.

There is a lot of overlap between what is available in HAT and what is available in the BizTalk Group Hub. HAT has existed since the original version of BizTalk Server and has always allowed for the core querying functionality that exists today. With the release of BizTalk Server 2006, much of the functionality of HAT was moved to the Administration Console, using the improved user interface to allow for more rapid document tracking. This being said, there are still reasons to use HAT, including the following:

- **Access to message content**: The content of messages (the actual message body in XML or EDI format), as it is received and sent, can be accessed and saved to files. While this is available on some result sets in the Group Hub page, HAT makes this available on all results.
- **Ability to search on additional criteria**: The ability to track messages based on values of promoted properties and matches on schema definitions is available in HAT.
- **Additional reports**: There are a number of reports that are only available in HAT and are invaluable when troubleshooting, especially when multiple documents across different solutions may have failed. The unique HAT reports are available via both the Reporting and Queries menu options. Running the reports creates a result set that allows access to the message details and content.

Note On the toolbar of HAT, one of the report options refers to *EDI Reports*. These reports shipped with the original base EDI adapter, released prior to BizTalk Server 2006 R2, and remain on the menu to allow continued support of solutions built around this adapter. These reports do not provide any reporting for the R2 EDI edition.

- **Orchestration debugging**: Orchestrations can be debugged through HAT. For example, if a service instance result is available in HAT, it can be right-clicked and the option for Orchestration Debugger can be selected. The orchestration can then be walked through, breakpoints can be set, and data values can be viewed (see Figure 6-15).

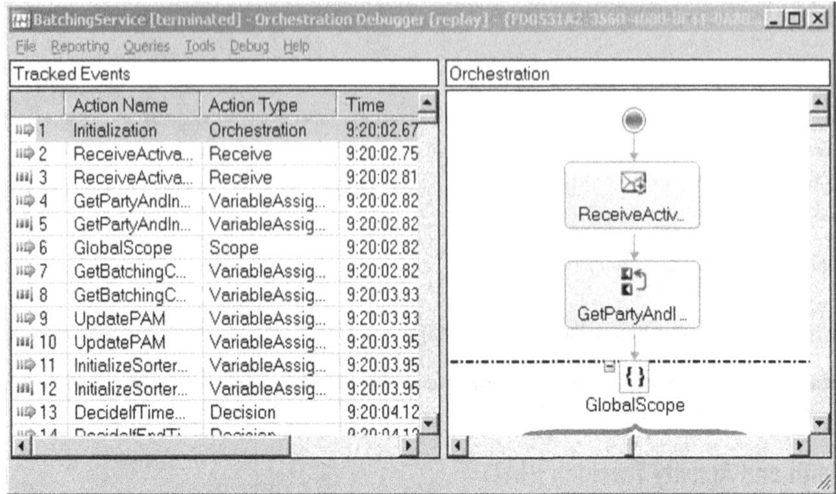

Figure 6-15. *Orchestration Debugger*

Message contents can be saved out of HAT by right-clicking any result in the result set and selecting Save All Tracked Messages. This saves the context and message body information to a file. When saving message contents in HAT, the message shown in Figure 6-16 may be displayed, indicating that tracking may not be configured correctly, or that the SQL Server Agent is not running.

Health and Activity Tracking -- Webpage Dialog

Service Instance ID	Message ID	Save messages status
{B72C13F7-593E-43F2-A44E-A9C65976EF8E}	{cc396ca1-01c9-4253-b4fb-47a860adea74}	The message was not found in the Message Box or the Tracking databases. This may be caused by one of the following conditions: (1) message tracking is not enabled; (2) the message(s) is no longer referenced by a running or suspended service instance; (3) the Message Box tracking tables have been automatically purged; or (4) the SQL Server agent is not running on the Message Box servers.
{B72C13F7-593E-43F2-A44E-A9C65976EF8E}	{25a8f35c-266a-400b-b487-5d0329a78a13}	The message was not found in the Message Box or the Tracking databases. This may be caused by one of the following conditions: (1) message tracking is not enabled; (2) the message(s) is no longer referenced by a running or suspended service instance; (3) the Message Box tracking tables have been automatically purged; or (4) the SQL Server agent is not running on the Message Box servers.

OK

Figure 6-16. *Tracking not configured correctly*

If the document cannot be saved, validate first that tracking has been configured on the ports or orchestrations where the data is passing through. If tracking has been configured as expected, the most likely reason that the error is being thrown is that the SQL Server Agent is not running. As shown in Figure 6-17, this service can be started in the services on the local machine. Open Administrative Tools, select Services, and start the SQL Server Agent. Run another message through the system and validate that the document contents can now be saved out to a folder.

Services (Local)

SQL Server Agent (MSSQLSERVER)	Name	Description	Status	Startup Type	Log On As
Stop the service	SQL Server (SQLEXPRESS)	Provides storage, process...	Started	Automatic	Network S...
Restart the service	SQL Server Active Directory Helper	Enables integration with A...		Disabled	Network S...
	SQL Server Agent (MSSQLSERVER)	Executes jobs, monitors S...	Started	Manual	Local System
	SQL Server Browser	Provides SQL Server conn...	Started	Automatic	Network S...

Figure 6-17. *Starting the SQL Server Agent*

Working with Document Tracking

To fully understand HAT, the BizTalk Group Hub tracking capabilities, and how to configure tracking, it will be helpful to work through the following set of exercises. Exercise 6-5 demonstrates how to work with document tracking as a whole, introducing the use of HAT and the Administration Console for tracking documents. Exercise 6-6 builds on this knowledge and shows how to track a specific document when the transaction set ID is used as the key unique identifier. In Exercise 6-7, accessing information about the status of the functional acknowledgment is illustrated.

Exercise 6-5. Introduction to Document Tracking

This exercise works with components created in Chapter 5—specifically the file receive port and FTP send port. This simple solution demonstrates how to turn on tracking and how to use the various BizTalk tools to view the message as it moves through the system:

1. Begin by setting up the components configured in Exercise 5-2 and Exercise 5-3, which consist of a file receive port and an FTP send port with a map. Check that these are installed and working properly before working through the rest of the steps in this exercise.
2. Set the tracking properties on the receive and send ports:
   a. In BizTalk Administration Console, double-click the receive port, named EDI.Demonstration.Example.SecureFTP.FILE.
      i. Click the Tracking tab. Turn on all of the tracking.
      ii. Click OK to save the settings.
   b. Right-click the send port called EDI.Demonstration.Example.SecureFTP.FTP and select Tracking. Set all of the tracking properties as shown in Figure 6-18. Click OK when this is complete.

Tracking

Tracking allows you to track interchanges and messages processed by BizTalk Server. Select tracking options below.

Track Message Bodies
- [x] Request message before port processing
- [x] Request message after port processing

Track Message Properties
- [x] Request message before port processing
- [x] Request message after port processing

Figure 6-18. *Send port tracking settings*

3. Run a message through the process:

   a. Copy the file Source 810 XML.xml from C:\Apress.Integration\Chapter 3\Test Documents.

   b. Paste it in the folder listened to by the receive location, which is C:\Apress.Integration\Chapter 5\Drops\Incoming - Secure FTP Demo.

   c. Validate that the message was delivered successfully by checking the FTP site at ftp://localhost/EDI.Demonstration/VAN - Outbox/.

4. Begin by using HAT to track the messages:

   a. Open HAT by clicking Start ➤ All Programs ➤ Microsoft BizTalk Server 2006 ➤ Health and Activity Tracking.

   b. Click Reporting ➤ Find Message.

   c. Click the Schema button and select `http://schemas.Apress.com/Common/810/v1#COMMON_810 schema`. This matches the Source 810 XML.xml document dropped on the receive location.

   d. Make sure that the From and Until dates cover a period of time that includes the current time.

   e. Click Run Query. This will return all of the documents that have arrived on the MessageBox that match the schema, as shown in Figure 6-19.

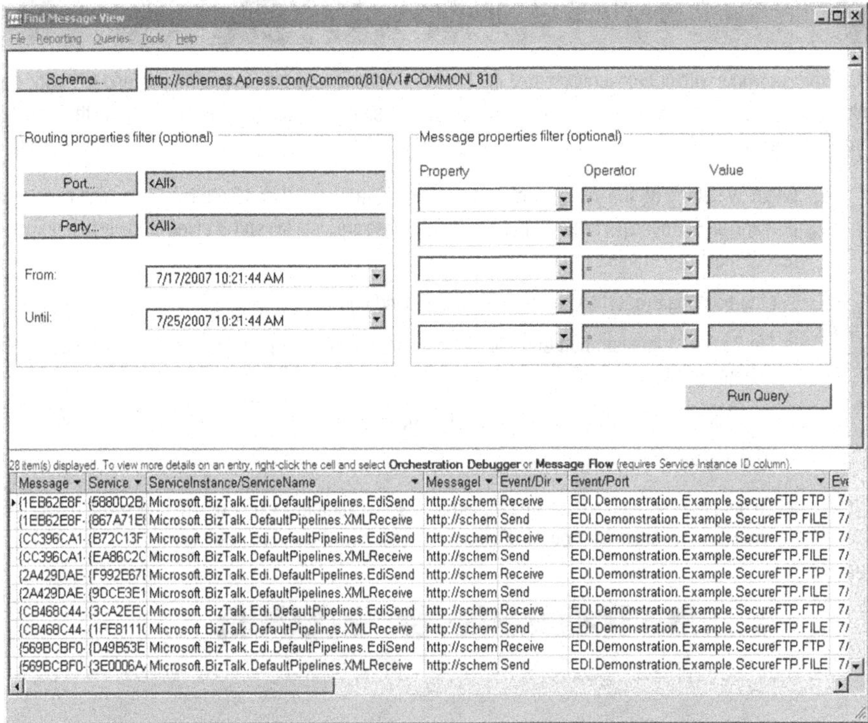

Figure 6-19. *Message results in HAT*

   f. Right-click the message that is on the Receive side of the EDI.Demonstration.Example.SecureFTP.FTP port and select Save All Tracked Messages.

      i. Create a folder to save the files to and click OK. If the messages are successfully saved, the dialog box in Figure 6-20 will be displayed.

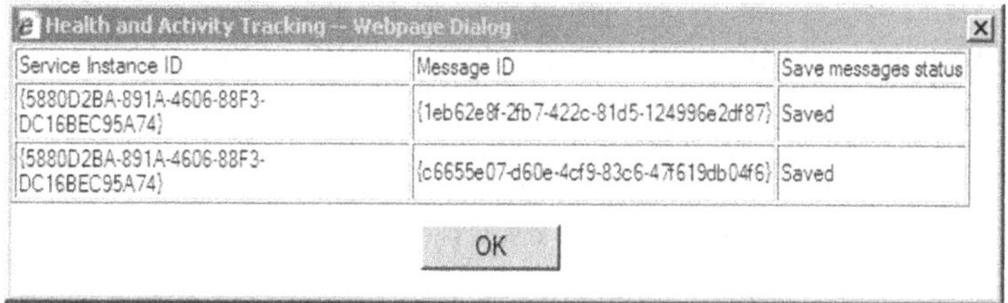

Health and Activity Tracking -- Webpage Dialog

Service Instance ID	Message ID	Save messages status
{5880D2BA-891A-4606-88F3-DC16BEC95A74}	{1eb62e8f-2fb7-422c-81d5-124996e2df87}	Saved
{5880D2BA-891A-4606-88F3-DC16BEC95A74}	{c6655e07-d60e-4cf9-83c6-47f619db04f6}	Saved

OK

Figure 6-20. *Successfully tracking messages in HAT*

ii. Open the folder where the files are saved. There should be four documents, one document representing the XML as it came in to the port, one representing the EDI document that came out of the port (after the map and the pipeline were applied), and two context documents. The files are shown in Figure 6-21.

Name	Size	Type
{1eb62e8f-2fb7-422c-81d5-124996e2df87}_{109A0643-CD42-4A61-B170-1498BDFBFBA8}_body.out	1 KB	OUT File
{1eb62e8f-2fb7-422c-81d5-124996e2df87}_context.xml	8 KB	XML Document
{c6655e07-d60e-4cf9-83c6-47f619db04f6}_{FB3A4EB3-A74F-4AA6-804D-D3A993F7F057}_Body.out	1 KB	OUT File
{c6655e07-d60e-4cf9-83c6-47f619db04f6}_context.xml	20 KB	XML Document

Figure 6-21. *Saved document list*

iii. Open each of the four documents in Notepad and look at the contents (as shown in Figure 6-22). One of the _body.out files will be identical to the XML dropped on the receive location; no pipelines or maps made any changes to it prior to the send port picking it up. The second of the _body.out files will match the EDI document and appear exactly as it was delivered to the FTP site, after the pipeline and map were applied in the send port. The two _context.xml documents contain information about all context properties used while processing the document they are directly related to. These can be helpful when trouble-shooting issues.

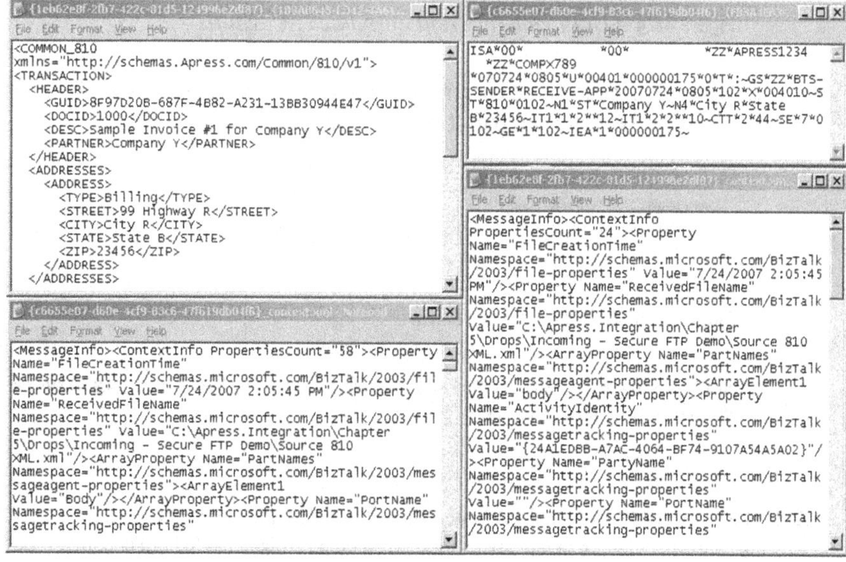

Figure 6-22. *Output messages from HAT (four documents)*

■ **Note** For full EDI reporting, ensure that the Activate EDI Reporting flag has been enabled for the party associated with the EDI documents being tracked.

5. Next, use the BizTalk Administration Console to view information about the message:

   a. Right-click the BizTalk Group and select View ➤ Group Hub Page. This is where all of the EDI reports are located, as shown in Figure 6-23.

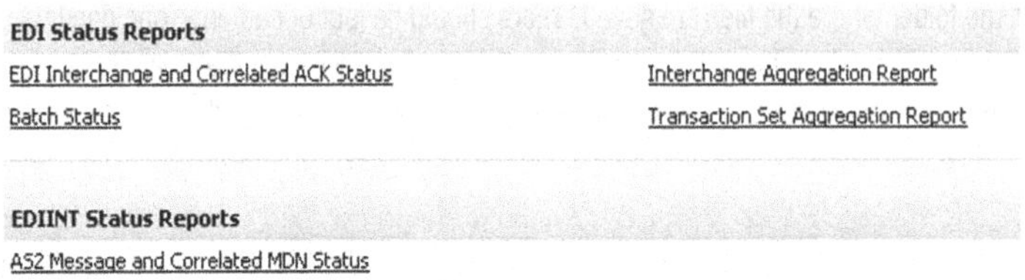

EDI Status Reports

EDI Interchange and Correlated ACK Status | Interchange Aggregation Report
Batch Status | Transaction Set Aggregation Report

EDIINT Status Reports

AS2 Message and Correlated MDN Status

Figure 6-23. *EDI reports in BizTalk Group Hub page*

   b. Click the EDI Interchange and Correlated ACK Status report. This will return a list of documents containing the document dropped earlier in this exercise, as shown in Figure 6-24.

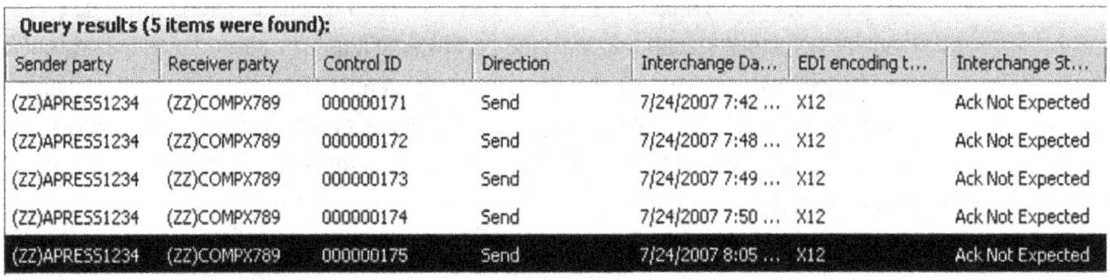

Query results (5 items were found):

Sender party	Receiver party	Control ID	Direction	Interchange Da...	EDI encoding t...	Interchange St...
(ZZ)APRESS1234	(ZZ)COMPX789	000000171	Send	7/24/2007 7:42 ...	X12	Ack Not Expected
(ZZ)APRESS1234	(ZZ)COMPX789	000000172	Send	7/24/2007 7:48 ...	X12	Ack Not Expected
(ZZ)APRESS1234	(ZZ)COMPX789	000000173	Send	7/24/2007 7:49 ...	X12	Ack Not Expected
(ZZ)APRESS1234	(ZZ)COMPX789	000000174	Send	7/24/2007 7:50 ...	X12	Ack Not Expected
(ZZ)APRESS1234	(ZZ)COMPX789	000000175	Send	7/24/2007 8:05 ...	X12	Ack Not Expected

Figure 6-24. *EDI Interchange and Correlated ACK Status*

   c. Right-click the most recent document in the list and select Transaction Set Details. A new report will appear with information about the transaction set itself (see Figure 6-25).

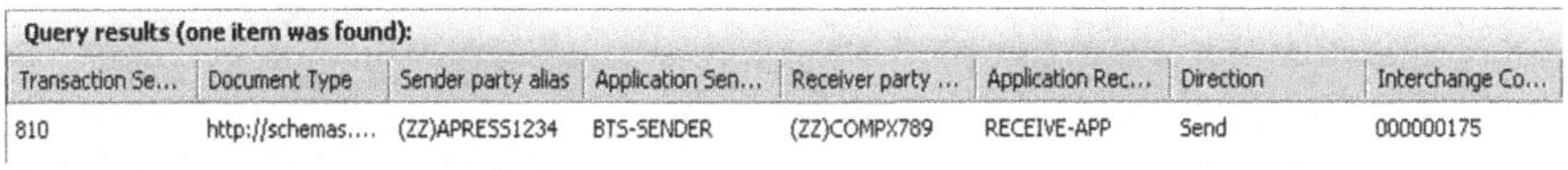

Query results (one item was found):

Transaction Se...	Document Type	Sender party alias	Application Sen...	Receiver party ...	Application Rec...	Direction	Interchange Co...
810	http://schemas....	(ZZ)APRESS1234	BTS-SENDER	(ZZ)COMPX789	RECEIVE-APP	Send	000000175

Figure 6-25. *Transaction Set Details*

   d. Right-click the single result returned and select View Transaction Set Content. This shows the content of the sent EDI message, as shown in Figure 6-26.

■ **Note** The transaction set content does not include the header and footer segments on the EDI document; it only contains the segments that are defined within the EDI schema. To see the full EDI document, HAT must be used.

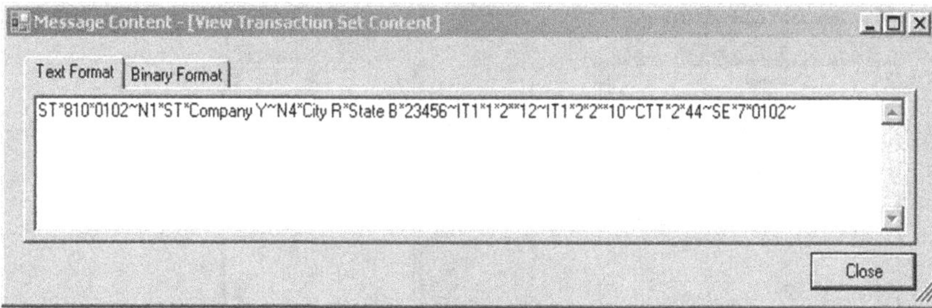

Figure 6-26. *Transaction set content*

The previous exercise shows how to use the BizTalk tools to track documents that have been processed by the system. Exercise 6-6 looks at how to track a specific document based on the transaction set ID. The transaction set ID is typically the only unique identifier that can be used to track a document from a source system, through BizTalk, to a trading partner. While this ID is not always used in this capacity, it is a useful technique to include when designing an EDI solution from the ground up, as this exercise demonstrates.

Exercise 6-6. Tracking Based on Transaction Set ID

Using the same project components as those outlined in Exercise 6-5, this exercise demonstrates how to track a message using a unique identifier from the source system, through BizTalk, to delivery to the trading partner. The ID that will be used is located on ST02.

1. Begin by looking at the input instance. This instance has been used in a number of exercises and represents the XML output of the call to the stored procedure and database outlined in Chapter 3. This XML document contains a node, <DOCID>, which stores the value that will be used to track this document through the system. Because this file is being manually dropped, it would be necessary to edit the value and change it to a unique ID each time that the document is dropped; this will simulate what would occur if it were extracting the data from a database where this ID is used as a unique identifier. Figure 6-27 shows this node on the document.

```
- <COMMON_810 xmlns="http://schemas.Apress.com/Common/810/v1">
  - <TRANSACTION>
    - <HEADER>
        <GUID>8F97D20B-687F-4B82-A231-13BB30944E47</GUID>
        <DOCID>1000</DOCID>
        <DESC>Sample Invoice #1 for Company Y</DESC>
        <PARTNER>Company Y</PARTNER>
      </HEADER>
    - <ADDRESSES>
```

Figure 6-27. *Showing the DOCID node*

2. The next step is to refer back to the map and see how the ST02 segment is mapped. The map (shown in Figure 6-28) sits on the FTP send port. Notice that the value in DOCID is mapped to the ST02 segment. ST02 is referred to as the *transaction set control number*.

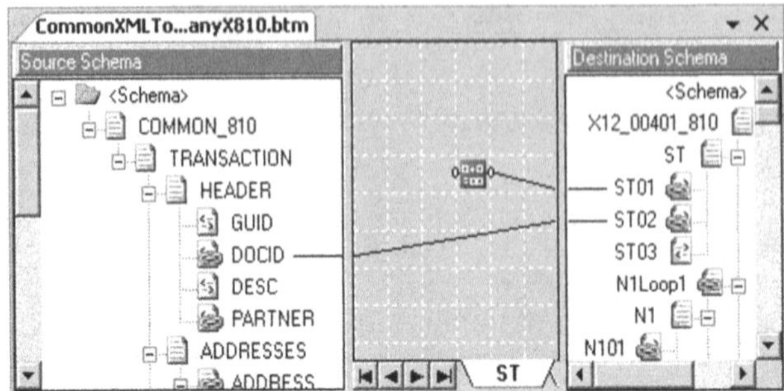

Figure 6-28. *Mapping the DOCID node to the ST02 segment*

3. Associate the FTP send port with a partner, such that the EDI properties are used on the delivered document by following these steps:

   a. Double-click the Company X party and click the Send Port tab.

   b. Add EDI.Demonstration.Example.SecureFTP.FTP to the list of ports. Since Company X has been used in a variety of examples, there will likely be at least one other port associated with this party. The final result of adding the send port is shown in Figure 6-29.

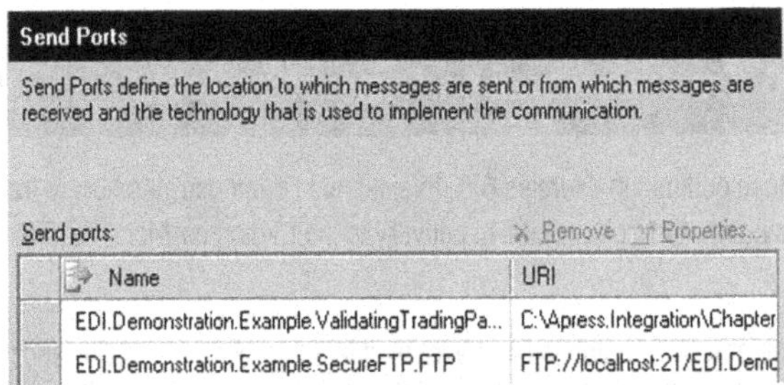

Figure 6-29. *Associating the FTP send port with a party for EDI formatting*

4. Unlike most fields, the ST02 can be set in a map or it can be configured in the EDI properties. In this case, ensure that the ST02 identifier is not overridden by taking these steps:

   a. Right-click the Company X party and select EDI Properties.

   b. Click the GS and ST Segment Definition tab.

   c. Under the Transaction Set Header section, uncheck the Apply New ID flag (as shown in Figure 6-30). This prevents BizTalk from overriding the value in ST02 with its own identifier. ST02 is one of the few EDI fields that can be set either in a map or automatically by BizTalk.

Figure 6-30. *Disabling the Apply New ID flag prevents BizTalk from overriding ST02.*

5. Restart the BizTalk host instance to ensure that all of the settings take effect.

6. Drop a copy of the test document to start the process:

a. Copy the file Source 810 XML.xml from C:\Apress.Integration\Chapter 3\Test Documents.

b. Paste it in the folder listened to by the receive location, which is C:\Apress.Integration\Chapter 5\Drops\Incoming - Secure FTP Demo.

7. Begin with validating that the EDI document was written to the FTP site with the correct value in ST02, as shown in Figure 6-31.

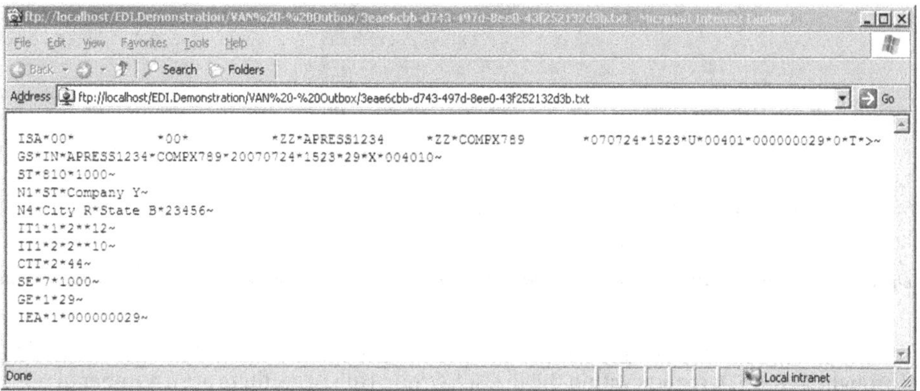

Figure 6-31. *EDI output with ST02*

8. Finally, trace the document using the BizTalk Administration Console and the EDI reports, using the value that is present both in the source document's DOCID node and in the target document's ST02 segment.

a. Right-click the BizTalk Group and select View ➤ Group Hub Page.

b. Click the New Query tab.

c. In the query window, enter the query shown in Figure 6-32 and click Run Query. Any number of additional parameters can be added to this, but for demonstration this will return all documents.

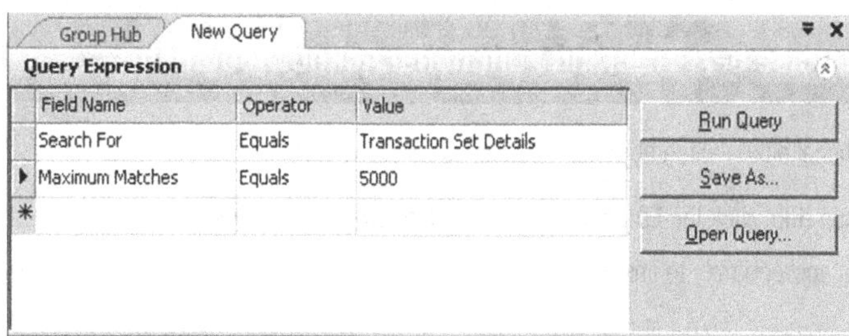

Figure 6-32. *Creating a new query*

d. Sort the results by clicking the Transaction Set Control Number column. This will order the results. Scroll down until the value of the DOCID is found (see Figure 6-33).

Query results (270 items were found):

Transaction Set ID	Sender party alias	Receiver party alias	Direction	Interchange Con...	Transaction Set Control Number
810	(ZZ)APRESS1234	(ZZ)COMPX789	Send	000000030	1000
810	(ZZ)APRESS1234	(ZZ)COMPX789	Send	000000031	8880
864	(01)2222222222I...	(01)3333333333I...	Receive	111111891	ST02

Figure 6-33. *Result set sorted by transaction set control number*

e. Right-click the record with the transaction set control number equal to 1000 and select View Transaction Set Content. This will open a window where the value of the ST02 segment is shown (see Figure 6-34).

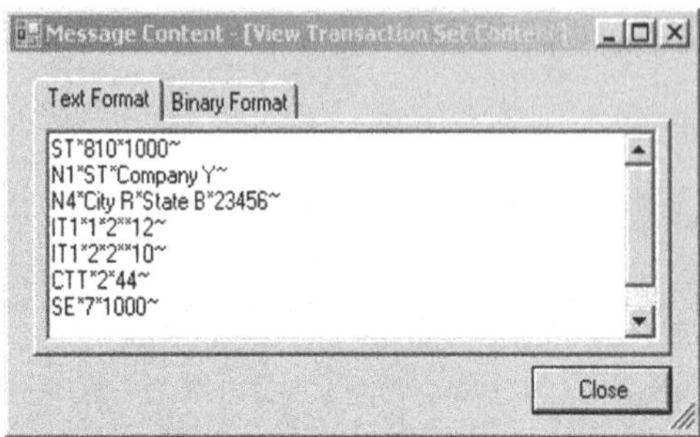

Figure 6-34. *Transaction set content*

The final type of tracking to look at is for viewing the status of functional acknowledgments. Throughout the EDI reports within the BizTalk Group Hub page, there are a number of references to the status of an acknowledgment. Many of these are misleading, as they do not refer specifically to the functional acknowledgment. There is only one report that gives valid information about the status of this acknowledgment (showing whether it has been received or not). Accessing this report is outlined in Exercise 6-7.

■ **Note** There are BAM activities that track functional acknowledgments, and these can be leveraged to create custom acknowledgment reports. BAM can be leveraged for a wide variety of solutions, but working with it is outside the scope of this book.

Exercise 6-7. Tracking Functional Acknowledgments

To see the status of a functional acknowledgment, use the steps in this exercise:

1. In the BizTalk Group Hub, click the EDI Interchange and Correlated ACK Status report.
2. Modify the criteria appropriately to ensure that at least one document is returned in the result set, as shown in Figure 6-35.

Query Expression

Field Name	Operator	Value
Search For	Equals	Interchange/ACK Status
Status	Not Equals	Accepted
Interchange Date Time	Greater Than	5/8/2007 12:00:00 AM
Maximum Matches	Equals	5000

Figure 6-35. *Query parameters*

3. Right-click any of the results (shown in Figure 6-36) and select Interchange Status and Ack Details.

Query results (249 items were found):

Sender party	Receiver party	Control ID	Direction	Interchange Da...	EDI encoding t...	Interchange Status
(ZZ)APRESS1234	(ZZ)COMPX789	000000024	Send	6/8/2007 4:09 PM	X12	Ack Not Expected
(ZZ)APRESS1234	(ZZ)COMPX789	000000024	Send	7/6/2007 1:35 PM	X12	Ack Not Expected
(01)COMPX789	(ZZ)APRESS1234	000000025	Receive	6/7/2007 3:55 PM	X12	Accepted with Errors
(01)COMPX789	(ZZ)APRESS1234	000000025	Receive	6/7/2007 3:55 PM	X12	Accepted with Errors
(01)AAA	(ZZ)BBB	000000025	Send	7/19/2007 9:31 ...	X12	Ack Not Expected

Figure 6-36. *Result set*

■ **Note** In order to see any data in this report, an exercise with an interchange that was received into BizTalk will need to be executed. There are several exercises in Chapter 2 (such as Exercise 2-4) that demonstrate how to work with acknowledgments and can be used to generate results that would appear in this report.

---

4. Click the Functional Ack(s) tab. The status of the functional acknowledgment will be shown (see Figure 6-37).

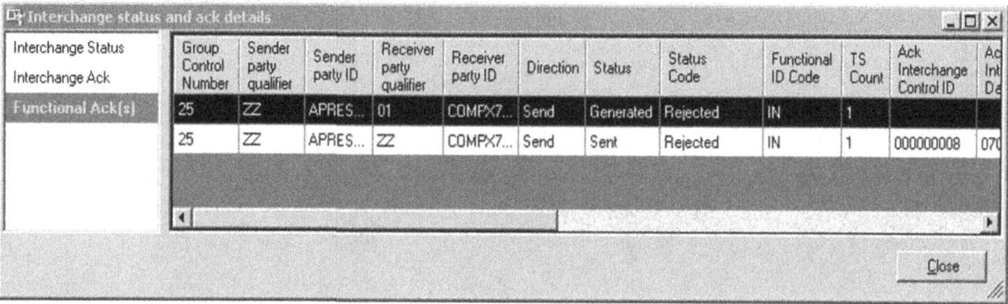

Group Control Number	Sender party qualifier	Sender party ID	Receiver party qualifier	Receiver party ID	Direction	Status	Status Code	Functional ID Code	TS Count	Ack Interchange Control ID	Ac Int Da
25	ZZ	APRES...	01	COMPX7...	Send	Generated	Rejected	IN	1		
25	ZZ	APRES...	ZZ	COMPX7...	Send	Sent	Rejected	IN	1	000000008	07(

Figure 6-37. *Functional acknowledgment report*

Final Discussion

The validation and testing of document content can often take a great deal of time and is something that should begin during the development of a BizTalk EDI implementation. As soon as a developer is able to create an EDI instance from source data within BizTalk and has taken steps to ensure the accuracy of the document based on the implementation guide, the content validation should begin. Depending on the complexity of the content and the responsiveness of the trading partner, this process can easily take a great deal of time, impacting development schedules. Trading partners often do not operate on the same agenda as the company working to implement the EDI solution.

As for the processing and delivery/reception of EDI documents, this is generally completely within the control of the architects and developers building the BizTalk EDI solution. Testing that orchestrations function as expected, that source data is queried correctly, and that maps function without throwing errors can be done without interaction with the trading partner. Unit testing the solution properly is an important step and should be fully documented.

Integration projects in general are often heavily weighted around testing. Development of components often takes far less time than the accurate testing of those components. BizTalk EDI solutions are no exception to this rule; in fact, the test phases of EDI testing often take more time on average because so much depends on the requirements and interactions with trading partners. This, however, is to be expected with any type of EDI implementation, BizTalk or otherwise, and should be planned for early in the business process.

CHAPTER 7

Deployment and Production Support

This chapter explores the details around deploying and maintaining an EDI solution in a production environment. Deployment during development is typically handled using Visual Studio, which allows a developer to quickly build and deploy code to the local BizTalk Server. However, production environments are frequently made up of multiple distributed servers, and Visual Studio is generally not an option. The key concepts for deployment are as follows:

- **Server architecture considerations**: In single server environments, the deployment needs to be done on one server only. In multiserver environments, the deployment needs to be done to all servers within the BizTalk Group that are to run the solution (not all servers within a group are required to run the same solutions; those that do, share the processing load).
- **MSI deployments**: When deploying an entire solution to a target environment that has not previously been deployed to, the standard approach is to use an MSI package. BizTalk allows for the import and export of MSI files to deploy all internal BizTalk components as well as any referenced assemblies and web services.
- **Manual deployments**: In environments that already have a solution deployed to them, a manual deployment may be necessary. For example, assume that a solution is operating in a production environment and one of the schemas for an EDI 810 needs to be modified. The only need is to redeploy the single assembly that contains the updated schema. Code updates such as this generally require a manual installation, rather than a full MSI deployment.
- **Use of binding files**: Binding files contain all of the information necessary to create, configure, and bind ports and parties. For a binding file to work correctly, any orchestrations, pipelines, or other components referenced by or bound to objects defined in the file need to be deployed prior to importing it. Binding files are most useful when deploying a solution to multiple environments, where the only difference between environments may be URLs, passwords, configured parties, or other configurable settings on ports. With this approach, an MSI is used to install all the components, and after this has been completed, the binding files with the correct settings are imported, overwriting the values set by the MSI package.

Once the solution has been deployed, production support begins. These tasks include keeping the solution optimized and up-to-date. Typical support activities include the following:

- **Resubmitting EDI documents**: Occasionally, trading partners may request that a document be resubmitted, either because the document contains bad data, or because internal processes at the trading partner require the reprocessing of the document. It is essential to understand how to resubmit a document with the least amount of impact and effort as possible.
- **Making code updates to EDI components**: Often it is necessary to update schemas, maps, orchestrations, and other assemblies that have been deployed to a production environment. There are varying degrees to the level of complexity associated with making these updates, ranging from a simple update to the Global Assembly Cache (GAC), all the way to a full unenlistment and undeployment of components.
- **SQL administration**: BizTalk has a number of administrative jobs and associated stored procedures used to keep the databases performing optimally, and it is important to understand where these administrative tools are located.

Deployment Options

There are three basic options to installing BizTalk solutions: a fully automatic MSI installation package; a manual deployment; or a deployment using a combination of binding files and either of the preceding two options. Prior to deploying to any environment, it is essential to understand how components are installed on the servers. This section begins by looking at a high-level view of installations on single and multiserver BizTalk environments. After these are illustrated, the different approaches to solution deployment are explored with detailed exercises.

■ **Note** For administration and deployment best practices, refer to the sections within the BizTalk Server Documentation in Operations ➤ Managing BizTalk Server ➤ BizTalk Server Administration Best Practices.

Server Architecture Considerations

There are two basic server infrastructures that will be described: single server and multiserver. The first topic to understand about BizTalk deployments is that there are components installed to the BizTalk Server(s), and there are components installed to the SQL Server. In a single server environment the installation needs to be run on only one box, whereas with a multiserver environment, the installation needs to occur on every server in the BizTalk Group.

A single server environment includes BizTalk installations that are on the same server as SQL Server, and also those that have one BizTalk Server and a separate SQL Server. Figure 7-1 depicts the two architectures that reflect a single server environment.

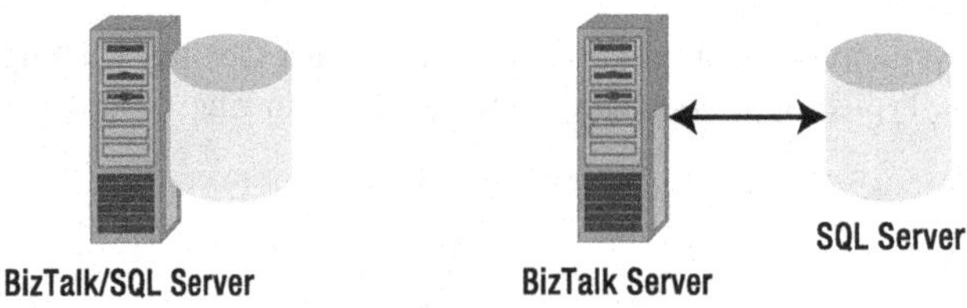

Figure 7-1. *Two options for single server BizTalk environment*

In a multiserver environment, components must be installed on each of the BizTalk Servers in the group, even though a number of the components are shared via the common SQL Server. Two examples of multiserver environments are shown in Figure 7-2.

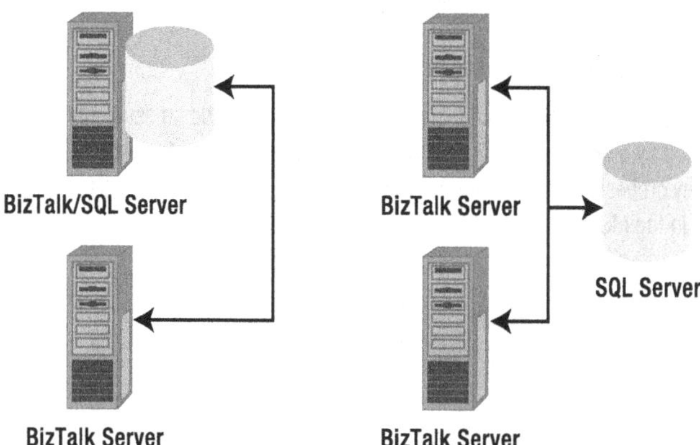

Figure 7-2. *Two examples of a multiserver BizTalk environment*

For MSI deployments, the MSI must be installed on each of the BizTalk Servers in the BizTalk Group. In manual deployments, the assemblies must be added separately to each server in the BizTalk Group. The sections that follow describe how to deploy using the different approaches. For a multi-server environment, simply repeat the steps on each server in the group.

MSI Deployments

Using an MSI package to deploy BizTalk solutions is the preferred approach when deploying to a new environment. The MSI is a single file that includes all of the assemblies, bindings, and other components that are needed for a complete installation of a BizTalk application. Installing the MSI may mean one or both of the following options will need to be worked through:

- **Import the MSI package**: Using the BizTalk Administration Console, the MSI package can be imported. All solution deployments require that the package be imported so that all of the BizTalk components are registered properly in the different databases, and so that the assemblies are properly installed in the GAC.
- **Execute the MSI package**: Often there are a number of non-BizTalk-specific components that may need to be installed for a solution; the most typical of which are any web services used to broker messages between orchestrations and external entities. Double-clicking the MSI package causes it to execute and run exactly like any other Windows MSI. The execution installs everything that is not registered as a BizTalk component in the appropriate locations (such as Internet Information Services [IIS] and the GAC), but it will not register anything internally to the BizTalk engine.

Exercise 7-1 creates an MSI package that can be installed on any BizTalk environment.

Exercise 7-1. Exporting a BizTalk MSI Installation

This exercise demonstrates how to export an EDI solution, along with all party settings and port bindings, to an MSI package. This example uses the EDI.Demonstration.Chapter3 BizTalk application as an example:

1. Open the BizTalk Administration Console and find an application to export.
2. To demonstrate how external assemblies are referenced and incorporated into an MSI, add an assembly to the application that represents a DLL called by an orchestration. For this exercise, it is not important whether the assembly is actually referenced by any orchestrations or other components. Take the following steps to include a "non-BizTalk" (resource) assembly in the MSI package (see Figure 7-3):

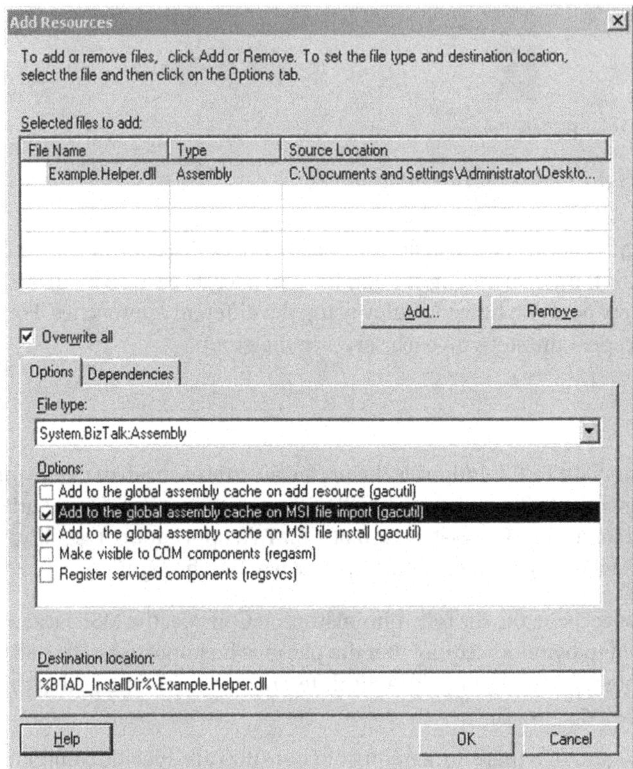

Figure 7-3. *Referencing an external assembly*

   a. Right-click the BizTalk application and select Add ➤ Resources (or Add ➤ BizTalk Assemblies).
   b. Click the Add button and browse to the location of the assembly being added. In this exercise, an assembly called Example.Helper.dll will be added.

c. Once the assembly has been added, there are several properties to set:

   i. **Overwrite All**: If the resource has been installed in the GAC (which it must be to be successfully referenced by an orchestration), this option will force it to be overwritten each time the MSI is imported. This ensures that the version of the assembly packaged with the MSI is the one that is installed in the GAC.

   ii. **Options**: There are two options that are set for this exercise:

      1. **Add to the global assembly cache on MSI file import**: An MSI can be imported into BizTalk, or it can be double-clicked and run (like any standard MSI). The most appropriate way to install a BizTalk MSI is to import it using the BizTalk Administration Console; this is how all of the BizTalk components are registered and installed properly (double-clicking the MSI will only install external components, never ports, bindings,etc.). By selecting this option, it ensures that the referenced assembly will be installed in the GAC, regardless of how the file is imported.

      2. **Add to the GAC on MSI file install**: This option is selected by default and ensures that the referenced assembly is installed in the GAC when the MSI is double-clicked and executed.

   iii. **Dependencies**: If the referenced assembly in turn references other assemblies, they will be listed on this tab. Often assemblies have dependencies that must be installed along with them to allow proper execution.

d. Click OK to save the settings.

e. The resource can be seen by clicking the Resources folder under the application to which it was added. It can also be removed from this location (as shown in Figure 7-4).

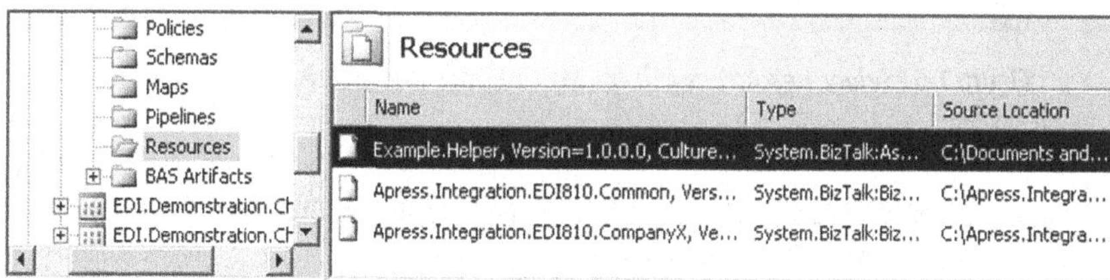

Figure 7-4. *The Resources folder*

3. Now work through the MSI Export Wizard. Right-click the BizTalk application that will be exported and select Export ➤ MSI File. Click Next on the Welcome page.

4. On the Select Resources tab, check the resources to be exported. Figure 7-5 shows that all of the BizTalk assemblies and resources for the given application have been selected. Set several of the check boxes as follows:

   a. Selecting the Bindings option indicates that all bindings associated with the application will be exported, regardless of which assemblies have been selected. Bindings include all ports, port settings, and other nonassembly components that make up a BizTalk application.

   b. Selecting the Global Parties setting indicates that all party settings will be exported. Once this is selected, click Next.

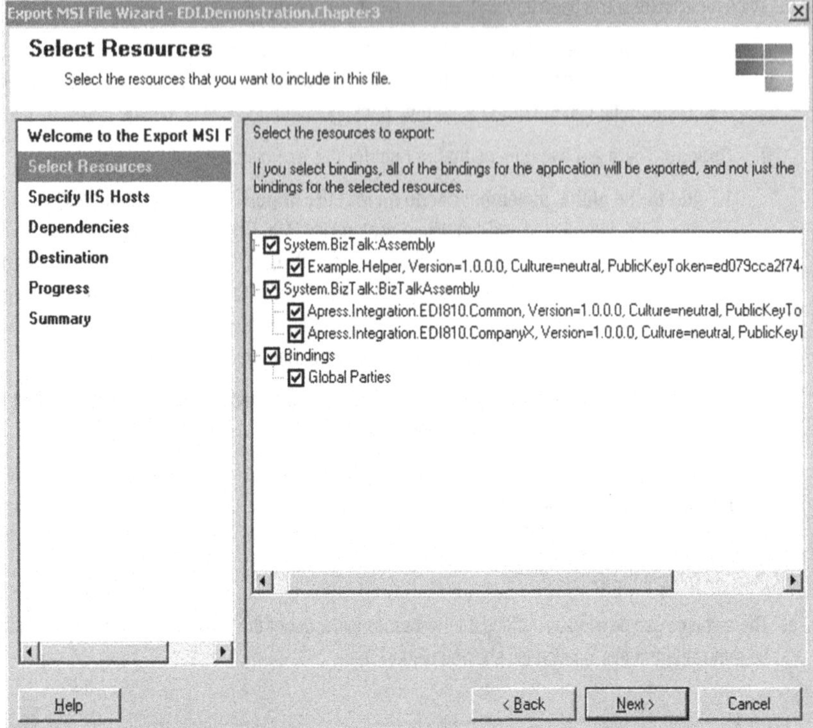

Figure 7-5. *Select Resources tab on MSI Export Wizard*

5. On the Specify IIS Hosts screen, the MSI Wizard allows for the selection of all IIS-related services. For example, if an orchestration or a schema has been exposed as a web service, the option to export the related IIS settings would be included here. Click Next to continue.

6. The Dependencies tab shows all BizTalk applications on which the currently exported application depends. If these applications do not exist on the target environment where the MSI is installed, the application will not run (i.e., any dependencies should be installed before installing the current MSI). All dependencies can be seen in the BizTalk Administration Console by right-clicking the application, selecting Properties, and clicking the References tab (as shown in Figure 7-6). Click Next when complete.

7. On the Destination screen, indicate the name of the MSI file and the location of the output directory of the MSI. This example names it EDI.Demonstration.Chapter3.msi.

8. Click the Export button. The progress screen will indicate the progress of the creation of the MSI file. Once the MSI has been fully exported, a summary page will be displayed that includes instructions for installing the MSI application, as shown in Figure 7-7.

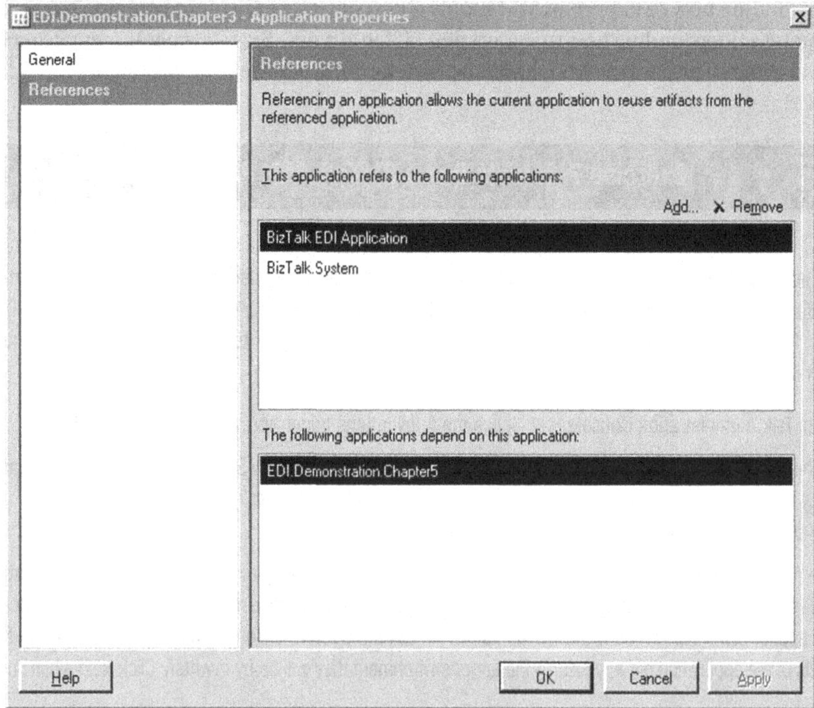

Figure 7-6. *Showing dependencies for the BizTalk application*

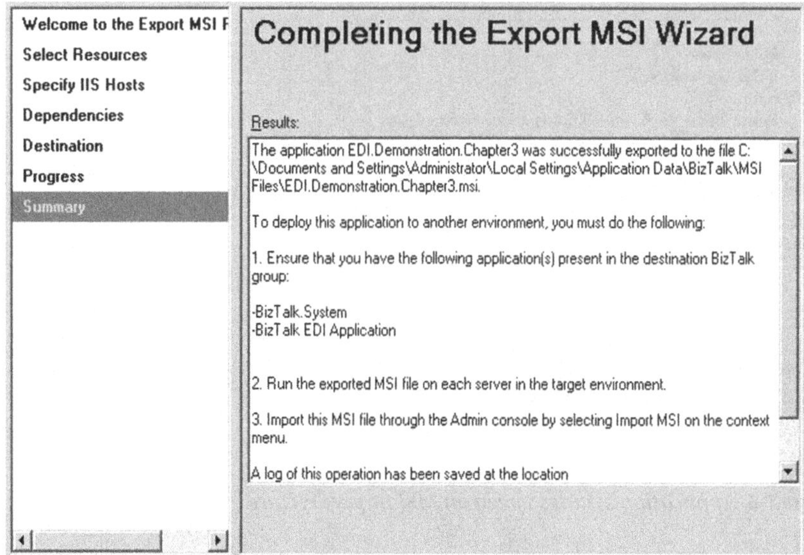

Figure 7-7. *Summary of MSI export*

Understanding how to export an MSI is only a part of the deployment process. The rest of the process requires understanding how to import that MSI into a new BizTalk environment. Exercise 7-2 demonstrates how to import the MSI, and how to determine whether the installation is successful.

Exercise 7-2. Installing a BizTalk MSI Package

This exercise demonstrates how to install and import a BizTalk MSI, specifically the MSI package exported in Exercise 7-1. Since this exercise imports the same application as was exported in the previous exercise, begin by removing all components such as the BizTalk application and all external DLLs from the GAC (unless a separate environment is available). If these items remain, the installation will still work, but the demonstration will provide a deeper understanding if the installation is run on a "fresh" environment:

1. In BizTalk Administration Console, right-click the Applications folder and select Import ➤ MSI File.
2. In the Wizard that opens, browse to the location of the MSI (under the MSI File to Import property heading) and click Next. In this case, the MSI will be the EDI.Demonstration.Chapter3.msi, accessible in C:\Apress.Integration\Chapter 3\BizTalk Application.
3. The Application Settings page shows all of the referenced BizTalk applications required for the imported application to run (these applications must be present). It also shows all of the resources (assemblies) associated with the application. This screen is shown in Figure 7-8. Set the Overwrite Resources option to ensure that if components of the application already exist in the target environment they will be overwritten. Click Next when complete.

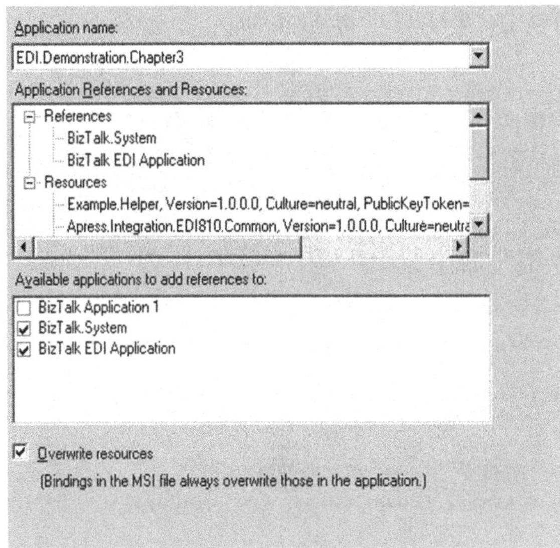

Figure 7-8. *Application settings screen on MSI Import Wizard*

4. Set the Target Staging Environment to Default. Click Next.
5. On the Summary page click the Import button. The application will be imported.
6. Once the application is imported, the Results screen of the Wizard will be displayed. Click Finish.

Note There is an option to Run the Application Installation Wizard on the final Results screen of the Import Wizard. Selecting this means that the MSI package itself will be executed after finishing the wizard. Not all BizTalk installations need to run the MSI package—only those that install components that are external to BizTalk and are not registered to the BizTalk databases. For example, if there are web service files and virtual directories that need to be created, the MSI would need to be run, not just imported via the BizTalk Administration Console. Additionally, if there are external components that were not added to the GAC during the import, the MSI would need to be run. In the case of this exercise, however, all of the BizTalk components and the single external assembly (Example.Helper.dll) are completely installed when importing through the Console, without the need to run the MSI.

7. Validate that the BizTalk components were installed using the BizTalk Administration Console. The ports and orchestrations will need to be started before the application will work.
8. Validate that the referenced assembly was installed in the GAC successfully by taking these steps:
   a. Open Administrative Tools ➤ Microsoft .NET Framework 2.0 Configuration.
   b. Click Manage the Assembly Cache.
   c. Click View List of Assemblies in the Assembly Cache. A list of all assemblies that have been installed in the GAC will be displayed (see Figure 7-9). Validate that the Example.Helper.dll, added in Exercise 7-1, appears in the list (this list can be sorted alphabetically by clicking the column Assembly Name header).

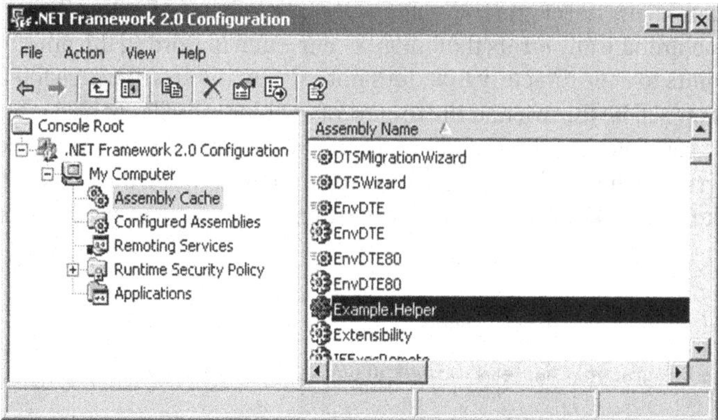

Figure 7-9. *Validating the installation of the referenced assembly in the GAC*

Manual Deployments

Deploying individual assemblies manually to a production system, when Visual Studio is not present, must be done through the BizTalk Administration Console. Deployments of this nature are generally very simple and consist of the following basic steps:

1. **Create the BizTalk application**: If the BizTalk application does not already exist on the target server, it needs to be created. Right-click the Applications folder in the BizTalk Administration Console and select New ➤ Application.

2. **Add references to other BizTalk applications:** If the components of an application require other BizTalk applications to be available (such as a reference to schemas/maps/orchestrations, or reliance on the BizTalk EDI application), references must be manually created. This can be done by right-clicking the BizTalk application and selecting Properties. In the window that opens, click the References tab.
3. **Add the assemblies:** Every assembly that is to be added can be added by right-clicking the BizTalk application and selecting Add ➤ BizTalk Assemblies.
4. **Import the port bindings:** Importing a binding file eliminates the need to create and configure any ports in the solution. It also eliminates the need to manually bind ports to any orchestrations or other subscribers (such as send ports). To import a binding file, right-click the BizTalk application and select Import ➤ Bindings.
5. **Configure, enlist, and start all components:** Once everything has been imported, and the ports are set up and configured, all of the components must be enlisted and started.

Use of Binding Files

As stated previously, binding files can be used to create and bind a number of BizTalk components. Before importing the binding file, it will be useful to manually edit it to ensure that any of the receive or send locations that may be included are pointing to the correct locations. For example, if a binding file is generated on a development environment and is being used to set up ports on a production environment, any file drops, SQL Server connection strings, FTP delivery URLs, and so on, will likely need to be modified from their "development" value to their "production" value. Doing this manually in a text editor will eliminate any errors that might occur when importing the bindings (e.g., if a file receive location points to a file directory that does not exist on the server where the import is being done, an exception will be thrown and the import of the binding will not be successful).

Figure 7-10 shows a subsection of a binding file that pertains to a file receive location. The <Address> node is an example of a value that will most likely need to be changed when the binding is imported into a new environment. The binding file can be opened in any text editor to modify the values.

```
- <ReceiveLocations>
  - <ReceiveLocation Name="FileReceiveFailedMessage">
      <Description xsi:nil="true" />
      <Address>C:\Apress.Integration\Chapter 4\Drops\Incoming - Failed Message
        Demo\*.*</Address>
      <PublicAddress />
      <Primary>true</Primary>
      <ReceiveLocationServiceWindowEnabled>false</ReceiveLocationServiceWindowEnabled>
      <ReceiveLocationFromTime>2007-07-05T06:00:00</ReceiveLocationFromTime>
      <ReceiveLocationToTime>2007-07-06T05:59:59</ReceiveLocationToTime>
      <ReceiveLocationStartDateEnabled>false</ReceiveLocationStartDateEnabled>
      <ReceiveLocationStartDate>2007-07-04T18:00:00</ReceiveLocationStartDate>
      <ReceiveLocationEndDateEnabled>false</ReceiveLocationEndDateEnabled>
      <ReceiveLocationEndDate>2007-07-05T18:00:00</ReceiveLocationEndDate>
```

Figure 7-10. *Manually changing binding files prior to import*

Production Support

Ongoing support for a production EDI solution includes monitoring processes and document delivery status, performing basic maintenance, and deploying code updates. Monitoring the solution using the different BizTalk tools and reports available is outlined in detail in Chapter 6. The following sections outline some of the most common tasks to production support that have not already been covered.

Deploying Code Updates

To illustrate the process of deploying code updates to a production environment, it will be useful to walk through an example scenario. This section looks at working through a change to a schema and applying the update to BizTalk Server. Assume that the schema shown in Figure 7-11 has been deployed to a production environment and that a change needs to be made to the maximum length of the N401 node.

X12_00401_810_CompanyX.xsd

- X12_00401_810
  - ST
    - ST01
    - ST02
    - ST03
  - N1Loop1
    - N1
      - N101
      - N102
      - N103
      - N104
      - N105
      - N106

Node	Description	Data Type	Min Occurs	Max Occurs	Minimum Length	Maximum Length
N3	Address Infor...		0	2		
N301	Address Infor...	X12_AN	1	1	1	55
N302	Address Infor...	X12_AN	0	1	1	55
N4	Geographic L...		0	1		
N401	City Name_19	X12_AN	0	1	2	30
N402	State or Provi...	X12_ID	0	1	2	2
N403	Postal Code_1...	X12_ID	0	1	3	15
N404	Country Code...	X12_ID	0	1	2	3

Figure 7-11. *Original deployed schema in production environment*

The schema shows that the N401 node has a minimum length of 2 and a maximum length of 30. Now assume that a document matching this specification has been delivered to a trading partner. The trading partner has responded saying that the city name has been truncated improperly and that the length of the name of the city should be extended to 100 characters. The first step to accomplish this request is to modify the schema. Increase the maximum length to 100 and save and compile the schema assembly.

Once the assembly has been compiled, it will need to be deployed to the production server. Whenever an updated BizTalk assembly needs to be deployed, consider the following:

- **Dependent assemblies**: Are there any assemblies that are currently deployed that depend on the presence of the assembly that is being updated? For instance, if a schema is being redeployed, and a separate assembly contains an orchestration that references the schema assembly, the orchestration assembly would be a dependent assembly. In cases where there are dependent assemblies, extra steps need to be taken to ensure that the update can be deployed properly.
- **Running or suspended instances**: If any processes are partially completed, it is best practice to allow them to complete prior to redeploying any related assemblies. For example, if an update to an orchestration adds additional steps to the flow, and an existing instance is already in process, the update will not necessarily execute the additional step. Also, if an orchestration must first be disabled and unbound prior to deploying the update, there is a good chance that the running instance(s) will be lost. Always take steps to ensure that all processes have completed before making code updates.

Note In production settings, it is often challenging to ensure that there are no running processes before making a code update. One way to ensure that additional processes do not start while waiting for existing ones to terminate is to shut down all ports that may be taking in new documents. For example, if a SQL receive port is polling a database, disable the receive location until the code update has taken place.

- **Impacts to other assemblies:** If multiple assemblies will be impacted by the change, those assemblies will also need to be recompiled and redeployed. For example, if a schema change includes a new field, it is very likely that any maps referencing the assembly will also need to be recompiled.
- **Versioning:** .NET allows for the versioning of assemblies, and it is possible to have multiple versions of the same orchestration, map, or schema deployed at the same time. This is generally done when there are long-running orchestrations that may take weeks to complete. During that time, an update needs to be deployed. Rather than terminating the current running instances, the version of the orchestration that the running instances are executing under is left deployed (as version 1.0) and the updated orchestration is deployed (as version 2.0). All future processes can be set to execute against version 2.0, and version 1.0 can be undeployed after all of the current orchestration instances have completed.

In the case of the schema change that is being discussed, assume that there are no orchestrations or maps that reference this schema. All that needs to be done is to redeploy the schema. This can be done through the BizTalk Administration Console and is illustrated in Exercise 7-3.

Exercise 7-3. Redeploying an Updated Schema

This exercise outlines the steps necessary to deploy a schema that has been updated using the BizTalk Administration Console. The same basic principles can be applied when redeploying other types of BizTalk components, such as maps and orchestrations. Work through the following steps for redeployment:

1. Open the BizTalk Administration Console and click the schema folder that contains the schema that will be redeployed. This exercise will undeploy the schema in Apress.Integration.EDI810.CompanyX, as shown in Figure 7-12.

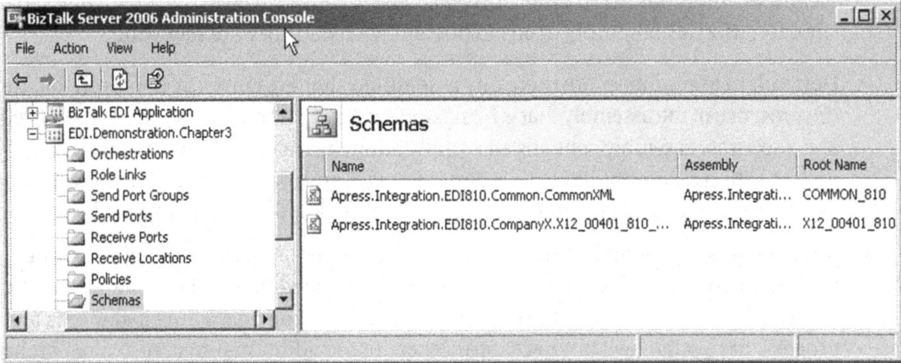

Figure 7-12. *Schema list*

2. Right-click the schema and select Remove. When removing an assembly several notification windows may pop up indicating that additional components will be removed along with the current item. For example, when removing the X12 schema from the EDI.Demonstration.Chapter3 BizTalk application, the associated map will also be removed (see Figure 7-13).

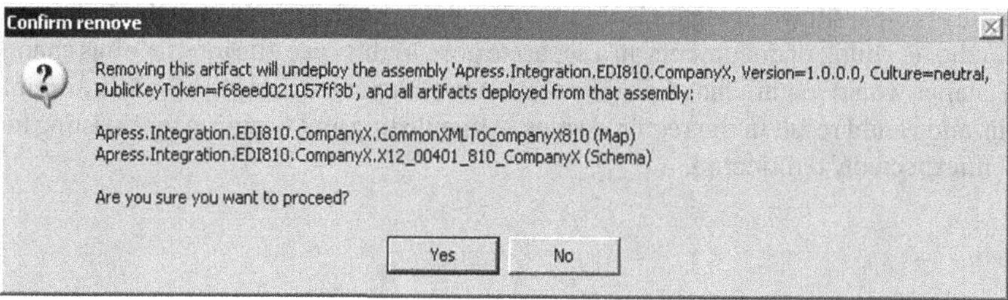

Figure 7-13. *Confirmation for removing a schema*

3. Once the schema has been removed, the new one can be redeployed by taking the following steps:

   a. Right-click the BizTalk application (in this case, EDI.Demonstration.Chapter3) and click Add ➤ BizTalk Assemblies.

   b. In the Add Resources window that opens, click the Add button and browse to the location of the newly compiled assembly that is to be deployed.

Note If the Overwrite All check box is selected, there is no need to remove assemblies before redeploying. Enabling this option will ensure that any existing assemblies are overwritten.

   c. Click OK and restart the BizTalk application host to ensure that the new assembly is fully registered.

Code Updates and Interface Changes

An interface is any external facing parameters or methods that interact with other components. When interfaces do not change, there is a shortcut to deploying BizTalk components. It is possible to deploy assemblies directly to the GAC and skip the registration of the assembly in BizTalk Server. Changes of this nature usually apply most readily to orchestrations, but can potentially work for schemas and other foundational BizTalk components, as long as the interfaces have not changed. To illustrate the difference between an interface change and a change that does not impact the interface on an orchestration, begin by referring to Figure 7-14, which represents the "original state" of an orchestration.

Figure 7-14. *Original state of orchestration*

In the example shown in Figure 7-15, a parallel shape has been added to the "original state" to allow for the reception of documents on a separate port. In this case, the interface has changed. This type of change would require that the orchestration be redeployed using the BizTalk Administration Console, and would result in the required steps of unenlisting and ensuring that existing instances are not unexpectedly terminated.

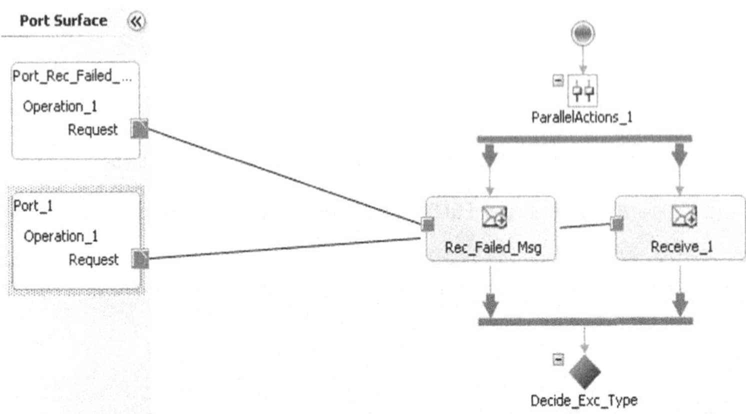

Figure 7-15. *A Change to the interface of an orchestration*

An example of a change that would not incur an interface change would be a new expression shape (see Figure 7-16); this could be deployed directly to the GAC using the shortcut method. In this case, only the code that is internal to the orchestration has changed; it does not impact external components that interact with this orchestration, and therefore does not need to be fully reregistered.

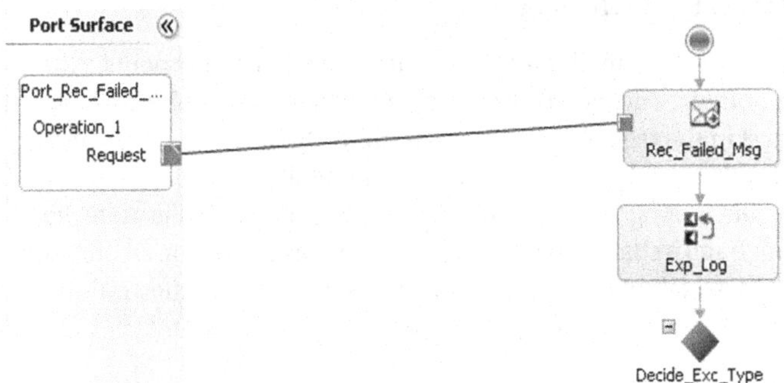

Figure 7-16. *A change to an orchestration that does not impact the interface*

The preceding figures illustrate the difference between a change that impacts the interface of an orchestration, and one that does not. Similarly, the same idea applies to schemas and to maps. Simple map changes, which do not require updates to schemas, can generally be updated using the shortcut method. A map, for example, may start with the implementation shown in Figure 7-17.

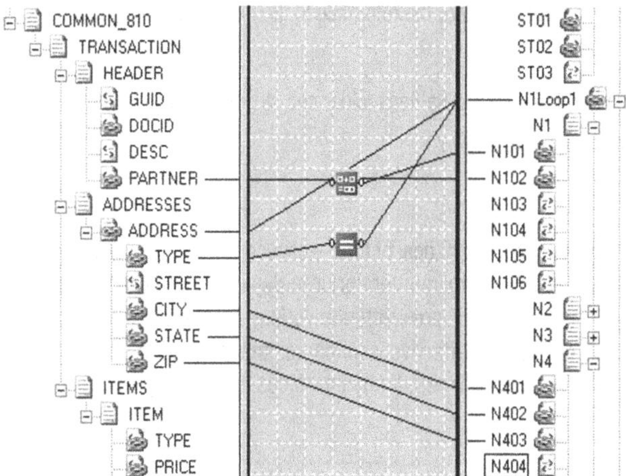

Figure 7-17. *Original map*

A simple change to the map, which would not cause an impact to the interface of the map, could be something like adding a constant containing the country code (hard-coded to a specific value), which would be mapped to N404. This map change is shown in Figure 7-18.

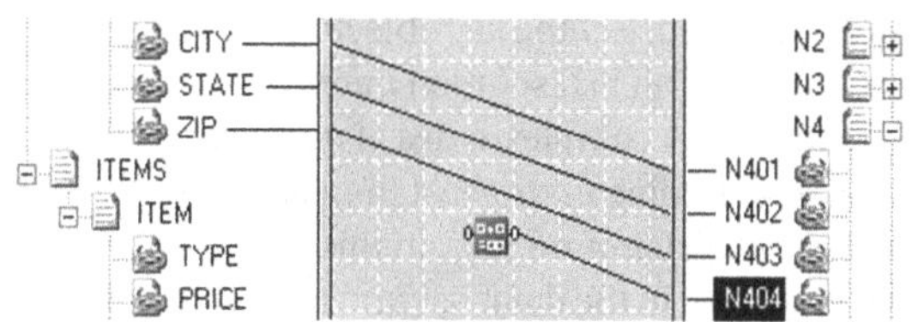

Figure 7-18. *A change to a map that does not impact the interface*

A change to a map that would cause an impact to the interface and require that it be fully redeployed using the BizTalk Administration Console would be any update to a schema referenced by the map. For example, if a new node, <COUNTRY>, were added to the source schema, and that value needed to be mapped to N404, the source schema would first need to be updated, then the map would need to update the reference to that schema, and finally the source <COUNTRY> node would need to be dragged and dropped on the target N404 node. The shortcut deployment method could not be used in this instance; a full redeployment would need to take place.

Exercise 7-4 illustrates how to use the shortcut method of deploying code updates.

Exercise 7-4. Shortcut to Deploying Updates

This exercise demonstrates how to deploy an updated orchestration assembly without having to undeploy or rebind any ports. This method should only be used when the interfaces for the updated component(s) have not changed:

1. Add the compiled assembly directly to the GAC, overwriting the existing assembly by taking these steps:
   a. Click Start ➤ Control Panel ➤ Administrative Tools ➤ Microsoft .NET Framework 2.0 Configuration.
   b. Expand My Computer, right-click Assembly Cache, and select Add.
   c. Browse to the compiled assembly and click Open. This will add the assembly and overwrite the existing assembly.

2. Restart the BizTalk Server application host. This ensures that the reference to the new assembly is made in BizTalk:

    a. In BizTalk Administration Console, expand the Platform Settings folder and click Host Instances.

    b. Right-click the BizTalk Server application and select Restart.

■ **Note** While this shortcut is extremely useful and can save a great deal of time—especially during development—it is essential to test that this technique works in a development environment prior to deploying to a production environment. When deploying BizTalk components, a number of items are written to various database tables; installing the actual DLL to the GAC is only one of the steps. This shortcut effectively eliminates the registering of information in the tables, which works fine as long as no interfaces have changed. If any interfaces have changed, unexpected results will occur.

Resubmitting Documents

When EDI documents encounter errors while being delivered to trading partners, or when trading partners receive documents with bad or invalid data, the need arises to be able to resubmit the document. There are a variety of ways in which to meet this need, but the key objective is to eliminate as many of the unnecessary steps as possible. For example, if an EDI solution queries a database for data, marks the data as "delivered," runs the data through a complex series of maps and orchestrations, and finally delivers the document to one or more trading partners at the same time, there is a level of complexity in resubmitting that prohibits rapid turnaround (e.g., in this case, an administrator would need to begin by resetting the "delivered" flag in the database and then ensure that the document that was originally delivered to multiple parties is now only delivered to the party requesting the resubmission).

Continuing with the scenario from the previous section, assume that the schema update has been fully redeployed and future documents will be delivered without truncating the N401 (city name) element to 30 characters. Assume that the trading partner that initially requested the change has now requested that the document with the truncated field in it be resubmitted to partner with the full city name.

This section looks at how to create a simple file drop that will allow for the manipulation of data and the resubmission of the document without having to modify the database where the data originally came from. The assumption in the current scenario is that the trading partner wants the EDI document resubmitted with the full city name, instead of the truncated value. Take the following steps to resubmit the document:

- **Retrieve document from HAT**: Begin with retrieving the original instance of the document received from SQL Server, the actual XML that exists before being run through any maps or EDI pipelines. Chapter 6 demonstrates the retrieval of an instance of a document from HAT and saving it out. The resubmission process begins by saving the instance of the original output of the SQL XML extraction document to a text file and setting it aside to be resubmitted.

- **Create an administrator file drop**: In cases where the document is received via any port other than a file-based receive port, there is no way to simply resubmit a text file version of the data. For example, in the EDI.Demonstration.Chapter3 solution, the receive port contains a single SQL receive location; it only accepts input from this adapter. A receive port can be easily extended, though, to allow for an administrator to drop a file, simulating the input from the SQL Adapter, as shown in Figure 7-19. The document being dropped must match the same format as documents being received via the SQL receive location. Since the data being resubmitted is extracted from HAT, and that document is an exact copy of the data as it was retrieved from SQL, it will match the expected format.

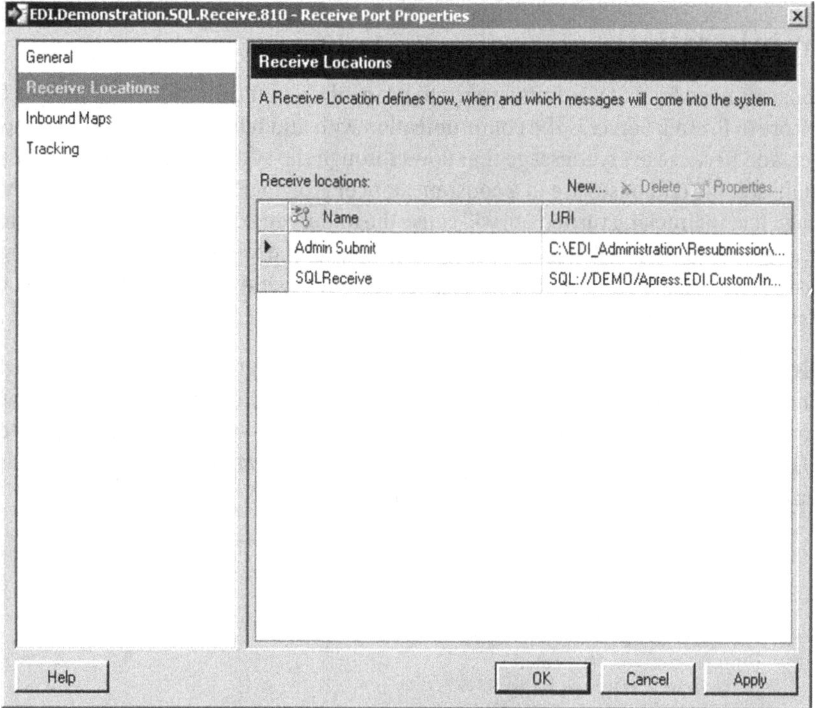

Figure 7-19. *Adding an administrator manual submission folder to a receive port*

■ **Note** Remember that when creating file-based ports on BizTalk environments with more than one server in a group, the source should be a shared network folder. If a local path is given (such as C:\), each server in the group will monitor its local C: drive and will not be able to share the processing load by monitoring a commonly accessible location.

- **Resubmit document**: The document saved from HAT can now be dropped on the new Administrator Resubmit file drop. The format of the document matches the document retrieved from SQL Server, so all of the BizTalk processes that would have been executed if the SQL Receive Adapter had executed will now be executed by the file dropped on the manual submission receive location.

It is a common request that when a document is resubmitted, some of the data should be modified. This leads to a question that must be resolved: Where is the appropriate place to change the data? In the case of a manual resubmission by an administrator via a file drop, a document is saved to a text file, and the text file is resubmitted to the BizTalk engine. It would be very simple to change the appropriate data in the text file prior to resubmitting; this would get the result to the target party. However, the data in the source system will still be the same as it originally was (e.g., if the data is from an accounting system, and the data changed is the value of an item, changing the value in the text file would cause a data integrity issue between what is delivered to the trading partner and what is stored in the accounting system). In some cases, it is fine to change the value in the text document; in other cases, it is necessary to resubmit the change from the originating system.

SQL Administration

There is a constant need for a SQL administrator to be involved in the operations of BizTalk Server. Because the core of BizTalk Server is the communication with and reliance on the underlying tables in SQL Server, and because every message that flows through the system writes numerous times to different databases, the databases are in a constant state of growth. EDI solutions, especially those that have a high level of tracking turned on, will cause the underlying databases to grow enormously. It is very important to monitor table growth, to ensure that a full database maintenance program is in place, and to enable BizTalk to operate at its optimal level. Several of the most common tasks for SQL administration are listed here:

- **Configuring and running BizTalk maintenance jobs**: There are a variety of jobs that are set up when BizTalk is first installed. However, all of these must be configured and/or started by an administrator. To access the BizTalk jobs, open SQL Server Enterprise Manager and expand the SQL Server Agent (the Agent must be started). Next, expand Jobs; all of the jobs related to BizTalk administration will be listed, as shown in Figure 7-20.

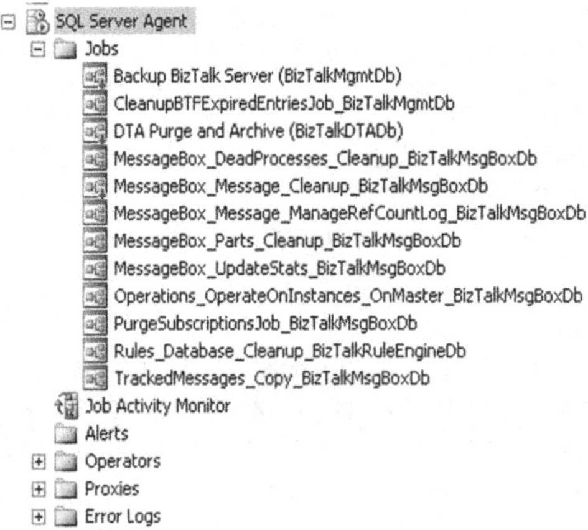

Figure 7-20. *BizTalk SQL administration jobs*

■ **Note** Most of the stored procedures that are called from the jobs can be run manually from a query window.

- **Truncating log files**: Log files can build up very quickly and take up a massive amount of space. A SQL administrator should create automated jobs that will keep the log files at appropriate sizes and archive backups at appropriate intervals. In a pinch, however, the SQL script shown in Listing 7-1 can be run; it will shrink the log for the given database(s).

Listing 7-1. *Shrink Log Files*

```
DECLARE migration_cursor CURSOR
FOR SELECT name
FROM sysdatabases
-- enter in the names of the database where the log files should
-- be truncted in the following 'where' clause
where name in ('NAME OF DABATASE','OTHER DABATASE')
OPEN migration_cursor
DECLARE @dbname varchar(40)
FETCH NEXT FROM migration_cursor
INTO @dbname
WHILE @@FETCH_STATUS=0
 BEGIN
  backup log @dbname with truncate_only
  dbcc shrinkdatabase(@dbname)
  FETCH NEXT FROM migration_cursor
  INTO @dbname
 END
CLOSE migration_cursor
DEALLOCATE migration_cursor
```

Final Discussion

Supporting EDI solutions in production is generally more straightforward than other BizTalk implementations. The EDI reports provide excellent insight into document delivery status. The fact that EDI documents are text-file based makes it easy to see the content of documents and resubmit documents when necessary. As with many BizTalk solutions, though, EDI solutions necessitate careful monitoring and administration. Often trading partners require that certain types of documents are delivered within a certain time period. If this time period is missed, either for technical reasons, or for bad data that did not pass validation, there may be major impacts to business processes and possible fines imposed by partners.

The key to production support is to make monitoring and administration an integral task to the life cycle of the BizTalk solution. Periodically looking at the reports defined in the BizTalk Group Hub view and monitoring the Windows Event Viewer on each server in a BizTalk Group will ensure that any errors or unexpected behavior is caught in a timely fashion. With careful planning during development, appropriate testing, and proper use of the reports and administrative tools provided, BizTalk Server R2's EDI components will result in a solution that is simple and cost-effective to develop, deploy, and maintain.

Index

C

D

G

H

I

L

M

N

O

P

UV

W

XYZ

Printed in the United States
By Bookmasters